Releasing the Light
A Journal of Caring

by

Carol Alma McPhee

Releasing the Light © 2023 by Carol Alma McPhee

All rights reserved. No portion of this book may be reproduced in any form without explicit, prior written permission of the author except for brief passages excerpted for review and critical purposes.

Published by

Coalesce Press

845 Main Street
Morro Bay, California 93422
coalescebookstore.com

Submissions by invitation only

Printed in the United States of America

ISBN: 978-0-9895234-7-9

Library of Congress Control Number: 2023905964

Book Design: Mary Hwass-Hay
Cover Design: Claire Norton and Peter Zell

For Ann and for Linna

Also by Carol Alma McPhee

Staying Under
A Small Town Women's Movement

with Bev Boyd, Joann Rusch, Bonnie Young:
Where Our Palms Rest

with Ann Fitzgerald:
Feminist Quotations
The Non-Violent Militant: Selected Writings of Teresa Billington-Greig

CONTENTS

1. A Necessary Background 1
2. Hoping for Hope....................11
3. Settling for Less....................71
4. The Tightrope of Stability.........105
5. Another Kind of Balance 149
6. A Steeper Path 203
7. Consummation 307

Note to Readers

The story I'm sharing with you in these pages is a deeply cut account of daily life during the last twenty-six months of my companion Ann's life. I'd kept journals off and on throughout my life, and when Ann and I were told she had lung cancer I began to write extensively about the days we spent together. I was trying to pay close attention to the options she had and the treatments she underwent, of course, but I was also doing my best to keep hold of what had been precious to me for twenty-five years – our relationship. Almost everything we experienced or that I was thinking and doing went onto the hard drive of my computer, with repetitions enough to fill volumes. These I've tried to eliminate, concentrating instead on the essence of our last two years together. I've allowed the words I wrote at the time, often hurriedly and with grim honesty, to remain unchanged.

Because of that honesty and because this publication is local – that is, under the sponsorship of Coalesce Bookstore in San Luis Obispo County, where I have lived all my life and where Ann and I and my family were known – I have used false names for doctors and for a few of Ann's friends. For her relatives, for friends that we shared, and for some of her internet friends, I've used first names and initials. For nurses and aides I've used only first names. My own family I've identified without hesitation.

In getting my journal ready for print, cutting thousands of words, thinking of a printed book of manageable size, I left out most of an email friendship with a man I'd known since university days. This exchange with Bob was an invaluable support during Ann's illness. Two more people who appear only here and there in the cut version were always comforting and helpful presences, Xiamara and Josef Weber, who relieved us every two weeks from the extra work that keeping a house clean entails.

I want to emphasize that I never intended the journal for publication. If I had, it might have made more sense from a medical point of view to do so closer to the time I was recording 2001-2003. Because treatment and the successes and failures of treatment are part of the story the journal tells, I did leave in the names of all the medicines and chemotherapies I recorded. I'm not aware of the treatment for Ann's kind of cancer now, but surely it has changed, as have the drugs used to treat her.

It's my hope that other couples on similar quests for peace, love and companionship during the ordeal of a final illness can find solace here.

– Carol Alma McPhee

The Third Hour

In memory of AFG

*It's noon below the back bay overlook;
the summer sun shines softly through the haze,
blessing me,
blessing the oriole in the wild rose bush,
blessing the blackbirds swaying in the reeds,
blessing the shallows,
where a multitude of shorebirds overflows
on mud flats and eel grass islands:
grey willets, marbled godwits, curlews,
all strangely alert, heads poised,
some stretching wings, some walking about,
waiting for a call, perhaps, a sign,
a visitation. Only the darker, smaller dowitchers
zealously beak the water surface,
and one lost sandpiper runs this way and that
among the longer legs.*

*You're not here to share the sense I have
that all time's been suspended, the way
it used to be when we were children
lost in the eternity of waiting
for the noontime bell to ring
and bring us to our feet to pray
– The angel of the lord declared unto Mary –
as if from somewhere beneath the sky*

would come – a tremor of earth or air,
a whisper under the water's surface –
a call, and we could rest in knowing
there can be release, there can be an end,
a surge into the air, a curve against sky.

Yet there are other moments that we shared
filled with such abundance, I could never
want release. Two days before you died, each
breath a pain made flesh, you struggled to sit up.
The effort left you gasping more than ever,
and I, trying to hold you, my tears
damp on your shirt, your face, cried Please,
and you lay back, smiling, generous as ever,
at peace,
as if the word I spoke had meant salvation.

That moment,
Filled with all the love I ever bore
ascends now with the birds –
a whirring of wings coursing into the wind,
a turning, now this way, now that,
circle upon circle –
a moment
when all moments fly together,
full of grace.

– Carol Alma McPhee

1
A Necessary Background

Between 2001 and 2003 I cared for my beloved friend Ann as she was dying of lung cancer. Nothing prepared me for this act of love. The journal of my experience I'm sharing with you here – after twenty years of hesitation – shows that I'm no model as a nurse for those who suffer, nor does it give suggestions on how to cope. Instead it describes what it was like for the two of us to live through this trial together: to fear all tomorrows; to desperately need to escape truth; to succumb to irritation; to regret mistakes, as well as to find occasional joy in love and laughter. It's also a record of Ann's courage and generosity in her care for me, even during the most difficult phases of her illness.

Our Relationship

I first met Ann in 1974. She'd sent a note of praise to the newsletter a friend and I were publishing, and so I'd taken notice a few months later when she turned up as a leader organizing a resource center for women. That same year when I was getting together a group to advocate a County Commission on the Status of Women, I phoned her with a special invitation to come to the first meeting, and as an enticement, asked her for suggestions on how to organize the campaign. She had plenty. Our first talk lasted thirty minutes, and she followed up with two typewritten pages mailed to me within one day of that phone call. That I took several of her suggestions, adding them (with thanks) to my own plan, maps the terms of the close relationship that began to form at that meeting

Once the Women's Commission campaign was over and it had been in place for a year, Ann and I began to collaborate as writers. Over the next several years we published two books based on feminist research, *Feminist Quotations* and *The Non-Violent Militant*. At the same time, she and I supported each other caring for our elderly mothers as they became ill and died; she helped me remain steady through the crucial years my three daughters grew from adolescence to adulthood; she opened a room in her house as an office where I could write after our collaboration as authors and editors had ended; she saw me through my bout with breast cancer in 1998. I couldn't imagine her enduring lung cancer without me. We were so close her last years seemed to me my last years also.

I'm still surprised at the way we seemed to fit together, for our backgrounds were very different. Ann was an only child, adopted into a wealthy southern California family. She had lived in cities most of her life – San Marino, Los Angeles, Pasadena, and southern California beach towns adjoining Los Angeles. Bold, forthright, and with a generous spirit, she'd been a natural as a student leader at Mayfield, a private Catholic high school, and at Stanford, where she was elected to Cap and Gown, a women's society honoring leaders. After graduation, she taught English, history and drivers' training at Mayfield while she helped her mother after her father's death. Then, after a solo tour of Europe, she took a graduate degree at Stanford and worked as a human resources administrator in Silicon Valley just a few years before it became Silicon Valley. Around 1959, she began to teach English literature at Long Beach City College. In 1969, unhappy with the strain of the leadership she'd taken on with faculty politics, she declined the presidency of its Academic Senate, took a leave of absence, moved to San Luis Obispo County, and soon resigned completely. She had inherited a little money from her grandfather, enough to live on frugally. Her mother helped her out from time to time, and she began to earn small sums as a stringer for Morro Bay newspapers.

On the other hand, I'd grown up in small town San Luis Obispo, the fifth of six girls. My home was the Cal Poly president's house, at that time close to dairy and horse barns, pastures, creeks and canyons, and more than a mile from the town. I was shy and my leadership qualities were in evidence only in small groups. Until I left home for Stanford and then Berkeley, my only acquaintance with cities came about on visits to cousins in San Francisco. After my four years of college and the two years I spent learning the hard way that I needed a fresh start, I came back to my parents' home in San Luis Obispo, got a teaching credential, and taught high school English for a year. Then I married a man seventeen years older than I, becoming, for the most part, a housewife and mother, staying home except for some part-time English teaching at the community college level. In general, I'd say that most of my worldly experience came from extensive reading – before I met Ann.

But we had both been raised as Catholics, both had left the church, and both stayed tangentially connected to it in order to protect our devout and loving mothers from believing we were condemned to hell. Our large, Irish extended families were clan-like, hers having settled in Los Angeles around 1850 and mine having landed in San Francisco at the same time. We both loved medieval and Elizabethan literature, read lots of novels and history, enjoyed political and philosophical discussions, thrilled to classical music, and most important, were in our minds radical feminists. Our routes to feminism were, however, characteristic of the differences between our life histories. I, because I was the mother of three girls and had myself felt discrimination in school, took notice of the movement almost as soon as it started and read everything I could find in newspapers, magazines and books about it. Ann had paid little attention to it, but converted instantly in 1973 when she came to the defense of a woman friend unfairly suspected of a murder by police who made assumptions because of sexual orientation.

At the time Ann was diagnosed with lung cancer – where the journal begins – we were six months past our celebration of the twenty-five years we'd been together. At this point, I believe I'd better explain exactly what "being together" meant. Basically, it meant we were committed to making each other a permanent part of each other's daily life – yet we didn't live in the same house. Before we turned from political activism in 1978 to putting books together, we saw each other almost every day, not only planning meetings and learning how to collaborate by writing letters and press releases together, but also learning how to make our love for one another the basis of our lives. Once we'd started working on *Feminist Quotations*, we were together every day except Sundays, sometimes at the house I shared with my daughters and my husband, sometimes where Ann lived in Morro Bay, more often at a summer cottage lent to us by a friend, and finally at the house Ann moved into in San Luis Obispo.

At the beginning of our relationship, all three of my girls, Noelle, Beth and Claire Norton, were teenagers whom I looked after almost single-handedly – that is, I helped with the homework, monitored social life, organized the household chores, and tried to be available for problems. Their father, then in his sixties (which I thought terribly old at that time), didn't interfere, except to help them get breakfast in the mornings. (To be fair, he was trying to keep an old-fashioned one-man pharmacy and drug store open in competition with chain stores and working ten or more hours every day except Sunday.) Ann gradually blended into the family. She joined my mother and the girls' boy friends at our family's ritual Saturday night dinners, became my ally in advising my daughters on papers they were writing for high school and university classes, helped me get them out of their occasional scrapes. (Nothing serious, but things like letting a car run out of gas on the freeway, or breaking a nose while driving a borrowed motor bike.) As they grew up, graduated from university, fell in love, married, had children, I sensed her presence in my relationship to them; I always felt she'd come to love them as much as I loved them.

My Husband

Though I shared a house with him, by the mid 1970s, my relationship with my husband Harvey Norton had failed emotionally. We hadn't been intimate for several years, and we weren't financial partners either. He invited no help in organizing the operation of his drug store, paid the household bills himself, and he'd refused to consider options I offered to solve the problem of the failing drug store and our lack of money. I had to argue forcefully to set aside money from the sale of a liquor license for the girls' university educations and insist, when the time came, that the store had to be closed permanently when he was having trouble meeting its bills.

Yet I couldn't bring myself to leave him. I've always had a difficult time breaking commitments and I'd come to see him as a much older brother, one I had to look out for. My initial attraction to him had been physical only, for we had no common interests. He didn't read or go to movies or date. He had done nothing except work in his father's drug store from the time he'd returned from World War II. It was as if life had stopped for him, or he wanted it to stop, because he'd lost his younger sister to tuberculosis in 1937 and his younger brother during the war, and he couldn't bear the idea of any more change. In a way he fit the stereotype of the Irish bachelor who lived his life in his parents' home. I had broken him out of it, actually seduced him from it, and so I felt that I had become responsible for him and as he aged felt I had to look after him.

Our Situation in 2001

In the 1990s, as Harvey passed his eightieth birthday, Ann and I began to make plans for our future. Ann had been suffering since 1989 from fibromyalgia as well as an autoimmune disease, Sjogren's Syndrome, that sapped her energy and caused widespread joint and muscle pain. She'd resigned from our collaborative book projects, and I didn't have the heart to pursue them without her. I started writing fiction instead, and by 1997 I'd finished two novels, one to be published in 1998 by a small California press and the other placed with a New York agent. Then Harvey fell and broke his hip, and just before publication of my first novel, I developed breast cancer. We began to recognize the perils of old age.

In late 1998 Ann decided to build an addition to her house that she thought would enable us to manage the changes coming: a large master bedroom suite with an indoor spa which she hoped would relieve her muscle and joint pain; and a studio apartment above it that I could move into if Harvey died. Or, possibly, she feared my having a recurrence of breast cancer and was providing a space where she could take care of me.

By 2001, when we learned Ann had lung cancer, I had made a practice of staying overnight at Ann's house two nights a week. These were Sundays and Thursdays, nights we'd traditionally had dinner together when we were working together. The other nights I stayed in the house I owned with Harvey, about one mile away. Our lives having settled into a satisfying rhythm, she and I were looking forward to travel, returning to England, perhaps, where we had made good friends while doing research there. Ann had developed a close online relationship with a national support group for Sjogren's Syndrome, saw old friends from Stanford from time to time, and kept in touch with several cousins and her one surviving aunt, Marge C, who lived in Montecito. I had formed a deep friendship with Diane W, a musician and former Unitarian minister, whom I met for lunch once a week for long discussions of philosophy and literature. Occasionally Diane would come to dinner at Ann's or Ann would join us at lunch, and whenever Diane had a bookshop appointment to play the Celtic harp, we'd both attend. Other good friends we shared were Anne C, whom we'd known since the days we worked for the Commission on the Status of Women, and Linna T, owner of Coalesce bookstore in Morro Bay. I also had three older sisters living in the county: Helen, Bernadette, and Jean, all of them closer to Harvey's age than to mine. Jean and her husband had moved in to San Luis Obispo from a ranch in 2000, and we had formed the habit of taking an early morning walk together three times a week.

 My daughters were all married and established in their professions. Noelle, a professor of political science, lived in Solana Beach with her husband Erwin Willis and their daughter Ellen, eleven. Beth worked for the federal government as a fisheries biologist stationed in Santa Cruz. She and her husband Chris Moore were hoping to have a child. Claire had set up a business as a speech-and-language therapist in Half Moon Bay, and she and her husband Pete Zell were parents of Ian, nine, and Annie, six. We visited each other as often as possible.

As for me, my second novel was still with an agent, I was finishing a third, and I was also working on short stories, writing and sending them out to small magazines. In odd moments, I wrote poems. I was also preparing myself to represent my family at a commemoration of Cal Poly's founding to be held in March. My father had been president of Cal Poly from 1932 until 1966 and had used his influence in the state to enable it to grow from a tiny junior college to an eminent state university; I was going to appear on a panel discussion to talk about his contribution.

Before Christmas in the year 2000, we'd both noticed Ann was getting out of breath on short walks. In January we were planning to take an overnight trip to Santa Barbara for Ann's birthday, but the shortness of breath had become alarming to me, and I insisted she visit a doctor.

I summarized the first visit to the doctor and the tests that followed in the January 25, 2001 entry. After that summary, the journal follows the life Ann and I lived from February 1, 2001 until April 1, 2003.

2
Hoping for Hope

January 25, 2001, Thursday

This, in brief, is what's been going on for a week. Last Thursday Ann's shortness of breath (increasing with activity since last December 15) became too noticeable to ignore. She went to Mission Medical, was x-rayed, was sent to pulmonary specialist Dr. James, and on Monday went through a thoracentesis. I accompanied her to the doctors, waited in waiting rooms. I also went on with two activities I felt took up too much time – making up a mailing list for Cal Poly History Day and visiting with Diane on Sunday noon – and an enjoyable one – having our birthday dinner out with Ann on Sunday evening.

My thoughts have been taken up with concern for Ann's health: with fear she may be discovered to have either a terminal illness or one that will make her a chronic invalid; and with dismay that I can't get back to work on "Manzanita" [a novel I was working on]. I also think I'm moving back into my reclusive self. Today I'm disturbed because Ann is angry about the hospital's having lost her x-rays.

Maybe people who write daily in their journals are

able to break through the ice around difficult times. Rather, the rocks surrounding difficult times.

January 31, 2001, Wednesday

Ann had a CT needle biopsy of her lungs yesterday.

French Hospital's long corridors, blue – thin carpet, long halls. I imagined myself striding carelessly, easily down the halls, as I worked against my stiffening back. Ann was at my side, at first. Then the tiny waiting room, people in line at the arched opening, the clerk seeing that papers were properly registered. A plump young woman with short, blonde, curly hair, glasses hiding astigmatic eyes, sat beside the arch. A couple was consulting the clerk. We stood until a nurse called an old man in, another nurse called another, and places to sit opened up. Ann and I sat down facing the arch.

There were nine chairs altogether in the waiting room. Padded seats, backs and arms rust and beige grey, but straight, sturdy. I opened my book, *The Constructivist Metaphor*. Ann said, "Go ahead and read – I will compose my soul in patience." We grinned, understanding words spoken to each of us by nuns long ago. My book would say we draw from our similar backgrounds to have similar understandings of the words.

When Ann was called in, I walked the long corridors again, bought a ham and cheese sandwich, a can of juice. Brought them back to the now almost empty waiting room. One woman was still there: white hair, full and pretty face, either tired or upset about what her older husband was going through or what might be discovered about her husband. She leaned on his cane and sighed, closed her eyes. After a while she left, then came back, then left again. I noticed she was wearing a handsome velveteen jacket.

Today was the waiting day, waiting for the biopsy report. All kinds of damaging fears arose – but I think I'm not really scared of terminal illness for Ann. I think we're early enough – that's why everyone was rushing to make sure it was not cancer. I fear the difficult problems of an operation and pain and long term painful non-recovery, where the chronic disease becomes worse.

February 1, 2001, Thursday

We heard from Kristy (at the pulmonologist's office) that Ann has lung cancer. Ann remained composed, asked many questions, while I wrote down answers. Tears came to my eyes, and I blinked them back, but I didn't feel frightened, nor that awful, despairing pain in my chest I've felt at times of failure. I suppose that means I'd been prepared. Every now and then I looked at Ann's face to see if she was having difficulty with the news. No sign – though now and then she wiped the corners of her eyes. Tears, like mine.

On the way out of the building in the elevator, Ann said she wasn't surprised. "My old bod's been telling me this for a while."

We went home and held each other and said we'd manage and I said, then Ann said, a lot about being together. I put my hand on her breast, the way I used to when I said she carried me there, and said, "Together, together."

We drank whiskey then and after went out to dinner, and talked about what Ann would do the next day. Making plans.

I phoned Noelle and Claire, who cried, and later Beth (who is sympathetic but scientifically willing to wait for tests), reassuring myself that the spot was operable or temporarily curable by reassuring them.

I woke several times during the night.

February 2, 2001, Friday

Ann had busied herself late last night writing email letters to her internet friends and cousins, and her rheumatologist and friend, Kay, and was at it already in the morning. Her nose was stuffy and she had been crying. We talked about plans – I'm concerned about learning how to take care of her business affairs when she's getting treatments. She wanted me to get a telephone installed upstairs, and we called and talked with Pacific Bell about it. They'll install next week. We went out to find an electric bed for her so she can stop having to find sleep sitting up in her reclining chair. We struggled through the problem of locating and getting in hand the x-rays. This is not an easy task, because the radiology departments tend to lose them in both local hospitals. We ate lunch at Hobie's because Ann wanted to go out for lunch, where we chatted mostly about present activities and a little bit about the news of the day.

Later, at home I stared into the computer monitor and felt a sudden existential dread – how we do everything to keep the possibility of death at bay, and plan as if it will never come, and suddenly, here it is. Damn it, here it is. I let myself feel it strongly, the awesomeness, the finality of death. The horror of loneliness. Pain. Suffering, in a beloved. Then moved back into necessary daily tasks.

I have to be sure I don't let myself go numb.

February 3, 2001, Saturday

When Ann and I sat down to talk after I'd arrived at her house, I mentioned that she and I may need a time to mourn our loss. To talk about what we are losing of our hopes, and grieve for those losses – then go on to our gains.

Kay [doctor, an acquaintance of Ann], came to visit Ann this afternoon. Ann met her outside and Kay showed off her new car while the dog, a short-haired border collie called Vinnie, ran here and there.

Okay, I don't like Kay because she doesn't attend to much beyond her own periphery. She's been insensitive to Ann, while trying to be friendly, and that bothers me. Seems to pity. Pity that's based on dominating? Controlling? I suppose so.

I joined them in the garden because Ann asked me to. Kay's words didn't provide hope, but then I didn't really expect them to. Effusion almost always means metastasis. That said, she drew curtains around it, saying colon cancer and brain metastasis were not likely. Unless the adenocarcinoma is on the periphery. Well, I recalled, Kristy suggested it might be... she suggested it might also be blood clots – those little spots showing around. She described the protocols now used by oncologists in treating types of lung cancer. Apparently they all use the same kind – yet new treatments may be available at research hospitals, like City of Hope.

February 4, 2001, Sunday

I took Harvey for a ride this morning, becoming tearful as I drove at the thought of not having Ann to ride with through the countryside. Harvey started tearing up too. In a few minutes though, he was speaking about my crying more for Ann than for him – meant kindly, no doubt, and it was understandable.

The rest of the day I paid bills and read email including one from Diane. She's taken us into her heart in that special way she has of nurturing and caring for people – her ministerial role – and is working hard at doing her best for us.

Noelle called, worried about people not understanding my role as care giver. Her friends, she said, aren't understanding the depth of Ann's relationship to me and our family and the consequent depth of her own grief.

February 5, 2001, Monday

This afternoon Ann drove me to the grocery store to market for her – her shortness of breath is bothering her whenever she exerts herself – and I went in and couldn't find this and didn't know what kind of that she'd prefer and time kept stretching out. I began to think of her sitting in the car, by herself, then thought of loss, loss, loss. When I came out I couldn't stop from telling her what I was feeling (trust me to be that kind of klutz) and then felt awful because I was simply adding to her burden. I mean, she could have done with some distraction, not my reminding her of the possibilities.

Dinner last night, the whole evening, normal. We rest in the past, in the routines built up over years. They give us a sense of walls around us, holding off the future. Long silence before bed, resting in peace, in peace, in peace, talking only of mantras. Dame Julian, *All will be well.*

But how Ann is I don't really know.

February 6, 2001, Tuesday

At eleven, Ann and I drove to Morro Bay to let Linna know that Ann isn't well. She took it well, without tears, but she didn't light the cigarette she'd brought out to smoke. Ann's voice shook: her hands were a bit shaky too as she told Linna. We were sitting in the garden on the bench facing the great Art Association wall, while gardeners plucked wilting cyclamen from a large bed.

Afterwards Ann and I ran errands. We tried to find a telephone answering machine at Staples, but Ann couldn't wait for someone to help us who knew anything about the machines on offer. I've noticed all day that her breathing was becoming more and more labored.

Late in the afternoon, after the MRI of her brain, (these words sound so damned invasive), while I was exercising, her aunt Marge called. Ann came in to me, needing to be hugged, and I needed to hug her when I saw that she had tears in her eyes.

It was sunset.

Then last night I finally went into Medscape and found that even if she has stage 4, there's hope – 20% at the high end.

February 7, 2001, Wednesday

The long, hard stretch has begun.

Dr. Doyle, the oncologist, a medium-sized, narrow-faced Irishman with dark blue eyes – young, early thirties, I'd guess – explained the options. Surgery, if cancer hasn't spread out of her lungs and Ann's quality of life afterwards would be all right – meaning enough lung power to make life livable. If cancer has spread, and there is a possibility since the pleural effusion isn't totally free of suspicious cells, then chemo – which he prefers, and then, at last, radiology. In the meantime, appointments, appointments.

I felt, I'm a little better now, because I'll have Ann with me for a while longer. But I began to think of the toll on Ann. She's pretty brave about her myalgia and Sjogren's pain, but to add this kind of pain on top of it may be too much for her. Then I began to think of the extra work I'm going to be into, and for a long time, and I realized that I have to work on my spirits too, find ways to be with people, to write, to get the writing out. At the same time, I'm going to have emotional problems both with Ann and with the decline Harvey may put himself into. Already he is having a difficult time hearing me – meaning he's having a hard time listening long enough to attend to what I say.

This morning I felt anxious because I promised an

article to the *Women's Press* and I haven't written it yet. Still, I had lunch with Diane today. Topic? The long, difficult journey through the dark at this point. Goblins and ogres ahead.

February 8, 2001, Thursday

Ann looked very tired today. Pale, and a slight blackening in the corner of her eye. The Webers came, and I barricaded myself in my office to work. Late in the afternoon, she walked by in the hall. Her face looked thin. I knew I couldn't bear her not to be here. I began to cry. Later, I cried again, this time sobbing. We held each other in the kitchen. I tried to stop. I said, "I'm sorry, I'm sorry."

February 9, 2001, Friday

I hoped the surgeon would be more decisive. Set things up. Get things going. Not have us drag on, waiting for phone calls, waiting. I don't think these boys look at the papers completely before they have to show up in front of the patient. At first, well, there are those nodules, then, well, with Sjogren's maybe the nodules aren't cancer. We'll have to find out. Biopsy of nodules?

Ann had more color today, but was really short of breath. I thought of how Maggie H. is supposed to have died – from lungs filling up. I wish I hadn't because when Ann turned down thoracentesis to Susan, Dr. Doyle's nurse, I'd hoped she'd take the opportunity. She doesn't feel it has helped her. I didn't tell her I hoped she'd do it today, because she is tired and must drive herself to Morro Bay to have her hair cut. But I did remind her of Maggie. Why? Because I didn't want her to pooh-pooh it if she really starts to drown.

I'm tense, but not tearful.

Some of the tension is from doctors' enclosed offices and hard chairs. When we left Dr. Oscar's (the surgeon) office we drove down to Santa Maria so Ann could talk to Dr. Henry [her gastroenterologist]. She was driving, while I twisted my hands between my knees.

"Don't fret," Ann said.

I asked her if she'd slept.

"I took a sleeping pill."

"Were you fretting? Or making plans?"

"I don't fret. I feel there's no point. There's nothing I can do about things. They're out of my hands. So I'm making plans. Trying to take care of people."

"I'll be all right."

"I can't overburden you."

"We'll take care of the hard things as they come up," I assured her.

I meditated on the feeling of having things in your body out of control and having to let life just take its course.

February 10, 2001, Saturday

Late in the afternoon I showed Ann the article for *The Women's Press*. I'd rewritten it as if she'd co-authored it. She demurred, briefly, but I said I wanted her to sign it for sentimental reasons, and she accepted that. We talked then about the plans – how I'd ask the children to take Harvey for the time immediately following her return home, if she has surgery. How I'd ask them to take turns coming down on a couple of weekends a month (one each) if she has chemo that debilitates her so much it puts a burden on me to take care of two households at once. I spoke of the need to teach me the ropes with her bills, and accountants Jane, and Mary and the lot. We decided we'd try to spend some time Monday afternoon.

Ann's difficulty breathing disappeared as she had a drink of whiskey. Is she just terribly tense?

I drank too much wine at dinner. The turkey I cooked turned out very well – a mixture of poultry roast and grill and Spice Hunter's herbs and butter. About equal with the spices. Brahms on the CD player, the lamp mellow on the wooden table – Harvey out to dinner – and Ann drinking a bit too much, but why not, since it made her feel better. We sat close together and watched a British comedy . . ." "Keeping Up Appearances," and Ann laughed.

February 11, 2001, Sunday

Inevitably, because I was home [meaning the house I shared with Harvey], waves of sadness, regret, fear swept over me. Music does it. In some ways it's an evasion of the reality, which is going to be at first total blackness. A sense of never getting out of where I bound myself. That is not nostalgia, regret, or even fear. It is enclosure. These last years have been terribly hard because of Ann's struggle with Sjogren's. I wish they hadn't been. I kept trying to bring peace and security into the relationship through slowness and steadiness, and slowness got us only tiny, tiny moments.

February 12, 2001, Monday

Yesterday morning. Rain during the night. Lightning on the other side of Bishop's Peak. I drove Ann to French at 8:30 and waited in the outpatient/lab waiting room until almost eleven while she had a CT scan of her abdomen. I was still reading *The Constructivist Metaphor* but I spent as much time watching the people. There was a woman whose husband's name was Loren; the paper they had in hand suggested a mammogram. She laughed out loud about it. I couldn't see if he was embarrassed or not. He was bald, sat upright. A son and his father, father bent over crutches, obviously hardly able to dress himself; son upright, a small compact man, black short-cropped curly hair, green sweat shirt, jeans that fit him the way jeans are supposed to fit, not tight but with a few inches to spare. A father, perhaps forty, and his teenage daughter, wearing a knit cap to hide her baldness. Her face looked as if she's had prednisone, too.

In the afternoon Ann and I worked on her bookkeeping software. During the work, a call came from the radiation/oncologist's office, and Ann became tense, her back stiffening. I believed it was a report on the CT scan, and became fearful myself. She admitted when she got off the phone that she was upset. Neither of us seemed to be able to shake the feeling. I was reluctant to go home, and when I did, was irritable. The irritability grew into serious pain, and I called Ann to see how she was. We agreed that we're both upset, and next time we'll talk with each other about how to cope with that – by planning, by getting ready for all eventualities. We told each other we were "catastrophizing." Nonsense. How can a lung cancer patient and her beloved catastrophize?

February 13, 2001, Tuesday

Rain. We saw Dr. Doyle, who told us the surgeon does not think Ann's a good candidate for surgery because of the pleural effusion, first of all, and second because – maybe – too much of lung might have to come out. I asked about the cytology of the pleural effusion. He said that the pathologists calling cells "atypical" plus the two clusters CEA – whatever that means – says probably the cells were thrown off from adenomatous carcinoma. The atypical cells are characteristic, he said. He presented chemo to Ann as a benign process, possibly successful for a long period of time. She felt encouraged. I don't, and don't want to tell her. Though it's true, as long as she feels okay about things, I can get along. It's when she is upset and frightened and hurt that I become troubled. I told her that if the cytology report on the second thoracentesis is no more definite than the first we should get a second opinion.

After Dr. Doyle, we drove through rainy streets to French, where the thoracentesis was done. Dr. Ferrana – handsome, dark hair. Short. Polite, careful. He wanted to do the job himself. We waited in the hospital until they were certain Ann's lung wouldn't collapse, eating lunch there, and then went on errands.

February 14, 2001, Wednesday

I have just about decided I'm not going to let these possibly last few days of Ann's being in reasonably good shape go by; I'm going to leave 67 Benton now and stay in my upstairs apartment at Ann's.

I told Harvey that I would be staying at Ann's for a while, but coming in and out at home. Then I left, walking past the camellia, feeling I'm leaving. I'm leaving. Though I've gone away a hundred times, this time I felt, I'm leaving. Nothing's going to be the same again, is what I think I was feeling. I worried a bit about how this was going to affect Harvey, and then realized *I've got to take care of myself at this point.*

February 17, 2001, Saturday

Claire is probably coming down next weekend, possibly without kids, though I said they would entertain Harvey and I would love to see them myself – if I don't need other kinds of help. At 11:30 Ann and I started out to look for some new sweats for her to wear, easy to get in and out of, mostly for chemo, but also for x-rays and so forth. We parked at Mervyn's, Ann telling me she felt not quite well. In Mervyn's we walked not far, and she was out of breath, said we had to leave, she felt queasy. Her face was flushed pink, I wondered whether that was a symptom of lack of oxygen, remembering my sister Jean telling me that there are two skin colors –

blue or grey and pink – in people without oxygen. Ann stood outside while I got the car. She told me it's her stomach, not lack of air.

Later, I was closing the garage door behind me as I returned to my office. I've been carrying cans, bottles, empties out to the blue recycling bin, which sits before flowers . . . there's netting down under an overhang where bats have dropped their prey, behind the netting a door into a storage closet. I don't know what's in the closet; I wonder if I should know. To the left of the bin are stacks of logs, unused for several winters now. Dry, waiting for cremation. I have lunch and breakfast groceries to carry upstairs to my apartment. Water to bring inside. Housekeeping, that's all I let myself think about. What must be done, will have to be done, will have to be accomplished. Not what is going to happen. We're rushing into this, eyes deliberately closed. Or sidling in, waiting for doctors to open doors. A long corridor door after door, and we walk, thinking only about the steps we're taking, the pattern in the carpet, the weariness in our feet, the occasional wish for a window. One small step after the other.

Solution to anxiety: constant work that gives no time for thought. Reassuring.

February 18, 2001, Sunday

The biggest struggle is conflict about Harvey, feeling sorry for him. Saturday night, Ann and I discussed my feelings of pity for him. "Even I feel sorry for him," she said.

"It's ourselves we should feel sorry for," I said. We

agreed we had been well-trained by our culture to put others first.

I took him to Avila in the morning and we walked on the pier. I told him again how serious Ann's situation is. I promised myself I'd try not to criticize when I'm at Benton Way [where he now lived without me]. Then I left at 3 p.m. after getting our income tax information together.

Ann was feeling strong enough when I arrived to go shopping for the sweats she wanted at Gottchalks, though I had to pull her out for fear she'd get too tired. We drove to Morro Bay, where she picked out two large crabs, later telling me why to pick large – they don't get overcooked. We went on to Sandy's to buy wine, where she chose Frog's Leap Sauvignon Blanc. Butter, French bread at Scolari's. She won't be able to eat and drink good foods, she's afraid, and is enjoying a "last meal," she said. Later, I fell asleep over Monty Python. Later still, we laughed and laughed at crab/crabs, quail/quails. Decided the singular or plural may have to do with how many you can get on a plate. She told me the story of how she and a Stanford friend had to use an outhouse on the way down to Pasadena when they were undergraduates and both got a case of crabs.

February 20, 2001, Tuesday

First day of chemotherapy and the day when we discover what the cytology report on the pleural effusion tells us. I didn't sleep soundly last night, waking up every hour or so. I waited for Noelle to call. I felt alone, thought of

Ann feeling alone. I told Noelle how people surrounded my mother when my father had his operation, and now it's only me.

Dr. Doyle was reassuring about the chemo. Made it sound much more restful than surgery – but I still wanted that second opinion because the cytology report is "not diagnostic." (When Doyle speaks of surgeons as aggressive, I do know what he means, but on the other hand – is he an aggressive oncologist, a true believer in his own medicines, his own ability to save? I was not convinced that the surgeon we consulted said definitely "no." Should Ann have called back, I wonder? Did he and Doyle decide no surgery? Why?) But Ann wanted to start the chemotherapy. They talked for some time about whether to start or not. I suggested that chemo might break down Ann's health so that she really might not be eligible for surgery. He seemed to think that's possible, but not probable, partly because when people lose ground with chemo it's often that the cancer is not shrinking. Ann wanted to begin – later she told me she was petrified that the experience would be too difficult to deal with. I remembered an email friend who's been filling her head with need for preparation – projectile vomiting, diarrhea you can't stop or can't get to the bathroom in time for – and wondered whether this kind of preparation might not be cruel, rather like the tales women tell each other about difficult births.

But Ann was okay. She drank a juice and protein drink for lunch and ate chicken and rice and fruit for dinner.

February 21, 2001, Wednesday

On Longing – I have to buy that book and read it again. But I believe that when I return to Benton Way and visit my room, I walk into all the old stories Ann and I constructed about our lives. I want them to be true. I long for them to be true.

Today when I returned to Ann's after my afternoon trip to Benton Way, she was suffering from burning face and eyes. Her mouth's becoming sore. Suddenly the sense of "it hasn't really happened" or "we're going to cure this somehow" disappeared, and I was fearful again. Resentful of the way things happen.

Only after dinner did I think of popsicles.

February 22, 2001, Thursday

Claire arrived at three. I went to greet her at Benton Way, hugged the children, missed them even while hugging them. Ian was already at work drawing cartoons. Annie asked me where she's going to sleep, and I showed her the futon and then my bed, and we discussed the possibilities. She wanted to sleep where Ian sleeps, she said. I told Claire my fears and worries. She wants to help out in physical ways; I assured her again and again taking Harvey off my mind for a few days was a boon beyond momentary gratitude. I have to thank heavens for the family sensibility my children have and the love they've nurtured.

At six-thirty, I went off to a poetry reading at Coalesce. I didn't want to go because I had to abandon Ann for an evening. Sometimes I think that's all we have left, our constant presence for each other. I wore my black pants, red sweater. Linna sat at the desk in the quiet bookstore. She was stunned when seeing me by myself. I wondered what she was thinking – I have abandoned Ann? Surely not. That I've come to ask for help, maybe. I told her I'd come to the reading. We talked about Ann. She offered help. Love. I received it, saying hold on, there's more to come. More to come that we don't know anything about.

The poets weren't bad. But the topics troubled me: no real rebellion, hatred, fear. Just nice thoughts about sad, lonely, pleasant, interesting things and relationships. I left after having coffee and a cookie. No one to talk to. Nice man said thanks for coming. On the way out I told Linna I was staying at Ann's most of the time. We hugged.

February 23, 2001, Friday

Ann woke up at 4:30, she said as we drove to Santa Maria to consult a second surgeon. Severe stomach ache, heartburn. Gas. Maybe the pyloric sphincter spasming. Rain terrible.

The doctor was obviously new to this office. There were two names either side of the desk, but not his. The waiting room was shabby, the chairs old, and not many of them. Paintings and posters on the wall were surreal, but not good surreal. Subdued colors, stupid combinations. After waiting half an hour, Ann and I were led into an examining room. One chair, one stool, and the table. Ann chose the stool to sit on, and after half-an-hour of my frequent suggestions we exchanged.

We waited another half-an-hour, assured frequently by an assistant that the doctor was on his way, he'd been in surgery here in the same building.

At last he stuck his head in the door. Boyish locks, thinning – just over his ears, dark brown. Wide blue eyes. Thin narrow face, a small man.

When all of him finally came in, he commented that it's a complex case. He has checked it briefly – but obviously hasn't seen all the papers, especially the one saying the pleural effusion is non-diagnostic. He didn't know about the nodules in the right lung. He hadn't seen that CT scan – the lost one.

What he did say is that a pleural effusion automatically stages at 3-B. Or worse. That only 10% of 3-B's live more than two years after surgery. He discussed the way the surgery could be done. But he was basically against it. Said chemo will do as well, in answer to my question. He promised to discuss the case with a group that meets at Sierra Vista in San Luis and get a few more opinions. If it's okay.

Ann teared up on the way out of the parking lot. Then my tears started. I asked her whether she had known those statistics.

"Not really, but subliminally, that's what I've been expecting."

February 25, 2001, Sunday

Ann forwarded a letter from Kay to me, suggesting other surgeons, other places like teaching hospitals and City of Hope. Kay doesn't think much of the surgeon we just saw, but prefers his office mate, an old Navy doctor. I said damn when I read the letter, and Ann's tears began again. She said she was afraid of letting me down by not pursuing aggressive tactics. I didn't know what to say, except to reassure her that I don't want her to put herself through the pain and anguish and difficulty of surgery for nothing but a recurrence. I let her know I was aware of the slim chances from reading the internet material.

All of today Ann spent working on her will/trust for the benefit of the lawyer she was going to see tomorrow. And on letters to people who don't have email.

February 26, 2001, Monday

Ann's mouth has been getting worse, as bad as it's ever been, she said. In the early evening, when she told me this and added that she didn't want to eat, I felt a surge of 'What do I do now? I have to make her better, have to.' It came as a kind of panic for me – I have to hold up the sky. (What an image! I've used the metaphor before, but never with a clear sense of the bent over, over-burdened, and now old, woman.) I have to let go, I have to allow her to make the decisions, I have to accept what she tells me. Most important, I have to refuse to become frightened. What happens, happens.

I did fix a liquid plus yogurt plus soft fruit for her and we ate in the ritual way, though without music.

February 27, 2001, Tuesday

Because Ann felt better and better as the day went on– even able to eat her dinner, I calmed down, feeling almost as if nothing was going on. I do think about ominous things – what if chemo doesn't work at all? What if within a few days the difficulty breathing returns? But I can't get myself to believe the possibilities emotionally.

I wonder sometimes whether when Ann feels comfortable she wishes I were somewhere else. The other presence in the evening, someone you might be cross with because you feel cross, but you cannot be. Yesterday she blamed me for leaving doors open. "Didn't," I said. "Someone else must have."

March 1, 2001, Thursday

This morning Ann said she woke up feeling depressed, and in our once or twice meetings in the kitchen, she was irritable. She apologized, and I said, and meant it, "Think nothing of it."

Her cousin Addie was coming, and she was having trouble finding the ring that had belonged to her grandmother, for whom Addie was named, so she could give it to her. Eventually she did find it. She also felt strong enough to clean out the closet where the stereo is kept so that the television people could get into it, if need be

In the evening, the television that was installed will not play VCRs. Ann was angry, in the same way she was with the computer four years ago. But I sensed a deeper anger.

"Yes, deeper," she said. "I don't have time for things to go wrong."

March 3, 2001, Saturday

Ann felt like going out today. She'd looked into the Friday *Ticket* and mentioned an orchid show. My heart sank – I have postponed any productive work – did nothing much yesterday. I'd planned to pick up my shoes, buy a belt, write bills, wash clothes, and get groceries, prepare the Saturday night dinner for Harvey. I hesitated. Ann noticed, and said, "Let's not."

I thought, but Ann has so few days, how can I deprive her, just because I want to make up for doing nothing much yesterday? I promised to go to the orchid show, reflecting that I'm too quiet with her these days. So much of my thought is taken up with concern about her becoming ill again with chemotherapy, I can think of nothing to suggest for entertainment.

We arrived at the orchid show in the late morning, admired the cymbidiums, the tiny delicate yellow flowers, the variegated ones – the flowers that look like someone's wallpaper or someone's LSD dream. Then to Trader Joe's up on the hill, where Ann enjoyed herself going about and buying things. Then lunch at Steamers' where she ate an enormous hamburger and had two drinks of gin and tonic while we talked and watched surfers.

Later, after fixing dinner for Harvey at Benton Way, I told her about the effect of the old routine on me. She didn't understand right at first, but did after I made a couple of tries. The old routine of fixing Saturday night dinner for the three of us makes me yearn for that time again. "The whole world has shifted," I said, "and when I'm in the new world, I can live with it; but when I visit the old one, I cry because the old world's story has ended. Things we planned in that old world have vanished."

Then should we not plan far ahead? I ask myself. But we tried not planning ahead once, long ago, and if we'd kept on doing that – that is, never making plans – but instead, for example, had never made the addition to her house – we'd have a hard time being together now.

March 7, 2001, Wednesday

Most of the day I spent preparing for the panel discussion set up for March 8th. [This was part of the commemoration of Cal Poly's founding in 1901. I represented the McPhee family.] I read Moody's book [about my father], read the interview I did with Dad. At noon, I grocery shopped for me and Ann. Picked up clothes at Benton Way.

Noelle arrived at Benton Way in the evening. She couldn't get my computer on and needed to do some work. I visited both to see to the computer and see Ellen. I miss her. I miss seeing more of her.

I found myself on the edge of tears all day.

March 8, 2001, Thursday

All day for me aimed at the afternoon program. Beth and Chris helped out by keeping me busy – especially after the curve thrown by Dan K., chair of the discussion, who wasn't clear about how the program would go.

Anne C brought Ann – Anne swinging the car around in a wild u-turn right in front of the McPhee Student Union, stopping in front of the Little Theater, Ann looking small, sunk into the deep seats. She walked up the slope to the theater okay. Dan K. came out to talk to her, standing among the empty seats. After a while, Dan and I went into a green room [back stage], where we sat by ourselves for a while. Dan told me of all his friends dying of cancer. I told him how it's hard to talk with Ann sometimes, because it's a constant undercurrent in my thoughts, and I don't want her to have to dwell on these thoughts all the time. He said, wisely, "It's in her thoughts too. Why not just put it out there."

The panel was good. Beth had told me the colors I wore were just right – a Victorian stage set was our background, for some Gothic comedy called "I Hate Hamlet." I didn't realize that I was going to do it – but I did! I did! I interrupted Bob Kennedy [president of Cal Poly after my father, and retired now.] My claque, daughters and sisters and husbands, plus Anne and Ann, sitting in front rows, all nodded. Afterwards even Bob's daughter said it was a good thing or he would have gone on and on. Which I sort of knew.

Many many congratulations afterwards, from people who knew me or knew my father.

I have a sense of myself wandering in a crowd of people, by myself but known to all, and all want to talk with me. Moment of triumph. Politics, power. Love, community. One is by oneself at a time like this, I'm aware.

But I worry about Ann. She left me a note – "Couldn't have done better," she wrote. Plus a brief letter saying the doctor had called. His protocol agreed upon. Two months of chemo, then more CT scans, and maybe surgery.

It took me a long time to calm down, yet at the same time I was feeling good about the fact that doctors have said, okay, this is what we do. Whether it works or not, still, this is the best we can do.

March 9, 2001, Friday

After talking with Claire and Pete at Benton Way, I went to Julie's [my younger sister] hotel. What's important is that Julie obviously wanted to spend time talking with me, expressing support. She was able to respond as someone who has been with a cancer victim who thought he was dying – Bill, her husband. (He bought a suit to be laid out in, he was so convinced he was going to die.) We sat in an alcove of the Quality Suites lobby in the right angle of a pair of blue-green couches. Dark eyes, dark hair, dark green jacket: "I felt panic at the thought of his illness and death, fear and loneliness."

I was surprised. "That means your bond with Bill still exists."

She didn't know what I meant, and I had to suppress telling her how it's probably been thirty years since I would have felt that about Harvey's illness. Instead, I compared it with how I feel about the possibility of losing Ann. "Yes, panic and an unimaginable isolation," I said.

March 12, 2001, Monday

Not much sleep for Ann last night. She read until midnight and then woke at 5. She was tired, she said, but was interested in Kay's having found a clinical trial that looks worthwhile: Iressa. She's heard that they want to start trying it out on lung cancer patients.

Otherwise an ordinary day with chores. Groceries. Ann's wash. Thank you note to Dr. Baker [the president of Cal Poly, who had hosted dinner], bills paid. Laughter with Linna over Ann's difficulties with Diane.

What was different about this day is that when I went to Benton Way to get the stew going for Harvey, he thought I was staying.

"You stay here Monday nights," he said.

I looked at him. "I haven't for a month."

"I'm worried about my blood pressure," he said.

The weekend had brought peace for me, with Beth and Noelle around, but suddenly there I was, fearful of his making himself sick.

March 13, 2001, Tuesday

This morning Ann leaned her stomach against the kitchen counter. She was wearing her black sweat suit, the jacket zipper open slightly at the top, a white t-shirt showing. Her face also was white. She looked at me, then down at the sink, her mouth a straight line. "My hair is falling out," she said. She took a handful of pills. "I've seen it on the pillowcase, but this morning I ran the comb through it and pulled out a wad."

I wasn't alert to her feelings. I thought, well, this was expected. She finished swallowing the handful of pills.

"How do you feel?" I asked. Not because I don't know, but because I wanted her to tell me.

"How do you think," she answered, shrugging.

I put my arms around her. "You'll be just as beautiful as ever. I wonder how you'll look in a turban."

Waiting for the doctor, we saw brochures with styles of hats, turbans and wigs in them. Bras and breasts, too. We went through a couple, and she laughed as I urged a wig on her. "Maybe it's because my mother always wanted my father to wear a toupee," I said. "Maybe I'd like to see you with red hair again. Maybe I'd like to wear one myself. I wouldn't have to worry about what to do with my hair, then."

When the doctor came in, they discussed Ann's pulmonary function test, the protocol suggested by the Santa Maria doctors. Chemo, then CT after two months, Dr. Doyle agreed. He discussed the change in chemo: gemcitibine only this time, because the navalbine may have caused the severe mouth sores. Next time gemcitibine plus carboplatin and then two weeks off. He still didn't seem to have decided for sure how to deal with this case. Maybe we'll do it this way. And then he shifted, maybe that way. I had to listen carefully to catch what he finally decided. I think, this time, it's the two chemos, then a week or two weeks off.

What is this day, in the series of days? A day of denial. A day when nothing bad is ever going to happen. I'm becoming accustomed to the non-future because I'm mildly depressed. The non-future is now, maybe.

Maybe I'm already in it. I want to reach outside this closed world.

Don't know why I call it a closed world. Because we can't get out? Or the ways out are not comfortable options – blank surfaces. How does place in the world affect vision of it? Constant problem of stories/myths. Ann and I are alone and in trouble. In a bog – the quicksand metaphor – with me trying to be present, be helpful when it's necessary. In a desert without water, but I'm stronger. Images of adventure stories pour in now, from the movies, comrade trying to help comrade. The comrade I play is desperate to help and cannot. No sense of peace in this comrade. Though we search the greater community for help – the medical community, the community of friends and relatives – it still comes down to the two of us, and finally, to each of us separately. Candles. I have on the table upstairs two candles we burned at New Years'. Ellen made them for me, and Ann got a pair of wooden candle holders, and we burned one, all the way to the bottom. The second is left standing.

March 14, 2001, Wednesday

This morning Ann was up before I came downstairs. "You should look at my comb to see the hairs that have come out."

Later, after I returned from checking on Harvey she said: "When will you learn to close the hall door?"

Offended (and I still feel offended, distant, feel a lack of concern for me), I objected quietly: "I almost always remember to shut the door. This time I didn't because

I didn't know the heater was on. What I wish you'd said was 'You didn't notice we needed to keep the door shut this morning.'"

I wanted her to apologize, to thank me, to say she couldn't get along without me. I've closed my own door, the door to my office. I feel like shutting myself off. I need to work through ways of handling her irritability, my response. I will just quietly point it out, when I notice it. I will withdraw as best I can. I will try to be brave.

March 15, 2001, Thursday

I am aware that my father's life has been haunting me the last couple of weeks. Obvious. But it has a mysterious quality. I seem to return to my youth, feel that I have years and years to live, yet I'm aware that I'm wrong in thinking that I have so much in the future. So in a way, I'm stretching out, expanding my present into the future more than I usually do. I'm also a little afraid to retreat to my youth. It beckons me, but the mix of then with now is painful as well as satisfying.

Before dinner I paged through Ann's history of Mayfield, the one written by Ave Bortz. Photos of Ann as a young girl – long hair, a little plump, the basic classiness of her face not yet established. I am far away from that child. I have a hard time connecting the Ann I know with her.

March 16, 2001, Friday

Because Ann was still troubled by the gradual loss of

her hair. I suggested we go up to the American Cancer Society – or call – to get a turban or hat today, if they have any. Or send for some today, if they didn't.

I added that they warn cancer patients about feeling worse than they thought they'd feel about the loss of hair. That's why they suggest shaving it off and buying a wig right away.

She felt vigorous enough to go outside and pick up the recycle barrel knocked over by the garbage company truck, then to call and complain to the garbage company.

By evening, though, she didn't feel at all well, as if she had the flu, she said. She wasn't hungry, but ate soup and toast. After dinner she read, but I thought she was worried. I'll try to assure her I'm with her, and concentrate on being in sync with, calming. It's practice. I have to work on it for the future. We go to bed at 9.

March 17, 2001, Saturday

Life becomes possible, again, with the thought that chemo may be bearable, if you can only wait until the end of the week.

March 18, 2001, Sunday

In the evening our conversation hit a rough spot. I pronounced opinions on an article Ann pointed out to me. The writer was conflating liberals' desire to preserve personal privacy from invasion with conservatives' desire to preserve invasion of individual rights from governmental interference. I pontificated, expressing anger. Ann wasn't ready for this; I was acting as if she disagreed with me. It robbed her of energy. I wasn't being gentle. Later, she referred to a shot put champion, a high school girl, as a monster. I corrected her, gently, but she didn't want to be corrected. What can I do about this? Not to respond is an invasion of our relationship; I shouldn't hide my reactions because of their effect upon her.

This problem is going to grow more troublesome. As long as I can, I must keep my honesty.

Later, when we held each other against the world waves, she said, "I'm afraid taking care of me is too much for you."

It isn't. It isn't. Not taking care of you would be too much, I thought.

March 20, 2001, Tuesday

This was supposed to be a chemo day, but Ann's platelet count was too low and Dr. Doyle postponed until Friday, if it's okay then. There's a strange method of determining blood count level. Ann has her blood drawn in the lab, a courier takes that sample directly to the hospital for analysis, and the results are returned within half an hour. We were talking with the doctor – I was trying to determine what he meant about giving Ann anti-biotics if she ran a fever, since she was already running one – how high – and he was not giving a direct answer, or at least his direct answer wasn't ours – when the results of the blood test came in. I guess carboplatin lowers platelet count so can't be given if the level is low.

Later that afternoon we drove out to Morro Bay together, where Fran clipped Ann's hair close to her head. She looks not bad – the strength of her features still attractive. On the way home we stopped to get a movie – a very bad comedy, it turned out. At bed time, Ann confessed she was made anxious by the irregularity of the chemo infusions.

I feel anxious too, but because of what may come as a result of not having chemo. And I can't tell Ann that. That's the separation between us, I think.

March 22, 2001 Thursday

Up at 4:40 to get Harvey to the train station for his visit to Noelle. Returned and sat in living room, thinking about isolation. Ann was having a good day for her. She cooked dinner – her special chicken recipe. We fooled around with the television set. Watched a disgusting documentary on prostitutes: really on the edge of pornographic: but I wanted to know what the life is like, what it is that attracts; what is the shadow side of our entertainment world.

The shadow side of entertainment. Perversion of connection.

We told stories about dragons before we slept.

March 24, 2001, Saturday

Ann had a few sores in her mouth, but nothing like the ones she got when given navalbine. She had energy this afternoon, and she not only drove me to the market, she came in with me and pushed the basket. At dinner, she advised the cook, fixed the asparagus. She remained alert and happy all through "Wit." Surprisingly, the story of a woman dying of cancer didn't frighten or depress her, nor did it me. I know that I'm in a form of denial, where the day to day activities overwhelm thoughts of the future. I think, what will I do when Ann is suffering with pain or severe discomfort? And I have no answers and no feelings about answers except a vague disquiet: am I going to be able to cope easily and well?

I don't know what Ann thinks about in the darkness. I trust her not to keep too much from me, but perhaps I shouldn't. Have we cried all our tears?

March 25, 2001, Sunday

This was a weak day, a tired day, a slow day – and a day when Ann's mouth hurt a little more and her stomach cramped.

I meditated after lunch and decided that's the time to work on the practice.

In the afternoon I was happy to read, content that Ann was content to be tired and sleep. Only mildly worried when she had a slight fever around dinner time.

I wonder if I'm going to feel restless as the months go on and the confinement increases. I'm not restless now. Does restlessness come when you're not convinced of the seriousness of what you're undergoing?

March 26, 2001, Monday

This, the fourth day after chemo, has been Ann's worst

day: a pattern, now, after the third infusion. As the day progressed, Ann became more tired, less energetic. At first she was willing to consider a trip to view wildflowers, but by late morning, she knew she couldn't.

Just before dinner we had a short discussion of Margaret Atwood and the class society she's describing in a small Canadian company town [in *The Blind Assassin*]. We both mentioned other books, American and Canadian of that period and the difference, if there is one, from books of English small towns. (Ann has been reading one: less tension about class.) Then we spoke of the woman who brought up the two girls. I believed Atwood was satirizing her and in doing so demonstrating scorn for the class. Ann thought it a naturalistic description. We stopped talking at that point, because Ann didn't want to go on. It felt too much like an argument to her, I think.

After dinner and putting dishes in the dish washer, I picked up Harvey at the train station and sat with him for a while before returning here. Ann said she's becoming spoiled: she misses my presence at night terribly.

March 27, 2001, Tuesday

After lunch I meditated. Shortly after one, I drove Ann out Highway 58 to see the wildflowers Diane raved about from her Sunday excursion. One solid bank of shooting stars. Baby blue eyes in the grass on the ungated part of the Sinton property. Lupine along the road, some phlox, some bright Indian warrior. Mustard, gold fields. Tidy tips. Sprawl. I noticed for the first time that Highway 58 is numbering the driveways. Property for sale near Creston.

Ann was very tired by six o'clock. She seemed short of breath. We're worried about the effusion returning. But don't say much.

March 29, 2001, Thursday

I've been listening to tapes by Weil on healing practices. So far nothing new. Discussion of food at length and health foods, like ginger and garlic. Believes the body wants to heal itself. Healing may not mean end of disease, but feeling whole in the body.

My sister Jean's birthday this weekend. Before I left to have lunch with her and my sisters Helen and Bernadette, Ann told me she was depressed. I guess I asked because I saw the grim expression on her face and thought I noticed tears in the corners of her eyes. I stopped, offered not to go, wondered privately whether it was because I was leaving her at lunch time again that she was upset. I reviewed notes in the care givers' book about depression. I sat down with her again before I left. I held her hand. I spoke about needing to get out. I promised that if no chemo Friday we might go out to lunch. I said if she does have chemo, then we'll have lunch out next week. When I returned, she was doubly upset because an earring she wore with her scarf had disappeared, fallen from an old ash tray she keeps on the chest near the heater. I helped her look for it, lying on the floor, searching with a flashlight, until she told me no, stop, and we went out on errands – library, stationer's, the drug store.

March 30, 2001, Friday

This morning Ann's tension was just under control. Yet we smiled, we joked. I didn't believe she was going to have chemo today, so I was okay. But Ann was probably concerned about her x-ray, fearful the effusion was back. I wasn't, somehow, believing that the effusion can be taken care of and that its reappearance doesn't mean failure of the tumor to shrink. I guess I'm not thinking from Ann's point of view – the process of thoracentesis hasn't been pleasant.

I let Ann off in the long, grey tunnel-like parking lot outside the lab, the white Presbyterian church building on one side and the varnished wooden structure on the other – pine trees here and there. You enter the waiting room up another tunnel that leads abruptly into waiting rooms and offices.

For almost an hour I waited in the oncology waiting room, sometimes reading, occasionally observing patients. Most come with partners. Sometimes I can't tell who's the patient – the companion looks older. A mother? I ask myself. A person who has suffered from cancer and is providing support? When Ann arrived, she was angry: the x-ray needed in order to compare today's x-ray with January 18th's is missing. All x-rays, they've discovered, are at Marian Medical center in Santa Maria.

We spent some time with Dr. Doyle discussing what a cycle is (two shots of drugs, one week apart) and the fact that Ann has sort of had two cycles, so that the next one will be her third. The doctor believes she's in good shape. She hasn't lost weight since the last time she was weighed and her platelet count is up from 103 to 147, even though she had chemo the previous Friday. He plans to start carboplatin in combination with gemcitibine in a couple of weeks – they decide on April 10. After two cycles like that – which would take us to the end of May – they'll CT scan and then consider the nodules in the right lung. If they haven't shrunk, then possibly radiation or surgery for the central tumor.

We were happy things had been explained, we both said. Then we had a happy lunch at 1865 considering trips for next week.

I continue to feel settled on the wrong side of reality. Now what do I mean by that? I keep thinking – actually feeling – that the way we are now is the way we always were and always will be. Isn't this the way I felt when the children were small? Each day was the same as the preceding day, you just try to keep on living, living, living. Time as the passage of years stays still. Only now, it's the passage of months. The days pass, because you have to count chemo, etc., but the month – it's still February to me.

April 1, 2001, Sunday

At bedtime Ann was tense and wide awake. I asked her where she would be if she could choose, and she began to think of traveling. I want to meditate on a place, I explained, and asked her to pick just one moment, even to naming the time of day. I reminded her of the walk over the Thames. She had seen much more than I – she remembered St. Paul's against the moon, and I couldn't visualize it. Finally at 11 when I left her – she was still excited.

April 2, 2001, Monday

This afternoon I shopped at two grocery stores, went to the post office, and the cleaners.

When I arrived at Harvey's, he rushed to tell me how he fell and couldn't get up. To myself I said, I can't cope with this. He's piling on responsibility, threatening me. Yet all he wants is to be first in someone's mind, a privilege few of us have at the end. Maybe, in the long view, none of us has that privilege, because we all tire of responsibility, even I do for Ann. It's rare, but just enough to know that it's going to be hard for me when it's hard for her. I have to remember that – we're sharing this terrible journey.

At night, lying close to Ann, I thought about how our whole relationship has been one of wanting to be closer, one of us always having to leave. Always. What would it have been like if no one had to leave, ever.

April 3, 2001, Tuesday

We left at five to meet the nuns, Ginny and her friend Elizabeth at the Texaco station on Los Osos Valley Road. Ann dressed in black slacks, a dark red – almost black – silk turtleneck, and a black velour top. With the chain bearing the women's symbol around her neck and her close cut hair, she looked like a figure from a Webster tragedy. Or a nun. Or both.

We decided on the way that I would ride with whoever

is driving the nuns' car. At the gas station, I climbed in with Elizabeth, who was wearing a long beige coat and carrying a silk scarf. I noticed her glasses, her forward ruff of hair, the bland but lively expression on her face. Her small mouth pulls in upon itself, so that when she talks, there's a sense of lisping.

Elizabeth half asked, half stated, "She's in remission now?"

I answered, "No, she had a fever of 101.5 on Sunday. She gets very tired."

Driving down Los Osos Valley road toward Ann's house, we discussed her treatment. Elizabeth has been seeing Ginny's emails from Ann. I described the chemo cycles. We discussed the prognosis, the statistics. Just as we arrived at the house, Elizabeth asked how her spirits were.

"Hard to tell. We have talked about how she felt when we thought I might be in serious trouble with breast cancer but . . ."

Then we considered the wall between cancer patients and others. I said I tried to keep that wall away.

Later, at dinner, the four of us shared our impressions of "Wit," the Emma Thompson HBO movie, which Elizabeth had seen as a play. She mentioned the play's use of the resurrection theme at the end.

Ann talked and talked. It's her old way of talking, and I was seeing it as an aberration, I'm afraid. I kept thinking she was overexcited. I asked her after the nuns had left, and she described how happy and relaxed she was, the first time in months.

April 5, 2001, Thursday

When we both went into the kitchen, Ann saw some plastic containers that I hadn't taken to the recycle bin last night. I was about to take them out, when she thought of emptying a file drawer in the cabinet in my office to make more room for my papers. I watched her pull folders from the drawer. "Aren't you going to look at them?" I asked.

"No. They're mostly school stuff. But they might have letters or writings in them. I don't want to keep letters – and" – as I started to flip through a file – "I don't want you to look through them."

I objected, but did as she wished.

Later, sitting with her in the living room, I said, "but letters or journals?"

"I don't want you to spend the rest of your life moping over my letters."

April 9, 2001, Monday

Another good day. Lunch in Paso. Rode back over Highway 46. Dark clouds, sun, on parts of the highway, making the damp pavement steam, almost thick as fog in one place.

I myself feel rushed. Partly because I'm beginning to make my writing and reading important instead of focusing on enjoying the moments shared with Ann. I'll regret this later,

April 13, 2001, Friday

"Is there a difference between the way older people and younger people view death?" Noelle said, asking me about Ann.

I'd been telling her we were hopeful she'd be able to take cisplatin, the next in the chemo series, because it might give us a little time. Or a few years. I'm not certain what I said.

Noelle's response puzzled me. "I thought she didn't want that."

She meant, to live in pain. She hadn't considered the possibility that Ann may have good days, weeks, maybe even good months ahead.

Then we began to talk about how older people looked at death. "You're still twenty inside, in spite of your body," I told her. "You still have things you want to do."

What is the difference? I thought later. There's not the great panic you might feel at forty thinking that you'll be gone in twenty years. By sixty you get used to the idea, though you do feel that there isn't enough time to get anything done when you can't see years stretching ahead of you.

April 15, 2001, Easter Sunday

When I looked out my window this morning my eyes homed in on a lawn on the street below where a little boy was hiding eggs. As soon as he put one out, his one-year-old sister would toddle, in her night suit still, to squat down and pick it up. His joy made the whole neighborhood radiant!

Ann did come to eat brunch out with the family, driving herself in case she didn't feel well enough to stay for the entire meal. She was wearing her leather jacket, and I noticed as I never have before, that she stoops now, leaning down like an old woman. Shoulders and head bent forward, not the upright firm stance she used to take.

After breakfast, we walked over the bridge that the hot springs people have recently built (how recently? I don't know.) Pleasant to look down at San Luis Creek, running like a small river, then water meadows beside the creek. And over the water meadows, in the flood plain, a set of cabins built up maybe six feet above creek level. I can't believe the creek doesn't rise to them. I can't believe anyone sleeping in them in the winter would not be worried every time the rain falls.

April 17, 2001, Tuesday

I often wonder how I'll react if Ann has severe pain. Will I panic? Will I sit with her, then become tired of sitting with her? Will I become used to it and try to manage her the way nurses manage patients in the hospital? What will this do to my feeling of being with her? Already I've had trouble concentrating at night, when I'm trying my hardest to send my power of good wishes to her.

I've been lucky in my children, or – congratulating myself – my best works of poetry are my daughters, who are loving, energetic, mildly but not heart-breakingly ambitious, sensitive and daily growing wiser.

April 20, 2001, Friday

I couldn't get over some desperately unhappy feelings. Result – I couldn't keep quiet with Harvey about messes in the back yard. He became upset, and when we went to move a flat from the back of his car he was jerking things around, and I fell, spraining my left 4th finger and twisting my knee.

Panic. I can't be injured. I won't be able to get the work done. Tears. Ice. Settled down only because Ann was feeling better.

April 21, 2001, Saturday

When I was close to Ann last night, I let myself feel first her anxiety, then her bodily suffering. I say let – because I think I bury myself in the daily chores and the far future too much, and dismiss the everyday pain of living as she must live. I wanted to make her a special place where all pain could be walled off, or passed through. And me to wipe carefully the lines from her face.

April 22, 2001, Sunday

I expressed this wish to Ann: not that we should spend these days as if they were the last days, but that we should spend them more closely together as we did when we were on trips. She replied she feels us to be close, that no matter where I am in the house she feels my presence. I didn't say I feel her absence especially when I'm upstairs, but I do think that her experience of having lived alone in the house makes her more sensitive to presence, no matter how many rooms away. She wants me to keep up my activities as I've been doing, because I must continue. I replied that I get lost in the quotidian.

"I don't want you to get stale, losing touch with what you always do."

I laughed. "It's sometimes good for me to draw back. While I'm working I keep adding this project to that, one after another."

"That's the way I was, once," She smiled that wide and generous smile – made brightly beautiful again by her loss of weight, her close-cut scalp.

Before I left to see Harvey, she said, "A necessary reality check."

Sweet Springs with Harvey was mercifully quiet. Song birds every where. At the bird watcher's outlook, I tried to find a bright singer; he wasn't in the tree 20 feet away, but in the coyote bush five feet from me. From there he flew over to the topmost twig in the rose and poison oak mixture, head tilted back, white throat ruffled, singing, singing, singing. Later, I saw swallows picking up mud daubs from the sand, flying like kites in the wind. Swooping, still, swooping.

April 23, 2001, Monday

Ann was pale and tired. I worked on the Shelley short story beginnings most of the day. I exercised, meditated in the hot tub, and rested briefly early in the afternoon, then at 3:30 went to the hospital to visit Bernadette [who had fallen and suffered a cerebral hemorrhage a week before]. Ann was expecting guests in the afternoon, relatives of an old friend; they had phoned from Santa Cruz to ask whether they could come by. She had a hard time showering and getting dressed, weakness overcoming her. But she was exhilarated by the meeting, even would have had a drink before dinner until I reminded her she was having a blood test the next day.

Images: her face, pale and thin, cheekbones prominent, above the pale green sweater we bought just after her birthday. Smile on her face, a bit mischievous, saying, "I think I'll have a drink."

April 25, 2001, Wednesday

When I returned from Harvey's, I learned that Ann had a call from her cousin Carmelita, who is at her house in Cayucos with Susannah and the two boys. Carmelita wanted us to come up to lunch one day, mentioning as an aside that she does have a cold. Ann became aware that I was distressed in the same way she had become aware on Tuesday. My tension shows in my face. A frown? I don't know, I'll have to think about my face, not my stomach next time. I didn't want to go, but felt I'd be depriving her of something she desired.

"Do you need me to drive you?" I asked

No, she didn't, not if she was feeling well.

I went upstairs. I'd hoped to have her to myself the next couple of days as the shots to build up her WBC count and her platelet count took effect. It occurred to me after a few minutes that my problem was this: I am short of time in general. If I go with her to see Carmelita and then also go with her on an expedition just the two of us, I've used up time that I need. I came downstairs and we talked.

"Carmelita," I said, "I'll lose touch with. She's not part of my future, and I need to use what time I have that I don't spend directly with you for the sake of my future."

We sat, I in the dark captain's chair, Ann leaning back in her beige Danish lounger, until I saw she was wiping her eyes. I knelt next to her, put my head on her chest, against the cancer, felt the soft flesh, the soft warm jacket.

At lunch with Diane, dipping into chips and dips, I discussed the problem of time. She listened well enough, but suddenly burst into tears and then said that Ann gets great pleasure from having me come along to watch her tell stories – perform – and that I should go with Ann to see Carmelita.

So later Ann and I took some time to talk over Carmelita's invitation more thoroughly than before. (This after Ann was told by the doctor absolutely not to come in contact with Carmelita's grandchildren and not to be in the same room with Carmelita, because of her cold.) That is, we spoke of the idea of the imminence of death and how it affects our use of time; of how we might use time if there's any possibility of remission (whether long or short); and if there's no remission, find ways to use well the good time that's left. We also spoke of the "practical" use of time, trying to decide together what's the best way to use it. Ann confessed that the reason she wanted me to go with her to be with Carmelita was that she thought I needed a pleasurable break from the daily round, not understanding that I might choose some other kind of break.

In March my concern was the taking up of time by former lives that moved like specters into the much different life Ann and I are presently experiencing. Now, it's the quotidian that eats up my awareness of where I am. Point is, I was pleased to see that there's a kind of progress in awareness of Ann and me and time. This means to me that there will be another progress, and another, and another, and if I'm aware and awake I can, if nothing else, become wiser. (But sadder.)

That night Ann complained about the severity of her "esophageal spasm." She opened her hand and placed it at the base of her neck, thumb on one side, middle finger on the other.

"It's like a ring here," she said. It came on when she exerted herself, and she felt breathless at the same time.

I was lying next to her, curled up, hip in the curve of the bed. "Have you tried your nitroglycerin?" I asked. I mentioned angina again. She took the nitro, and I waited until she felt better before I went upstairs.

April 26, 2001, Thursday

Images–sitting on hard chairs in doctor's office, the last room on the left. The restroom door across the hall made a moaning sound whenever anyone went into it. Ann in her black. She'd forgotten a book, and I offered to read to her. I also offered to go out and get one of the office magazines. We laughed. When Susan came in, she said Ann didn't need a shot. Her blood test showed that levels had gone up.

Ann asked to talk with the doctor, who came after we'd waited a long time. She told him about the pain and the shortness of breath she'd been experiencing, even in walking the fifty feet from the lab to his office. He tossed possible courses of action about, in his usual way. I'm beginning to see that he starts with one idea and then improves upon it. He began with sending her to get a blood transfusion as an outpatient, then changed to having her admitted to the hospital and having a cardiologist see her, then switched to calling the ER at French himself, getting her admitted, and then having a cardiologist see her. She agreed, and the doctor asked me if I'd drive her. Of course I would.

She was ushered right into the emergency room with only a few papers to sign. They attached her to the blood pressure machine, the oxygen in the blood measurement clip, and took blood and took more blood – for typing, they said – and provided, eventually, oxygen.

All of this without a book to read.

I sat, she reclined, we waited. When the same processes take place around my body some time in the future, her non-presence will fill the chair where now I sit. We exchange places, in my imagination, but her shade won't stay.

I said, at one point, "Would you like me to be closer, to hold your hand, to stand where you can see me?"

"Not especially," she answered. "Sentiment won't do." We laughed.

Her hospital gown – white, with the small blue bows or butterflies on it, the same pattern is everywhere, my mother twenty years ago, my father forty, wore one – she wore over her sweats and black shoes. She had a white pillow. The table on which she lay had the head propped up.

Approaching one o'clock, she was hungry and bored – no book. I'd been been making a list of things for her, but I offered to drive home and get a book and then to stop for a smoothie. I drove off, snatched the book, stopped to buy the smoothie, listening to Janet Baker sing Schubert lieder on the CD. We'd left it in the car for about three weeks. When I returned, we waited longer. She sipped at her drink, I chewed pieces of the bagel I'd bought at the same time.

Since they seemed about ready to move her – that is, she was in a wheel chair and a room had been assigned – I left to buy coffee and milk in the cafeteria. But when I arrived at the door of Ann's room, 102, and started in, a nurse stopped me. I saw Dr. Doyle's slate blue shirt above Ann's bed so I said I had Ann's power of attorney for health care. Still I wasn't admitted and stood in the hallway watching an attendant help a very sick woman walk down the hall. Eventually I heard Ann telling the nurse I had her power of attorney.

The nurse apologized, patting me on the arm. "Were you the person who was with her in emergency?"

Ann told me that they were going to transfuse her and send in a cardiologist. She suggested I have the staff xerox my power of attorney. "Then hold it up so they can see it! Say I have no next of kin."

The experience of having been pushed away combined with leaving Ann in a hospital bed reminded me of the future without Ann, filling me with self-pity. The lonely drive down barren streets. Most of all, not having anyone I could go to and cry with. No one to hold me. Too much as in childhood, where I had to swallow pain and suffering without comfort because my mother wasn't present or would try to help me by telling me to behave in a different way in the future, as if I were responsible for my pain.

I spoke with Ann later in the day about how she feels when in the hospital: isolated, she said. I said that I don't, I feel taken care of. Out on the streets, alone, no one to go to, I feel isolated, not really a person.

I tried to call Diane, but she wasn't answering, so I emailed her. Then I phoned Claire, and told her how I felt.

Crying relationship. I have crying relationships with a few people.

I phoned Harvey to tell him I wouldn't come by Thursday afternoon. I called Jean to say I wouldn't walk the next morning. These are my responsibilities. Not crying relationships.

April 27, 2001, Friday

I found Ann receiving an IV of potassium solution and angry at having been kept awake all night by noise, then awakened at 4 a.m. by a blood taker. She was, however, getting along very well with a nurse she had almost become angry with the day before. The nurse had been patronizing in her explanations to Ann about why the IV was beeping – when Ann was becoming angry because no one came in to fix the problem that made it beep. At that earlier time I had caught Ann's eye and put my finger to my lips – and afterwards said you don't want them to write anything on your chart. I reminded her of what had been written into Harvey's a few years ago because he'd objected to a pulmonary function test when just waking up.

The cardiologist came and explained to Ann clearly and without any condescension (noted because of the way the nurses treat the elderly) that though her heart wasn't perfect it was the chemo and consequent anemia that caused the angina and that she'd probably be okay with the nitro and a careful watch on her blood.

Ann was told she could leave as soon as the potassium drip was completed and Dr. Doyle had released her. Privately she told me she was leaving whether he released her or not. We were home by three.

April 28, 2001, Saturday

Last night, Friday, I was falling asleep at eight o'clock. Ann wasn't ready to go to bed: it wasn't time for pills or she hoped the gastric reflux would simmer down after dinner, or perhaps she wanted slow time to finish her drink. I said I'd either have to take a nap or go to bed. We talked.

I told her I was exhausted. She repeated her "thank you's" to me, and I said just hearing "thank you" made me even more tired, for it brought to mind what I'd been doing. She understood my emotional weariness compounded by the physical. I kept to myself, however, how "thank you" was a bond, a constraint, a reminder that there was no relief. My sense of her pain was evaporating in my weariness. Regrettably, I said, "I wish I could say "thank you" to someone."

I hope those words didn't keep her awake. I hope she didn't perceive them as my failure to want to accompany her. They were, rather, a deep wish that we - I - had succor here in town, a reaction to my Thursday afternoon discovery that all help – my daughters, my sister Julie – resided out of town. Or like Diane, seemed to be sometimes unreachable. And my responsibility to Harvey weighs heavily upon me. It's not just that he continually laments, but that it is a constraint, something I have to do, and no matter how easy it is, I dislike the requirement.

One problem I've encountered before: every day takes planning, every act requires planning, so that I don't dream or mull over new ideas as much as I usually do, I have to think of the next step, the next bit of shopping, the next arrangement of time. When will I pay bills? When will I exercise? When will I take notes on a book?

This morning Ann was just getting up when I got back from walking with Jean: the royal blue, soft robe, the cropped head, the grey face above it. Thin – and she stoops a bit. We decided to wait to see how she felt later before deciding to go to Trader Joe's – this had been the plan for the day. After she showered and dressed – gaunt black figure like a shadow – she looked peaked, and I proposed not going. With some reluctance she agreed. I went on to say, I wanted her to rest, to get stronger. I spoke of how maybe she'd get better, and we could go to London. I said this lightly – but it made her weep, because she said, when I held her, she knew she can't even think of that. I assured her that I wasn't going to insist on her getting well. I held her for a long time and said that I was content just to be with her, and I am.

May 1, 2001, Tuesday

Last night Harvey phoned during our dinner to ask what he should eat with the ham he was going to cook. I suggested lima beans or potatoes. I told him we were eating and then we hung up. I assumed that he phoned me in order to imply that he wasn't able to look after himself and that I should run to help.

I think it's important for people to speak out about what they want, both for their own sakes as well as for the people whom they ask for help. If you speak out, there's no backing away from hearing someone deny your request. If you speak out, the person you ask for help has to face her refusal to help and, maybe, the reasons for it.

I don't always know what I want. Trying to be clear for others makes me clear to myself.

The consequences of last night sprouted this morning, when I went down as usual to visit Harvey and do a little housework. Harvey began his lamentation about the night as soon as I came in the door. I listened for a while, but then felt I must say: if you don't want to cook for yourself you have a few options. You can go to the senior meals at French and Sierra Vista hospitals; you can go to the Elks' Club and to the Mission's senior meal on Thursday noon. You can have a tv dinner, or you can go and live in the Village. He squinted at me over the last option. "I can't come and fix dinner for you," I added.

This afternoon Claire phoned, and I described for her the stress I was feeling because Harvey seems in a downward spiral.

What I didn't say was that part of the difficulty is seeing my future self in him.

May 2, 2001, Wednesday

Yesterday (Tuesday) a good day for Ann, best yet, though she tired in the afternoon.

She's at the computer, looking up at me. Dark jacket. Hair about an inch long now. "You're brave," I said.

"What else can I be," she said with a smile.

"It just needs to be said now and then," I replied.

May 5, 2001, Saturday

As soon as I arrived at the house, Harvey told me he'd fallen and sprained his wrist. He implied it was my fault because I'd left a stool in my old room where he or someone might fall over it. He'd broken the window too. I looked at the broken window and marveled that he hadn't cut himself badly. Long sharp, pointed splinters have come out of the frame. What if he'd been seriously injured, how would I manage?

May 9, 2001 Wednesday

I'm taking notice: now is a period of hope. We hope the chemo works, we hope the right lung is clear. All symptoms can be ascribed to the chemo. But after the chemo is over, every symptom will become a return of the cancer. It will be more a period of fear. If I let it. Also a time of grabbing time.

We spoke today of the lists of household and family goods to be given to her relatives – how to handle, how to leave the house more or less intact, yet hand on family heirlooms to those who might want them. Ann added, "And some things need to be picked up."

May 10, 2001, Thursday

Ann was feeling fairly well this morning. She read my story, "The Invitation" and wrote commentary on it. In the afternoon, I went down to see Claire at Harvey's, later phoned Ann to see if Claire could come up. She agreed, though she worried about her appearance, and suggested we warn Annie that her hair is gone. Annie told us about her sharing at school. She also described for Ann her drawing in my guest book – a fish in honor of the fish that Annie hoped to find in Ann's pond.

May 13, 2001, Sunday

After Claire was packed and ready to go, she said she wanted to visit Ann again. When they arrived, she and Annie stood near the brown chair, side by side, a bag in their hands. After apologizing for not wrapping it, she pulled out two presents for Mother's Day, one for me, one for Ann. Ann's she presented with the words, "my second mother." When I opened my card with her loving words, calling me a "perfect" mother, I really had trouble not letting tears flow.

May 17, 2001, Thursday

The white driveway as I backed up, avoiding the agapanthus. Into the sun, spread through and over the windshield by speckles of dust, the spread made even worse by the moisture in the air. The drive down Chorro. I almost turned on Morro, but Ann reminded me it's Osos. I thought, curve and curve again, shuttling back and forth between Monterey, Higuera, Marsh. Shall I let you out here? Pausing before the ramp up to the back door.

The long room, Venetian blinds on the windows that looked out into the trees of Pacific Street, the parking lot, the title company across the street. The chairs, two lines of ten or more down the wood paneled walls. Pastel colors, blue, pale green, blue mixed with a kind of pink and mixed with a kind of green. Morning light, dusty – a subjective sense of freshness because it comes in from the east.

We walked back to a room where there were no pictures on the wall – the room two doors down from Doyle's office. Ann asked me how she looked, she believed she looked terrible. I examined her face. Pale. She pointed out that there's no color in her fingers, and I asked her to turn her hands over. Pale, pink only around the periphery, the thumb, the margin under the little finger.

The doctor sent Ann for an x-ray and a blood test.

We returned to another room this one next to the doctor's office, Ann holding her x-rays.

Dr. Doyle entered – nice brown shirt and pants today, not the Friday dress down, and straight on he seems thinner. Silk shirt even? He had the blood count in his hand, and after going over it generally, he decided that she'd have a blood transfusion that afternoon. He wrote out the orders. Then he began to look at the x-rays in the window facing Morro Street, snatched them down, took us into his office, put them up again.

I'm not sure whether his face showed expectation, then flattened out, or whether he showed disappointment. The signs are subtle. There may have been a flash of disappointment in a glance at Ann or at me. As I looked at the x-rays, it looked as if the cancer had grown smaller, but I didn't know what he was seeing. When Ann asked, "what's this?" he showed us the picture of the cancer and we could see that it hadn't changed much since the last x-ray. He outlined it for us, and we saw a triangular area equivalent to the lower lobe. He said the white streaks – and the white streaks were plentiful in both pictures – were the cancer. We had rather imagined it as a golf-ball sized tumor – but it isn't – it is like a root and it's got hold of a large part of Ann's lower left lung. He wasn't sure, but perhaps one of the small blobs in the right lung has shrunk. Generally not good news.

I was numb.

I sensed Ann's discouragement as we left the building. I had a moment of cold fear and pushed it away before I reached the car. On the way down Morro

Street, in the shady part, where it looks like a tunnel, Ann said, "I hate putting you through this."

"Oh, it's no problem, the blood transfusion."

I was already on Chorro Street driving down past the 1920s stucco bungalows when I said, "You mean the cancer is no smaller."

"Yes."

On the way up Ramona to the house, we spoke of the size – bigger than we first thought – of the "golf ball" description, of our reaction to Dr. Doyle. Not then, but later Ann said she heard the signs of disappointment in his voice.

3
Settling for Less

May 18, 2001, Friday

Ann was not feeling well this morning. She woke at four, her stomach bothering her. At eight thirty she felt nauseated and took atavin. I sat down with her a minute before I left to walk with Jean. I rubbed her toes and her hands, offered to rub oil into them. When she apologized for making my day difficult with her feelings, I said she must tell me so we can be together, so I can stay close to her heart. I put my hand on her chest, "Right there," I said.

By nine-thirty, she'd arranged herself to get some work done. Dressed. Gone to her computer. Left early for the doctor's to get her shot.

In the afternoon she felt nausea. She worked on her bills, nevertheless, sitting at the desk behind me as I struggled with a problem on the program where she keeps her accounts.

May 19, 2001, Saturday

During the afternoon, Ann spoke briefly to her Aunt Marge, who was describing her packing chores. Marge is moving and is giving away some of her treasures to her children. Ann told her she had the same problem – making a list and deciding who's to have what.

Later, Ann became pensive. We began to discuss the lists we'd planned to make on Monday. Ann had already begun her third list – things not to be given away immediately, like the china. I suggested she stick to the first two lists – the things to be given away now and the things she wanted me to make sure in my will go to the right person. Early in the day when I was putting library books in a row, she said she wanted to give the pair of glass horses, a set of bookends, to Ellen. She had been given them by her grandmother.

May 22, 2001, Tuesday

I can't say this morning that I feel depressed. I have energy and desire to work. I'm sad, I'm anxious, I'm worried. I recall mistakes – harsh words, minor neglects, times I didn't hold up the world. I think of all I don't know.

On the other hand, I understand suddenly a way Ann and I have of being together now and then: we take on roles, she is the precise and fussy person requiring that things be just so. I'm the one who messes up, like a child. We both laugh; it's not serious. Funny, I never thought of it before as role playing. But it is, and it's one of the only habits of fun from our earlier life we've brought with us to this one.

May 24, 2001, Thursday

Before I got home from my trip to see Harvey this morning, Ann had heard the results of the scan from Dr. Doyle. She believes he's going to switch to carboplatin. She doesn't know whether he mentioned paclitaxel. She did tell him that her condition may not be as good as it seems to him, because she isn't able to do much. She told him that I'm doing almost all her household chores.

This morning we did talk about options, hopes, what question to ask. I said I wouldn't be satisfied unless I knew how the treatment she is going to receive differs – if it differs at all – from what she would have received if the nodules could be defined certainly as the result of Sjogren's syndrome. It's just that I need to know that the best is being done for her. I don't want to have regrets later.

May 25, 2001, Friday

Last night, Ann asked me how I was. I answered, living day to day. Then, thinking how this week I'd been upset by remembering the past, I thought how living day to day keeps you from absorbing the past into the present. And was silent. She noticed my silence, and I asked her how about you.

"Living day to day myself." Waiting for me to say more, I could tell. So I told her what was on my mind. She said, in contrast, she's able to remember scenes from the past she enjoys.

May 26, 2001, Saturday

Noelle phoned in the late afternoon. I'd been at peace until then, enjoying a day with Ann. But Noelle wanted to know when if ever I was going to be able to come down in the next two years. "Ellen's changing so much. You're going to miss it."

I fell silent for a few seconds, thinking how to tell her I've made my decision. I've set priorities. "I don't know. I have no idea when Ann will be well."

"Yes," she said, "I guess you can't leave. What if she has a heart attack in the middle of the night?"

I tried to answer, "That's not the problem. It's not fear of a heart attack or leaving Ann by herself – we could hire someone to take my place. It's just I don't want to leave."

June 3, 2001, Sunday

As we were reading the paper in the living room, Ann mentioned that she'd emailed Addie requesting her to make a reservation for two nights for the Keller family reunion to be held in Danville. She asked whether I'd be staying with her or going to visit Claire and Julie. I answered, "Claire and Julie." We went back to reading for a moment but grief was welling up in me, and I said, "You know, if we make that trip, we're going to have to go down to Noelle's for a visit. I've been telling her we can't travel."

This notion took Ann by surprise. I tried to elaborate, describing how I feel to miss Ellen's recitals.

"But the trip is much worse, going down there," said Ann. "A harder trip."

"No harder than the north is any more," I pointed out.

"Addie has a quick way of going. Over the Pacheco pass, up Highway 5. I can't go with Harvey."

"Harvey wouldn't be going. Just you and me.'

"Noelle misses you and keeps pulling."

I said, "No, I'm the one who feels bad. I'm torn. I want us to go, but know that I can't. That's what I've told Noelle. She understands. She didn't even tell me about the recital yesterday, I had to find out from Erwin." The tears were really falling, but I had to hold them back to say, "I crossed over a line last January."

"I did too."

"Yes, of course. I said I'd be with you as much as possible, but there are losses. I don't want to go to Noelle's without you. It's all loss." Then I felt sorry for myself, and said, "All I have is one great big loss because when I lose you I'm going to lose everything."

I didn't have to say it was unfair for her to be able to go to this reunion and not accompany me to Noelle's. She understood and apologized.

Later I thought how narrow the choices become as you age and become ill. Then, but narrow choices aren't necessarily bad.

June 4, 2001, Monday

At five, when I returned from visiting Harvey – I should say, listening to Harvey's complaints – Ann told me she was breathless, that walking from one room to another caused the breathlessness. I asked about the pain in her throat. Yes, she'd been having that. In addition, after she sat down, as she caught her breath, she had a flowering sensation in her chest. You mean a pain. "Well, yes," she said.

I suggested she call the doctor, who had us meet him at Sierra Vista, where we discovered that her platelet count was extremely low. He tried to get her into Sierra Vista, but the hospital had no beds, meaning they didn't have enough beds staffed. We had to walk down the corridor from the outpatient lobby to the main lobby and back, and he walked with Ann, seemed concerned she might faint or fall. At French, he got a wheel chair and pushed her to the room himself. She stayed overnight there, but the platelets were late, the blood later. No one ever gave her the oxygen he ordered. At one point, she had a severe chest pain and asked if anyone had brought the nitro patch she was supposed to have. The nitro patch did improve the pain.

I'm not reacting with grief any more, I noticed as I went home, nor panic. But a deep melancholy and a concern about whether I'm going to be able to manage.

June 8, 2001, Friday

I sat all morning with Ann in the hospital. She was irritable, having had no sleep at all last night. Finally, they let her go at 12:30. Everything moving like a mud slide, slowly.

June 9, 2001, Saturday

I woke early. Ann slept until noon, she told me, then went to work on her mail. She's talked with her cousin's child, Peggy, about giving her grandmother's jewels to Mary this weekend, and she's also had a long talk with her friend Jean [from Silicon Valley days] and a shorter one with a friend of ours from England who wanted our email addresses.

June 12, 2001, Tuesday

We went up the coast to Ragged Point for lunch. I drove, Ann quiet, a small figure, drying up in the seat beside me. She seems shorter now when she sits. She's much leaner.

The grass has turned yellow-green, but wildflowers abound on the road above San Simeon. Yarrow, mostly, but some poppies, silver lupine, bush lupine, and what are probably California violets, golden, hugged the borders of the road. The wind blew fiercely, and the sea was dark under threads of fog, dark from underneath too, kelp, but light over sand, light over rocks. White caps, even small rollers close to shore.

We sat outside at a table with a view of pond and flowers. On the lawn was a bright red shrubdeep wish that we - I - had succor here in town, a reactionwe called them fire-something – reminding me of my childhood home. I remembered the ants that infested them because of a sticky syrup that oozed from the individual pod-like petals in its crown.

June 13, 2001, Wednesday

After all, the discussion with Ann the other day – my sense that I'm responsible for a part of her depression – brought change: she asked me last night what to say to Sheila about her funeral. She wanted a script. I provided her with this: tell Sheila first of all that you're no longer a Catholic and haven't been for some time. Then tell her that when Carol is ready, she will have a memorial service, and she will ask you to read then.

In the evening, suffering from a neck and spine ache, Ann said it felt like her old fibromyalgia, but worse. Her scalp tingles and burns. I suggested my microwave hot packs again. Finally, she accepted, and went to sleep, a canvas ring around her neck.

June 15, 2001, Friday

Quiet, productive day. I worked on Ann's bookkeeping program in the afternoon. She felt well enough to prepare a handsome spread for Anne C, who arrived shortly after five – and a little bit before I'd returned from seeing Harvey. We gossiped about Anne's neighbor who tried to kill his wife the other day, and about Anne's work. At one point, Ann was talking about the list she was working on to provide gifts to her family, and Anne interrupted, kindly, yet directively – a little shakily maybe – "Now let's not talk about dying." Ann protested that she wasn't, not really, just thinking through getting rid of things.

June 17, 2001, Sunday

A bad Harvey day: that is, he didn't sleep "a wink" he said, and complained and complained. He'd spent all his awake time going over the slights and deprivations he's suffered. It does no good to tell him how all of us suffer this way. My problem is that I can't just listen and let it happen, but think I have to fix it for him.

A good Ann day, though. We spent twenty minutes in the morning before Ann got up holding hands and chatting – rather I chatted, my ideas about the impressionists' film, my ideas about capitalism and commodification of art stirring her up until she has to say her usual "You've been up a lot longer than I have," and then we laughed.

June 22, 2001, Friday

I visited Claire and Annie [who had come to stay with Harvey for the weekend] from 8 until 9, making arrangements to meet them at Barnes and Noble to buy Annie some books while Ann had chemotherapy. It turned out Ann didn't have chemotherapy, though, because her platelet count was pretty low. But I think Dr. Doyle had already decided not to infuse her on that day, preferring to check a new CT scan, then go on with – we hope – a stabilizing dose of gemcitibine for a while. He told us he'd received word from the company that makes Iressa and that he'd received the forms to fill out for joining a protocol. He wasn't totally clear on what will happen – whether they'd determine whether Ann is eligible for a protocol and then do a lottery to see if she can be one of the patients on it. He was excited about the possibility.

Then Annie, sitting on the floor in the bookstore, poring over the book she'd chosen: she's quite determined about what she wants, and she wanted one with well and realistically drawn animals in it. She pointed out to me the picture of a cockatiel in the cover art for the book – animals were depicted in circles, as if in a family album. At some time this day I told Claire I'd learned from my journals that I knew at the time I was making a mistake when I married Harvey.

"Why did you?" she asked.

"Cliff jumping," I said, "then too, a sense of responsibility. I thought of myself as unfair to an older man whom I was flirting with . . . and this was stupid of me. But he had gained from it. He'd be pretty much alone now if it hadn't been for me."

June 25, 2001, Monday

Again, last night I woke twice in the first two hours of sleep, desperately restless. I had taken aspirin. Tonight I'll try ibuprofen. I hate to start taking benedryl, because I think it increases the runny nose I have during the day. Or, perhaps, dries up my nose too much.

Ann and I drove up to French for Ann's CT scan before seven. We sat together in the waiting room, Ann a bit impatient and possibly tense. When she was called, I asked for a wheel chair to help her get down the long pair of halls that lead to the ambulatory patient's section. I watched the carpet as I rolled, blue, figured, leaned on the chair to save pushing stress on my right hip, recalling the happy day Ann and I went through the Chinese archaeological exhibit in San Francisco a little more than a year ago.

Once inside the Ambulatory Patients' section, I followed the nurse in. Small, dark-haired, wearing lavender scrubs and thick soled athletic shoes, she faced Ann to begin the procedure for affixing a tube for the CT injection.

June 26, 2001, Tuesday

In the morning Ann expressed impatience while waiting for Dr. Doyle's call. We talked over whether she should have gone ahead and made an appointment for today – since he had told me she should see him right after she went through the CT scan. Some time before noon she called the office, hoping to get a return call in time for us to go out to lunch. But at noon, Addie phoned from Paso Robles. She'd like to bring her daughter Lisa by, and Ann agreed, hoping to go through pictures with her and give her what she likes for the Keller family reunion.

June 30, 2001, Saturday

Jean had heard from Julie yesterday. Julie's to arrive at around three. "Some time in the evening she will come over and have a glass of wine with you," said Jean. "How will she get home after the glass of wine,?"

Laughing, I said, "Just one?"

"Do you want to come have barbecue with us that afternoon?"

I said, no, I'd better stay with Ann.

Then I felt socially uncomfortable. Did Jean want to be invited for a glass of wine too? But why should she, when the point is for me to have a visit with Julie?

July 1, 2001, Sunday

In the evening Ann shared with me an email from her cousin Mary, thanking her for the dressing table set and her great-grandmother's jewelry.

It took me a while to understand that Ann was dissatisfied with the letter, believed Mary should have written more enthusiastically, or, perhaps, have phoned her. At bedtime she talked some more, letting me know that it was specifically the casual thanks for "Eliza's jewelry" that bothered her. She said she'd gone to a lot of effort to get the things together for Mary, and expected more effort in the reply, adding, "Why bother? I might as well let you give them to your kids."

I answered the question, "Why bother?" this way: "Because when Mary gets older and is giving her things away, she'll say, as she gives the jewelry to one of her daughters, 'This belonged to your great-great-grandmother. I got it from Ann, who got it from Ruth, the eldest of Henry Keller's children." Well, I didn't speak quite so formally, but I did image a small scene. I think it made her feel better. She said so before we exchanged good nights.

July 2, 2001, Monday

As I worked on my journal, aware of Ann lying ill on her bed, I slipped over into an area of mild tension. The house is silent. It's filled with Ann's things, remains of Ann's life, responsibilities she's not able to tend to any more. They make a heavy wall.

July 6, 2001, Friday

I woke up anxious again. I think the problem of Beth's pregnancy and my inability to help is bothering me, as well as the feeling that it's so much better with Harvey visiting her that I wish he wouldn't ever come home. Not so much because he's hard to be around – though that is often true – but that he takes up time and work I don't feel particularly generous about giving.

July 7, 2001, Saturday

When Diane arrived to go out to breakfast with me, I wasn't quite ready. I'd been sweeping up after Harvey's bird (which I'm caring for while he's gone) and I had to change my shirt. While I was changing, Ann told Diane she hadn't slept much the night before. Instead, she'd listened to a mockingbird and created words for his song, thinking of a TV program she'd seen about a blackbird. "I'm Tony, then I'm a wonderful fellow, wonderful Tony. And variations. Then on to I'm here on the telephone pole. Just look. Tony, Tony, Tony. And variations, Then see me turn cartwheels, here I go."

Diane was delighted and charmed.

July 8, 2001, Sunday

I spent time on the computer rereading some of the lung cancer sites I'd bookmarked last January and February and faced the reality of losing Ann again. The reality is hard and right now frightening because I've been denying it in the day to day tasks for several months now. I think Ann does too.

Hope and denial of the truth fit together like a dowel and a drilled to measure hole.

July 10, 2001, Tuesday

Since Sunday the threat of coming face to face with Ann's illness hangs like a bat – I see it crunching on my bones the way the bats hanging on Ann's porch used to crunch on scorpions – right under my surface thoughts – my surface thoughts that pretend we're living in the forever. I still feel anxious often. At noon I soaked in the spa, ate my lunch, then shivered in my bed until two. When I was ready, Ann and I went on errands – papers to her bookkeeper, me to bank, and then I went into the Cal Poly library to retrieve books Ann thought would tell her what she wanted to know about the history of Kansas.

Although Ann has developed a UTI – perhaps – or at least feels as if she has – the day was quiet and ordinary. A day of eternal presentness – except when talking to Beth. Her nine month connection with new life parallels Ann's waiting for death and severe illness, and I'm all too aware . . .

July 11, 2001, Wednesday

I ate lunch with Diane at Le Patisserie, then returned to her house afterwards for about an hour. Mostly, I talked – I spoke about the denial I'm aware of. It's easy for me, I told her adding that on Sunday on my old computer at Harvey's house, I summoned up articles about cancer that I'd bookmarked on the internet, and felt lost. But as soon as I came home to Ann I felt fine.

"I do feel anxious from time to time, but it's easy to slip into denial. The way we live now will go on forever, I tell myself."

Diane agreed that denial is good for you.

"But I don't feel right. I don't feel human. I don't feel that all of me is there."

"That's right, it's not all there," she said.

Today Harvey was generally happy, planning to take the bird down to get his toenails clipped at the pet shop and preparing to go to the American Legion dinner tonight.

July 13, 2001, Thursday

In the morning Ann took out the vacuum for me so that I could suck up the dust bunnies in her bedroom. She dusted the living room furniture, and later she vacuumed some of the carpet in the dining room. In the evening we changed the sheets on her bed, then at dinner time, she took over starting the rice when I was busy talking with Claire on the phone.

At the same time, she was mildly irritable. Maybe the irritability was caused by an episode of forgetfulness in the morning and she needed to prove to herself and to me that she was all right. She'd read out to me in the morning the story of an Atascadero woman with C-J disease, having forgotten that I told her about it on Tuesday. Later, I noticed that the hall toilet needed cleaning and asked her if it was okay to use bleach in it. She stood in her bathroom, trying to remember the word for Lysol, and I interrupted by trying to explain what needed to be done. This irritated her, and she told me so. I don't give her enough time as a general rule, come in on her too soon when she's having trouble remembering words. I got the sense she was asking for special concessions to her illness – and I didn't think it was her illness causing this problem. We 've had the problem since we first knew each other – each getting mad at the other for stepping in before the other's ready to give up the floor.

I said, "We just have to be patient with each other."

She accepted that, but I wasn't sure she wasn't still irritated when I went upstairs to bed.

July 13, 2001, Friday

Ann felt comfortable, cared for, and listened to at the doctor's today. He had phoned Dr. George, who was reassuring about the eyes: since a treatment for the Sjogren's problem was to sclerose the lacrimal ducts, maybe this would help. Dr. Doyle also was concerned about her veins and suggested providing a permanent under-the-skin port. The port is rather like a computer port: blood may be taken from it or infused, drugs may be infused, IVS, etc. Before she left, after the infusion of taxotere, he'd made an appointment with her for a surgeon, who is going to put one in. This will save her arm veins, which are becoming difficult for lab techs to deal with.

The steroid she took this morning plus the infusion have lifted her energy level up. She was funny, excited, articulate, loving during a lunch with her Aunt Marge.

July 14, 2001, Saturday

We'd arranged to do the grocery shopping at noon so I could nap before going down to cook Harvey's dinner. While I was in Scolari's – almost an hour – she became impatient, having started a headache. Upset and tired when I came out, I said, "We've got to find another way to do this."

My knee hurt, my hip hurt when I climbed into the car so I complained half the way home. After I'd carried the groceries in – not all, for Ann carried some – I got tearful and ashamed of myself for complaining. Ann reassured, "Don't be sorry, don't be sorry."

Later, I thought we're going to have to change the plan. We'll have to stop at grocery stores on days when we do other errands.

July 16, 2001, Monday

This morning Ann and I went to see the surgeon to prepare for having the port placed under her collarbone. He outlined what he was going to do, naming the difficulties, the changes of intention at the last minute from one collarbone to the next, the risks. Then we made the appointment – it's to be Thursday at noon. Ann became tense as we drove downtown later. I asked what the matter was. At first she said it was my driving, then admitted it was all the procedures that she was going to have to go through again. She is becoming tired of hospitals and procedures.

In the evening, discussing Noelle's visit, I said that Noelle was interested in bringing Ellen to hear the full symphony orchestra at the Mozart Festival. Would Ann like to go? No, she didn't think so. But she approved of my going.

We were quiet before going our separate ways to bed, just trying to feel close. I wonder if the surgeon's quiet "I'm sorry" about her having lung cancer brought the reality nearer. Sometime today I mentioned Noelle's arriving when she was having the port embedded as beneficial.

"Why?" Ann asked, eyebrows raised.

"To remind her how sick you are." Eyebrows still raised. I felt disapproval – not a lot, but a flickering.

"You and I living from day to day sometimes don't think of it either."

July 19, 2001, Thursday

Back to Sierra Vista again, this time to see Ann through the embedding of the port catheter. We appeared at 10, Ann nervous enough to fuss at one of the volunteers who was stupid enough to think she was a man – Ann? My former neighbor Betty was there, pleasant, and I thanked the volunteer for volunteering – a big surprise to her.

The lobby of Sierra Vista is rather like a heavily used main room in a medium sized hotel, filled with sofas and arm chairs, most hard, for people to sit on and wait, some of them sleeping. This appears to be the only room for meeting surgeons. Ann's had promised to come out when the surgery was done and tell me all about it.

The room upstairs was shared by a youngish woman enjoying a rapid conversation about family, friends, dogs, opinions. The light was graceful, bluish – the curtains were blue, the gowns were blue, pleasant against the white. Clean. Warm. Comforting. I remained with Ann until she was taken out.

I waited in the lobby then until the surgeon appeared in green coveralls looking more youthful than usual at about 1:15. Ann was fine. He'd put her out because of her GED and fear of getting acid into her lungs.

July 20, 2001, Friday

I rose already tired this morning, and felt even more tired after my back and knee ached all through my walk with Jean, even though we didn't go far because Ellen was with us on her skateboard. I was home setting up the errands I might run after going to the dentist: how I planned to go into New Frontiers after picking up my prescription at the drug store. Ann said she needed some sourdough bread. I grimaced at the idea of having to make a second stop at a different grocery store, then noticed Ann's distress – a kind of flattening out of all expression in her face. I began to dislike myself for letting her down. She used to tell me how bad she felt for letting me down, and now, in a minor way, it was my turn. I was sorry, so sorry. We blamed it on my tiredness and on the ache in my knee.

July 21-22, 2001, Saturday & Sunday

Off and on during the two days Noelle was here I spoke about her father – how she and her sisters' coming makes him feel part of a family, not so isolated. She agreed. At one time he praised me for being such a splendid mother to have produced such great kids. She thinks he's not as bad as a lot of men are these days; I say, well, my father's generation were not so self-centered as Harvey's generation and besides, were taught to take care of women. He's never taken care of anyone by accepting what they need. My way or no way, has been his motto and that of my brothers-in-law, who were his age.

Then we talked about the situation with Ann. Until Ann is stable, I said, I can't leave town. Stable means not receiving dangerous chemotherapy, not reacting badly to treatment, and the cancer is not growing. Goal? Getting the cancer to shrink or to stop growing with minimum side effects.

July 23, 2001, Monday

Dr. Doyle is pretty sure he and some other local doctors will be able to take part in clinical trials of Iressa. Let's hope the permission comes soon, before the cancer begins to grow again. He said he heard wheezing in her chest. They chatted about asthma, the use of a medication for it.

July 29, 2001, Sunday

During the afternoon, Ann had read through her will and the material surrounding her trust. In the evening she wanted to make sure I wouldn't support Harvey with her money, or my girls would not. As she tried to bring out the words, she called herself paranoiac.

I said, "No, distrustful."

"No," she said, "Maybe cautious." We considered ways of making sure. The upshot is that I'm to make my will as soon as she signs hers – in fact, I should ask questions on Tuesday and make an appointment. Later that night I assured her that by himself Harvey had enough to keep him in an expensive nursing home for twelve years.

July 30, 2001, Monday

Hope continues. Dr. Doyle thinks he may get the go-ahead on the Iressa trials soon, within a few weeks, and will get Ann going if she qualifies. In the meantime, next week he wants her to have an x-ray so he can see what's happening in her chest. Neither of us asked what he meant by "qualify."

July 31, 2001, Tuesday

In the afternoon, Ann and I went to her lawyer's offices on 9th in Grover Beach – Ann missing the turn, I pointing out the way. Though she hesitated to take my directions, insisted that the office was behind us, she did follow them – seat of the pants – and we arrived swiftly at the office, and just where I thought it would be.

Ann had a number of corrections she wanted to make in the wording of the document/will. Then we began working on the power of attorney for health care, and while struggling with some phrases, began to imagine scenarios where Ann would be dying and I would have to take action. And, we were laughing and making jokes. I couldn't picture Ann in those circumstances – denial, denial has taken me over.

I asked the lawyer about whether what I might inherit from Ann was protected from Harvey as separate property, and she said yes. We agreed that I would make a will with her next week.

August 1, 2001, Wednesday

I spoke with Diane about my desire for community in religious experience. Why, do you suppose?

Her answer led to circular argument: to establish your humanity, leading to the statement – community leads to community. Doesn't answer at all. Diane was low, had a generally, low level of energy. She said she'd failed to stop smoking and had retreated to five cigarettes a day. After lunch we sat on her porch while we shared poems and she smoked.

I'd asked Ann to come with us, but she refused, planning to get work done instead. An old friend, a close one, from Stanford phoned her. They were talking just as I left. When I returned, Ann told me her friend is worried about her state of mind. Her husband believes or tells her she is forgetting things all the time. One whole episode in her life was blanked out, she says, something about a gate open that she must have opened: but how is everyone so sure she opened the gate?

August 3, 2001, Friday

At bedtime Ann and I talked about how I'd been absent from her for the last week. I don't know what is the matter with me. I'm afraid for her, I think, with this low-dose treatment. Maybe I'm just looking forward to the x-ray and am troubled about it. Ann was upset because she thought I might be getting more pleasure from exchanging emails with an old college boy friend than I do with her. Not so, I said. I write about once a week, and it's recreation because I'm thinking through things spiritual.

"We never discuss things spiritual," she said.

"Sometimes we do, after we experience something aesthetically pleasing" I replied.

But I don't discuss these things with Ann – I feel she's too practical, not willing to go off in wild directions and that I have to catch her with the experience, not the words.

I felt guilty for having deserted her this week.

August 4, 2001, Saturday

This morning still fussed about deserting Ann, not giving her a wonderful summer, with outside drinks and all. I think, I was ragged last week, but I had no one to tell except Ann how fussed and worried I am living on this kind of tight rope of a disease.

August 5, 2001, Sunday

Ann and I went out to dinner to the Galley tonight, where we enjoyed a bottle of Chalone Pinot Blanc and finished dinner with a mousse torte. Mostly we talked with some excitement and insight about Smiley's *The Adventures of Lydia Newton*, its failure to explore the intersection of violence and ideology in any person's head. Several seals swam up and down outside the window, patrolling, it looked like. No sign of the otter. Was she chased away?

Sometimes Ann still jumps in where she assumes she knows what I'm going to say. No point in repeating the episode here, but she was irritable and I have to think about ways to be comfortable about her irritability.

August 6, 2001, Monday

The doctor had an x-ray taken. The pleural effusion is about the same. He thinks that's "good." Ann felt fine and took over some of the dinner prep. I began to wonder what I'm doing here. It's becoming another world – where I am Ann's companion, not her caregiver.

August 7, 2001, Tuesday

We saw a pair of goldfinches when we sat outside for drinks in the evening. They sway together in flight, as if they're in a flock – the curve is wide, like a pair of skateboarders going downhill on a street.

No birds are singing these days, though there are mockingbirds around. I thought I heard a meadowlark yesterday morning ... strange.

The crows have left the neighborhood.

August 8, 2001, Wednesday

We decided because of Ann's feeling tired this day that we might not make the planned trip to Nepenthe on our anniversary the next day. I kept assuring her that it would be okay with me, and laughed to myself at my superstitious notion that just because I hadn't signed my will – just made with Nita – that my old dream of our driving off a cliff together would come true.

That is a strange dream, and probably represents the chances we took in entwining our lives. I must say, too, that I had it long before the Thelma and Louise movie made it part of American woman's symbolic system.

August 9-12, 2001
Thursday, Friday, Saturday, Sunday

Ann has been feeling so well the last few days that I begin to lapse: she will remain this way for a long time, years maybe, and I won't be alone. Though my feelings don't shift drastically – that is, I remain comfortable, generally – I do experience a shudder together with a reminder that one of these days we may have to go through the entire experience again. We may learn it's growing once more, Dr. Doyle may say no Iressa. Iressa may not work, we will have to watch Ann decline again. I fear even as I write this. Then put it out of my head.

Thursday we drove out to Creston just to see what was there. I think we did drive over the "Heilman" hills once before, but Ann didn't remember. Smell of oak and dry hay in the summer time. Golden California, long straight roads, hills, horses and cattle, and highway repair trucks and steamrollers. We brought a Brahms quartet to play, and had to turn it off and on because we were talking. Nothing new and wonderful, just the usual desultory exploration of news and ideas.

In the evening we ate at Windows, enjoying a placid bay, a superb (expensive) wine, and more and more talk. The couple right in front of me were having an anniversary too. I was amazed at how much talking they didn't do, though they ate carefully, quietly, lifting their forks sensuously.

A quiet, easy, contented anniversary.

August 14, 2001, Tuesday

This evening Ann and I discussed chronic fatigue, whether her fatigue was different when experiencing chemotherapy from her experience of Sjogren's. I wanted to define – Ann said that her definition of fatigue meant that you didn't want to start something you couldn't finish. I felt that wasn't enough – I referred to how I would start something after my 1998 surgery, knowing that I wouldn't be able to finish, yet willing to put in fifteen or twenty minutes as long as I didn't have to finish. Put in fifteen or twenty minutes until I was exhausted, I mean; I described the sick feeling in my stomach and limbs. She described something entirely mental, or so it seemed to me.

Before we went to bed, Ann and I spoke of what we would do if she were well again. Well, she won't be, but IF. Of course I can't return to live with Harvey. Of course she doesn't want me to. "What is different?" she asked me.

"It's more companionable. I spend more time in company of someone I love," was my answer.

August 15, 2001, Wednesday

I'm thinking about the subjectivity of pain and fatigue and other states of illness. The practice now is to ask a person to rate his fatigue or pain on a scale of one to ten. That way, they measure against their own states and imagine the fiercest pain or greatest fatigue they might feel. Thus the observers have an objective –

more or less – standard for the particular person. Then the observer must accept that the personal expression is correct, that the sufferer is experiencing extreme fatigue or pain if he says so.

This brings up ethical and/or cultural questions. First, for the sufferer. How much pain is debilitating? How much fatigue says, I can't work? Should I listen to those who encourage me not to take pain medicine, but to bear with it? Should I try to work because others think I'm malingering?

Second for the caregivers. How much care must I give? How many tasks must I take over? When does my pain – caused by tethers and other kinds of burdens – equal his pain? Which sufferer must I choose?

I think the answer for the caregiver must be first, that the sick person's own evaluation must be accepted. Then, the caregiver must evaluate her own pain/fatigue/sense of waste – and this is hard. How do you measure a burden of time and patience and energy? Against what? Against ability to eat and sleep? Yes, there could be a ten here. A person keeps me awake all night – an Alzheimer's victim, perhaps. I don't have time to eat. Against ability to earn a living. Yes, definitely, there could be a ten. There can also be shades – the loss of a job after a certain amount of time, the loss of a career, as a woman who must stay home during crucial years,

Against loss of health – tension, stress, weariness, arthritic incursions, time to see doctors, etc.

Now, in each case, do we measure caregivers against one another, and say, this one's a saint because she gives up everything to take care of her husband, and say this one's not because she's leaving the old man? No. We have to allow the caregiver the same right to say – this I cannot do and accept what she says.

Suppose we enter a community, bond with others, continue a relationship, aren't we saying that both sides in a situation of illness have to be fair to the other? Does this mean that levels of refusal to feel capable or to help are adjusted by community standards?

All this is not to say Ann and I are in trouble about who feels what – not at this point. Earlier I was restless and often pained, not as a caregiver because I wasn't one, but as a companion because our/my activities were circumscribed. The above thoughts derive from experiences with Harvey, who exaggerates his pain.

August 15, 2001, Wednesday

Ann was tired today. She slept at noon time, then at 3 was willing to go out shopping at Trader Joe's with me. But by the time we got home, she was exhausted again. Nevertheless, she pulled herself up to the computer for an hour, spoke to a neighbor about another neighbor's heart condition. Before dinner she worked to fill out an application for a bracelet identifying her as someone taking coumadin. She was so tired, this was a major effort for her. Possibly the conversation from last night, when I said that I'd start a project when I was tired if only to get fifteen minutes of it out of the way, motivated her. This morning she also paid much attention to my arthritic rigidity and joint pain.

Sometimes it doesn't work to talk things out, because the effects come up on us in surprising ways.

Later on, right after dinner, Ann's cousin Matthew called. He's coming to visit her tomorrow afternoon and evening. She'll go out to dinner with him and his wife.

I wish I knew how to improve life right now for both of us. I can't think of anything, except to fly far far away from here.

Other than that – as for my quality of life – I'm not connecting with people at all.

August 19, 2001, Sunday

Just before time to sleep, Ann was impatient with me. Harvey had phoned, making me aware of how depressed he was. I thought of the anti-hero, and the right men seem to have to play tragic heroes when they suddenly wake up to the human plight, after years of hiding from it. (Even ridiculous tragic heroes like Bloom.) And how women when they try to play tragic heroine are victims – and they're not allowed the role of savior. I was trying to explain this to Ann, but she pushed me forward – yes, yes – and I became tense – and told her so. I told her this was harmful to me. I felt terrible, telling her this, possibly in her situation making her insecure – or defensive because insecure. But I must. As an ethical person, I can't let her think all is well in what goes on between us when all is not well.

August 20, 2001, Monday

This morning Ann was sad and I, noticing moisture in

her eyes, was also sad. We didn't talk about the previous evening though, but of the day ahead. What errands will I run while Ann receives her infusion? What time must we leave for the doctor? Plans made, I went to work, finding it difficult to get back into my story. At the last minute, I had to rush to eat and get ready. Dr. Matthews attended Ann, checking the sore spot on her tongue, later telling her that her platelet count was a little low, but they'd go ahead with the infusion anyway, give her Procrit, and then postpone the following infusion. This sequential infusion would have been the last in this cycle of taxotere, and should have been followed by a CT scan.

I left Ann at the doctor's, bought myself new shoes – hoping to stop the soreness above my right hip – and visited Harvey and phoned Beth.

Beth was excited, pleased with herself for having gone through the amniocentesis without flinching, and happy about seeing the embryo (we're still having to call it the embryo) kicking and with its tiny hands folded (in prayer, she said). She and Chris know the sex, but aren't telling, and Noelle is not to know that they know it.

Late in the afternoon, Ann and I drove to Cambria for dinner with an old friend [who had written the history of Mayfield] and her husband. Ann's friend, round-eyed, her hair in a sort-of just below the ear page boy, entertained. Grandmother, student of Latin America, traveler, story-teller – and her husband is entertaining too. He looks at her frequently with love. She steals the show, at least with me and Ann, and I found myself listening to her while trying to talk with him.

Ann, high on prednisone, had a wonderful time, the best she's had for a few months.

August 25, 2001, Saturday

During the night anxiety. In the morning, I was sleepy and nervous. I felt stiffly arthritic, my right hip very sore. I felt tired. I didn't even notice how Ann was feeling. I slept a bit in the afternoon, went to the grocery store, felt more sore as the evening progressed. After dinner I felt as if I might be sick. This was frightening – what will happen if I am sick, really sick, and can't help Ann. I have had some twinges in my left arm this week, just mild muscle aches, but I've thought of what it would be if I developed at this point a recurrence of my breast cancer.

August 26, 2001, Sunday

After dinner we spoke – really, Ann spoke – of a review of her life she's been doing for the last several months. I thought, yes, this is what Diane says should be done. I didn't make as good an audience as I'd have liked to, though, because the theme from which we started was that of failed promise. Ann had been reviewing the biographies of her Stanford classmates, finding among most of the women hopes and promises that hadn't been fulfilled. Her own failure, she thought was changing the direction she took initially – medicine – when she discovered she couldn't do math or science. Then, she descended into English, but she really felt she should have become a scholar of history. She would like, if she could start over again, to be like Barbara Tuchman. She praised me as a scholar, and I had to correct her, describing for her the time I wasted doing nothing, absolutely nothing. I directed the conversation, disagreed with her, and was altogether not the person I would like to be. I was honest. I said, "I don't want you to mourn the failures of the past, that's what Harvey does. You've published two books and taught many students, and led people into feminism. What more?"

August 28, 2001, Tuesday

We went to a movie, "Under the Sand." Afterwards, Ann and I discussed how people whose loved ones have disappeared keep reawakening to their presence. We puzzled over the ending in which the woman whose husband has disappeared views a body, says it's her husband, but then decides that she can't live with that and insists that the watch found on it was not her husband's – so that she can continue to think she is accompanied by his spirit?

August 29, 2001, Wednesday

I asked Diane about people wanting to record their lives before they died, wondering whether I'd done the wrong thing in trying to tell Ann Sunday night that she mustn't go into the past. At first – we were driving along Foothill by then – Diane couldn't remember.

Then, finally, when we got to the light at Patricia, she did say that people need to work through their regrets. "You don't want to carry that with you," she said.

August 31, 2001, Friday

Chemo, the yellow room, the green chair – Ann had pushed back so she reclined with a pillow behind her head when Janet came in to take her blood and clean the port. We talked about construction, about student housing. Janet lost focus, concentrated. In order to draw any blood, she had to push the chair back so that Ann lay flat. After she left, Ann and I chatted. It was cold in the room, with the door open. I put on my sweater. Finally Dr. Doyle came in, a little giggly: he turned to me, his eyes sparkling, every time Ann said anything. After he listened to her chest, he fussed a bit about the wheeze but when he ordered the CT scan, he said he thought she'd stabilized. Then he told us he had four patients on Iressa, those who can't take chemotherapy.

4
The Tightrope of Stability

September 1, 2001, Saturday

Morning, facing the window of the computer, the colors bright and unreal. Depth and shallowness combined. Ann felt energetic – effects of prednisone. Her mouth, she said, was still sore. I reminded her she hadn't told the doctor about her sore mouth. She agreed; she was concerned lest he stop the treatment.

In the afternoon, before I went to spend the evening with Harvey, we were sitting in the living room, she in her beige chair, I in the yellow armchair. She spoke with me about writing my autobiography, urging me. I said no, I wasn't interested enough in the writing.

"I have journals," I said.

"Not the same, too inward. Your family won't know who you are."

Later, I thought, well, perhaps a set of essays.

Lying side by side on Ann's bed, we began to talk, and talked late. Rather, Ann did. At first, Ann thought I was saying she was getting quieter – that is not talking so much – and she explained that she couldn't remember as well as she used to and felt hesitant. Sometimes she had to search for words. It became easier to let me carry on the conversations.

Then I explained – I meant socially quieter, not

seeing as many people as she had as a young woman. We talked about whether people seem to change but really haven't – myself, for example, searching for friends thirty years before must have seemed social, but I wasn't. I was isolated and looking for connection. She wasn't clear – about hers – but did say that in Pasadena when she was in her twenties social activities with alumni were expected of her.

I thought of my own lonely and isolated twenties.

In the end, I had to tell her I was getting too sleepy to talk any more.

September 3, 2001, Monday, Labor Day

I woke up feeling guilt – or whatever it is that makes me feel I have to keep Harvey happy. (In truth, it's fear he's going to cause worse trouble for me than he does now, fear he's going to become a burden.) Since keeping him happy makes me unhappy much of the time – his complaints and messes are burdens I yearn to do without – I asked myself, what about me? I haven't asked that question of myself for some time, not since Ann has been reasonably well and I've been able to write as much as I want. I have what I want, temporary as it may be, so when I consider Harvey, I'm looking at someone who is in need. To fulfill that need, I would have to give up so much I'd become needy. I decided to create a moment of grace for myself, taking a mantra or a prayer, calming myself, putting myself first. I began to think about whether I am just expecting myself to take care of everything, expecting not to be loved if I can't take care of others, expecting incorrectly. I am almost seventy now, and most people don't expect me to take responsibility for anything, certainly not for the community. Many people this age just manage to take responsibility for themselves, like children or young people, preparing for the difficulties to come. I want to be like a child, expected to take care of my soul and no one else's. When I returned from Harvey's house, I talked with Ann about how to stop expecting anything more from myself than a child does. She agreed with me that it would be very hard to stop. She thought women were hard-wired by the time they're ten to take care of others.

September 5, 2001, Wednesday

I phoned Annie to acknowledge her phone call Tuesday afternoon. Claire said she was teaching her to use the phone. Annie decided she wanted to tell me about her day at soccer. "I almost hit a goal. I kicked it really hard. Do you know what number I am? Eleven! Do you know what I am? A Golden Eagle."

September 7, 2001, Friday

I rose at five thirty, Ann at six. We were on our way to French for Ann's CT scan. Neither of us is nervous any more as we drive through the almost empty streets. We don't expect much change. We've learned the ropes. Wheelchair. Tell them we want to keep it. We sat in the outpatient waiting room for half an hour. The nurse wanted to follow protocol and couldn't get Dr. Doyle's office on the phone.

In the afternoon, the doctor's office. I've assured Ann that I believe the CT scan won't show much change, since he believed the taxotere was holding the cancer – at least he'd heard nothing new to be concerned about when he listened to her chest. We waited. Blood taken. Typed for transfusion. We waited, reading. The doctor came in. Blood all right. No transfusion. No word from CT scan. If stable, may go on with taxotere. If not, try new drug, or Iressa.

September 8, 2001, Saturday

The afternoon with Harvey was easy enough. It began with my discovery of an envelope in the mail box, a letter telling me that South Dakota Review has accepted my story, "The Invitation." I called Ann, she wasn't home. I waited for her to call back. She was delighted. I was happy. Afterwards, the happiness went flat, as if we'd opened a bottle of champagne and then hadn't drunk it. I began to think of my age. How much can I do between now and physical defeat? Ann's situation. My not writing a novel now. My hard time with the Christabel story. Ann expected me to have been more excited and joyous. I said I wouldn't be joyous unless I knew she was well. I went to bed feeling troubled.

September 9, 2001, Sunday

I tried to sleep in this morning, but couldn't make it. Instead I read, trying to finish John Mortimer's *Sound of Trumpets*. Then I went down and lay beside Ann. We decided I'd been troubled the night before because we hadn't had the celebration we usually have had for any of our successes. "Maybe you have celebrations," I said, "so that you don't think of all the negatives."

September 10, 2001, Monday

When I returned from walking with Jean, Ann had already had her call from the doctor. At first I couldn't take it in emotionally, not even as we decided to go ahead with the train trip to Chicago we'd decided to try, but later, when I went upstairs to get dressed to go down to Amtrak I began to feel surges of joy. The cancer stabilized, the blood test down from a 10 to a 5, just one point above normal.

A ticket agent at the Amtrak station worked out our trip for us, setting us up to leave on the 19th. This was more than a travel agent was willing to do – though she had told us things weren't possible as far as she could see from Amtrak's central office. He sympathized, giving advice about insisting on getting help, asking for it. About staying all night in Portland to keep ourselves from feeling stress. About how to get hotel reservations.

We ate lunch at Mosaics, afterwards, in a sort of celebratory mood. Then I slept easily for the first time in days.

September 11, 2001, Tuesday

Noelle phoned at 7:15 to inform me that two jet liners had crashed into the twin towers of the World Trade Center in New York City and another had plunged into the Pentagon in Washington. Already dressed, I hurried downstairs, woke Ann, and together we went to the living room to turn on the television. Horror. The curtains remained pulled. The room, shadowy green. CNN was breaking the news at the same time it was showing reruns of the second jet hitting the second tower. Ann and I were watching when the first, then the second tower collapsed. The voices of the newscasters were trembling.

September 12, 2001, Wednesday

All day yesterday I'd been distancing myself from the terrible deaths. Not allowing myself a personal response, but pushing it back. Yet I woke up during the night, and again early in the morning, feeling anxious. When I went to Harvey's, I began to feel extremely anxious about the mess in the yard, and tried to mention how I felt to him. He, too, probably feeling the national depression, horror, fear, anxiety, reacted more defensively than usual.

In the evening, news about two of Ann's Stanford friends: their daughter, son-in-law and grandchild had been in the plane that crashed into the Pentagon.

September 14, 2001, Friday

Ann became involved in an email argument with her small group of Sjogren's Syndrome friends. One, who lived in Scranton, was angry and afraid and wanted instant retaliation. In the evening, Ann showed me the letters she'd written. I was impressed by her eloquence and percipience, and I hope my words conveyed that message to her. Amazingly, she's feeling well and strong, though mildly concerned because she's used up so much time on her email. I've told her it's good, she needs it and they need to hear what she has to say.

I mailed a second short story in the afternoon. No more until October.

September 18, 2001, Tuesday

Packed. Lengthy job, difficulty deciding what was to go where. Organized first by use, then by possible necessity. Finished by early afternoon. Ann exhausted from bending over. I had put mine on the table. Back hurt though. Pleased with myself because I'd cut down the number of books and tapes I was taking.

September 19, 2001, Wednesday

Went to bank to get cash for Harvey. Talked about how much he'd need while I was gone. Decided where to hide it – under the ceramic head of the Chinese woman painted by his mother.

Diane came in to drive us to the train. She sat on the couch, face long, troubled. Just the day before she and her friend Barbara had decided not to go to France. She told Ann she felt "fragile."

But she was brisk, helping us get suitcases into the car. They're too big and bulky. She used her musician's strength to lift – I didn't have a chance. At the station, she helped us unload then left, sweeping off in her green car.

Ann and I waited inside the station, sitting on long brown benches, facing the tracks. Then Harvey arrived, wearing his yellow sweater. He sat next to me, Ann on the other side.

At last the train rumbled in, we found our way to our compartment, one on the lower floor, set aside for handicapped. It was troubling almost immediately. The seats were uncomfortable, only a curtain separated us from the wash stand and toilet. If we left the door of the compartment open, we would be viewed by every person coming down the stairs.

Worse – air from the train's circulation system was blowing into our faces.

What follows is a joint email from Ann and me written to some English friends after we returned from the trip.

Dear Florrie and Meg,

You did receive the first, brief version of Ann's tale about our aborted train trip, I hope. She's resting today, so we decided I should forward/copy the first installment of the longer story she started to tell on Sunday. I must confess I have (with some difficulty) dissuaded her from a mile-by-mile account of the Columbia River Gorge, the peculiar street arrangements in Astoria, Oregon, the view of the bridge to Washington State, what Cannon Beach looks like in heavy rain, the best book store for dining in Newport, how to find Triple A (our version of the automobile club) in Coos Bay and notes on Arcata, California, after dark. I'm sure she'll fill you in if you ask, however, as soon as she recovers from the effects of this week's chemotherapy. So here's Ann's unabridged version of the first few days of the trip that wasn't – or was, but in unanticipated form:

As Amtrak and my Aunt Marge promised, Carol and I and our baggage were treated like Waterford crystal in San Luis Obispo, being driven to the door of our train car on the baggage golf cart and being welcomed handsomely by our (bless him!) excellent car attendant (what were used to be called "porters") and plopped in a downstairs handicapped suite. We sat down in the seats which become the lower berth when you're ready for that. These are not designed to accommodate the human back and buttocks, but we thought, "Aw, heck, for one night, we can take it," AND we had agreed to this accommodation when we made our hasty reservations the day before the World Trade Center disaster.

We sat unmoving for an hour in the San Luis Obispo station. Even Harvey Norton (Carol's husband) had left the station. This minor delay (one of the reasons why Amtrak suggests you stay overnight in a hotel in Portland, OR, before continuing your journey by connecting with a train that goes to Chicago) was occasioned by the fact that the sprinklers – yes, dears, sprinklers – had mysteriously gone off on a timber trestle RR bridge just north of town (Carol swears it is THE original bridge from early last century), so the southbound train waited on one side, while we waited on the other as RR folks checked out the bridge. Finally we left.

Then there was dinner. We had been handed reservation slips for 5:40. Reaching dinner involved a climb up to the second level of traindom and through several cars. We were seated so close together that it was almost impossible to deal with our food, delivered by a waitress who was rude, loud, and altogether obnoxious. Our table-mates were a nice couple, and conversation was required but difficult. From them we discovered that the first-class accommodations were almost all taken up by people like them who were on some sort of tour. We found out from others later that most had made their reservations months before, an explanation of why we were unable to get rooms in hotels that offered Amtrak discounts.

So we come to Wednesday night. I had started a bladder infection on Monday but, since this is a common experience in my life, I'd been taking the usual Rx's for this and had plenty of pill-ish help with me. But, as Wednesday progressed, my symptoms had become rather more severe. At the same time, Carol had become more and more distressed since we'd boarded; we think now that the air conditioning in the lower level of the sleeper cars may not provide the air exchange that we experienced in the upper levels. She didn't tell me that she was getting pretty queasy. I had elected the upper berth because I don't have a problem with tight spaces, nor a bad knee. Let me say that the upper berth in this particular accommodation was rather like an

MRI capsule open on one side. Both berths had all the comfort of resting on a gurney. Yeah, we got extra pillows and propped up knees and did all the things we know to let old bods sleep. No go. The roadbed hasn't improved since we rode the trains to Stanford and Cal in the late 40s – and it wasn't just us – everyone complained all the next day. For one thing, the train was trying to make up for the time lost sitting in SLO, and lost another hour and a half before it reached Portland. Sometime in the early hours, Carol confessed her physical distresses and put down one of my Ativan (it's a relaxant and anti-nausea drug I have for chemotherapy – can't imagine why I took it along) and that helped. Nothing was helping my urinary tract, however.

Thursday morning. No reservations for breakfast and lunch. At 8:30, there was an hour's wait. We ate an adequate buffet thing and the lukewarm coffee offered at what is normally the bar in the parlor car. In the parlor car, there are 8 sittable chairs, as well as benches at tables. At the first opportunity, Carol and I grabbed two of the chairs and hung onto them until lunch, taking turns to return to our stateroom for the necessities of life while the other piled books and the like in the vacant chair. While I'm whining, though, I must tell you that these chairs are the ones that people cling to as they stagger down the aisle and, if the train lurches while they have the back of your chair in their grip, you get whipped 90-180 degrees along with your fellow passenger.

You want to know about the scenery? The forests of southern Oregon are a disaster. Thursday afternoon gave me the most reading time I had on this luxury cruise during which, if you will remember my earlier press releases on this topic, Carol and I planned to read and rest a lot.

Thursday, evening, arrival in Portland about 1 hr. and 45 min. late. Total breakdown in the promised assistance at the station. Our porter ended up delivering our baggage inside the station, accompanied by Carol, while I tried to pace myself for what turned out to be a walk of about 4 long city blocks. (I have trouble with one block and, by this time, my infection was blooming.)

Carol checked on the next leg of our journey – Portland to Chicago. Either we had misunderstood from the git-go, or Amtrak screwed us, but we were scheduled for the next 48 hours in exactly the same kind of handicapped "suite" on the lower level, and nothing else was available.

We schlepped our baggage to a surly taxi driver outside; he drove us to the Holiday Inn across the river, deposited our bags IN the driveway and left them there after I paid and tipped him rather well. According to Carol, who dealt with the baggage from there, a great deal of outrage at the taximan's behavior was expressed by a group of young Blacks, about whom more later.

The hotel people coped with two pretty uptight old besoms rather well. Harvey had called and left as his identity "HTN," and I almost lost it, saying that I didn't know any "HTN" and what sort of message was this?! So everyone got nervous until I realized that it was our own Harvey being funny. (He still thinks these are the sorts of hotels that we had in San Luis in say 1935.) Yes, we got help with the baggage from the hotel folks, the room was just fine, we got what we needed to eat (not much) right there, and crashed.

Digression: The African-American kids were students from Grambling State University, LA. At first we thought they were there for some sort of band competition, but no. On Saturday their football team was to play Portland State University. We were never able to find out how they came out, but I noted today that they whopped somebody 40-6, and it made me feel good. They were THE nicest bunch of kids of that age I've been around in years – and remember, I live in a college town. They were having a good time, but they were considerate of everyone else; their respect for their adult supervisors was complete but "easy."

Apparently, Grambling is a self-segregated school.

And so, after an uneasy night, we come to Friday, 9/21 (in case you've lost track). ASAP, I called my SLO urologist and got the right people right away. BUT, doctors can't do much about a new Rx – even if he can guess which antibiotic might work when Cipro hasn't – from out of state, and he says I must see either a urologist or get to an ER. Remembering how very ill I became about two years ago when a bladder infection suddenly turned into a big-time urethral infection, Carol and I realized that we would have to stop the train trip right there. We cried a little. We got another night at the hotel. We rented a car and got picked up at the hotel almost instantly; we cashed in our Amtrak tickets; I called urologists' offices and found out which ER to offer myself to and found our way there by 11:00 a.m.

At 2:45 a doctor saw me, asked a few questions, listened to my lungs, and sent me off with an Rx for Cephalexin 500 mg. 4x daily for ten days. He said he hoped it would work and to call them after 72 hours for a report on the culture.

Shortly after he left and I was just about dressed, the nurses allowed Carol to come in because she had finally raised a rumpus. I treated them to a lecture on the illegality of not allowing a person the adult wishes to accompany her into the examination room to do so, especially when that person is the patient's "agent for health care," a point I had made when they refused Carol admission. One unfortunate Nurse Nellie first responded, "Are you unable to make medical decisions for yourself?

I said to the entire brigade that I had not made a more strenuous objection because it was clear that they had been having a very heavy day and that it was not the time to try to educate them and their doctors but, now that the pressure was off, I thought they ought to get this matter straightened out with their doctors, the hospital, and themselves.

About 5 we had my Rx filled, we had a snack at an interesting shopping center, and returned to the Holiday Inn, praising God and our intelligence that we were not on the train, and the doctor for having apparently hit the right medication, and found a good place for dinner.

Tomorrow (if you're still with me): A trip up the Columbia River. Night. *Ann*

Back to Carol:

From my point of view, once Ann began the antibiotic prescribed by the Oregon emergency doctor, the trip became marvelous fun. On the first couple of days, Ann was full of energy, her sense of humor in good form, and she even ventured down a path or two to see some of the famous waterfalls that feed the Columbia. We stayed an extra day in Astoria because we had a comfortable motel and we liked the funky town. (To Californians this was like visiting a foreign country – a town whose population has shrunk instead of grown, from 20,000 to 10,000.) Luckily we did stay, because Ann had a "tired" day. When she recovered her energy, we sped down the Oregon coast, suddenly having realized we had no idea how far away California really was. (Not that we wanted to get back to California, but on the other hand, we did have a rental car to turn in.) The long, narrow road, the rain, and the sparse population brought back happy memories of a drive we once made from the far north of Scotland down to Littlehampton in order to reach Fiona B-G on the day we'd promised.

I've been reading your emails over Ann's shoulder and enjoyed with her your post cards. The computer correspondence has been a wonderful boon to her

– and to me too, as I slog away on short fiction. (I have a novel ready, but am holding it back in case it sells – in which event publicity and travel connected with it would become a major problem as long as Ann is ill.)

I hope you are both well – and worried, as we are worried, about what may become of civil liberties in this terrorist world. Love, *Carol*

October 1, 2001, Monday

Chemo this morning at 10.

The long, paneled room at Mission Medical felt like home after we climbed the stairs and Ann presented herself to – is Ginny the receptionist's name? I'll have to make sure I know it by next week. Two blonde women were waiting together. I examined them to figure out which was wearing a wig, but failed. Janet called Ann's name. She was weighed – back to her original weight of 158, she told me. Janet wasn't sure what was to be the procedure for the day. Ann told her "Infusion." I had the feeling she thought Ann was well enough not to have to come in, a false feeling, but confirmed later, when Dr. Doyle asked the same question. He was thumbing through his notes. "Can't read your own writing?" I teased.

He gave me a real grin.

"You were going to give her six to eight weeks more of taxotere," I said.

Ann agreed.

He agreed, looked at Ann, decided he didn't need a blood test.

I went to the library, marketed, picked up Ann. Bought the protein berry smoothie she likes to treat herself to after chemo. At home, after a while, she felt a bit queasy, but that was gone by dinner time.

Galleys from the *South Dakota Review* arrived, with instructions to have them back by October 4.

October 2, 2001, Tuesday

In the morning, Ann and I proofed the galleys. She stumbled as she read out loud. I think her mouth felt dry and sore, and I was immensely grateful for her help. I was still sleepy, tired, not quite myself.

October 7, 2001, Sunday

Harvey prepared to go to the Poletti Barbecue this morning with his pictures of previous barbecues pinned to the easel his father had made for the children in their finger-painting days. When I returned home, Ann had gone out to breakfast. Around one o'clock, she returned, telling me she'd been such a long time because she'd met first, her urologist, at Frank's, then Shirley H. [who worked with us for the Commission on the Status of Women]. Shirley was woeful – cruise missiles and B52-bombers were plastering Afghanistan.

My feelings: I'm puzzled about what to think about Afghanistan. I don't have all the pieces ready in order to form an opinion, and therefore, I remain ambivalent. Not numb. Just puzzled. I don't want war. I want to get rid of the Taliban. I don't want terrorism. I don't want

Bush in power, leading the nation. My opinions won't change anyone. Maybe that's a clue – a child whose feelings weren't right for her family (as mine were not – not quite) loses sense of a voice. Shirley, though, was upset.

After I'd eaten lunch, Ann and I sat down to watch CNN for a while. Only airfields, they say. Bread rained down for the people. I hope the Taliban remains true to its religious principles and does not move women and children within range of targets.

October 8, 2001, Monday

Ann was in fairly good spirits this morning as we went to chemo, Ann driving. She felt sleepy, enjoyed resting in the chair provided in the therapy room. When Doctor Doyle came in, she didn't try to get up – I mean sit up – but lay there, laughing. She told him she was fatigued, and he agreed that chemo does take its toll that way. She showed him a cyst above her left breast, apparently attached to a rib. I'm not sure he felt it, but he said they'd x-ray it if it was there next week. I was surprised she hadn't told me about this, and I don't know whether she didn't tell me because she was afraid I'd worry or because it really seemed inconsequential to her. She slept a little in the afternoon. Then, as I was working on her accounts for her, I heard her bustling about – in the kitchen I thought. When I went out to the kitchen, I found her outside.

"What's up?"

"We don't have any parsley," she answered, adding

something else cryptic, about John cutting too soon or not watering.

"What are you doing?"

She was heading the rose bush. "That should be obvious," she said.

"But why?"

"That too should be obvious."

"Are you feeling the prednisone the doctor put you on?" I asked.

"No, I still feel tired."

But manic, I said to myself.

October 9, 2001, Tuesday

Dr Karl's office called. Ann didn't have a UTI, but she had a high amount of glucose in her urine. The news had frightened Ann, though it didn't me, really. I thought of the possibility of the cancer spreading to the liver or the pancreas. Then I thought of prednisone, as a cause, and told Ann. I think she was mildly comforted, but not as much as I would hope.

October 11, 2001, Thursday

Ann called Dr. Doyle about sugar in urine, and he ordered a fasting blood test. She seemed more worried about her situation after this – or was she more tired? I couldn't figure it out, and so worried myself – a funny kind of worry, where I think about how she's feeling, then apply back to myself. I'll have to think this one through.

October 13, 2001, Friday

Claire phoned, and we chatted about world troubles, whether she should be concerned about driving across the Golden Gate Bridge, what was happening as the media drove people's fears towards violence and repression.

October 14, 2001, Sunday

In the morning Ann was up early because Manuel from Charter was to restring the cable. Before he arrived, she came upstairs to see the kestrel that can be seen out my window atop the cypress. She seemed to be breathing all right climbing those stairs.

October 16, 2001, Tuesday

We discussed our mutual tendency to bury ourselves in email or writing of some sort or other – or my exercise necessities – just as it's time to sit and enjoy each other. Both of us feel we are so dull that there's not much to say. Life passes as if for children, long, slow and steady, when at its best, I think. Nothing left to do, nothing left to worry about.

October 17, 2001, Wednesday

I left to bring Harvey money, waited for him for more than an hour, stirred up Ann because I phoned to see if he'd left a message about where he was planning to go. He arrived, just as I began to drive away, a ticket in his hand. He'd tried turning left on Los Osos Valley Road to visit a friend's ranch, then found he hadn't turned at the ranch road, and began to drive down the side, in the bicycle lane no doubt, looking for the road he'd missed. A highway patrol officer frightened him by horning him to stop, and, when he got out of the car, by ordering him back in. He tried to explain what he was doing and she told him to be quiet and listen. He had to tell her he was hard of hearing and then threatened to have a heart attack. She threatened to have his license pulled.

I tried to calm him down by telling him to ignore it, not to think of it. We'll pay the ticket.

October 19, 2001, Friday

Ann still feeling well, though we fuss about blood sugar. I'm worried that her pancreas or her liver is being affected by the chemotherapy. I told her so. I have always in the back of my head these days, we're too content. Things are going too well. It's going to be awful when – is there possibly an "if?" – the cancer comes back. This isn't quite the fear I have about Harvey having a difficulty that makes him more dependent. This is more a fear of my world coming to an end. For the second time. How are we going to make ourselves deal comfortably with that?

Claire and I talked for a while in the afternoon, about Pete's upcoming birthday and parties and plans. More than that, though. Claire is concerned about Pete, who goes to his meeting at the Pentagon in the week after his birthday. Ian will worry, what can she tell Ian?

I answer, the truth, and assure him that plenty of people live with and have lived with fears that never come true. His grandfather was in a war, was in an area being shelled, and he's here.

October 20, 2001, Saturday

We drove to Parkfield, an exploration within the county we'd never made before. The sky was overcast as we found our way into a long valley, narrowing as we climbed up, up, slowly to 2600 feet, where the road then descended into another valley. Ranches, fields of alfalfa, miles of them. Bright green against the greyish brown hills. Stands of oaks, strong, healthy, pines. The valley we were seeing hadn't burned for years, I guess. Down in the second valley, the ranches were more frequent – or perhaps they were just small places where people working in Coalinga or Shandon lived. Or maybe they worked in Parkfield, though I don't know where.

It felt like a day we might have experienced in Oregon or in England or up the coast, the driving for me taking the place of hiking, exploring, discovering. Illness forgotten, the present became all, movement taking the place of life, in a way, or life becoming only movement, becoming only vision, a willing suspension of disbelief in this world, the only world, strong as an ideology, a religion, a place to be when other parts of experience bring or threaten, like waves coming in on a beach, terror.

To get to Parkfield itself you have to turn off the road. The settlement has a motel and a a cafe, both in log cabin style – or rather the log cabin style of the toys we used to play with, the ones that preceded Lego. Green shutters on the motel. A big porch and rough-hewn tables at the cafe. A fountain made out of what looked like old boilers graced a small park in front of the cafe and another beside the motel. A gift shop, an ancient house or store, was closed, but clothes were hanging outside in the wind and dust. I noticed the library – a small shack, almost like one of those sheds you might keep tools in. The school neat, tidy – I thought of a boy I'd taught in high school, who now teaches there or who did, driving bus to pick up kids, sweeping the floor. Teaching all day. Field trips. Manual arts. There was also a small fenced enclosure labeled US Geological Survey and containing a large trailer and some very scientific looking equipment. Everyone seemed to be in the café watching football on television and chewing on what smelled like southern (not western) US barbecue. We drove on toward Cholame instead of driving back the way we came, and saw the Jack ranch up against the eastern hills, a long tree-lined drive leading to the buildings. We went on to Highway 46, on through Shandon, wine country, then south and home on US 101.

October 22, 2001, Monday

Dr. Doyle didn't seem too excited by Ann's blood sugar levels, suggesting she receive counseling from Dr. Borda, her primary care doctor. He did speak of a conference he'd been to over the weekend, letting us know he was feeling pleased with himself for the way he'd been dosing Ann with taxotere in small increments, allowing her to live a normal life and still hold the cancer back.

October 25, 2001, Thursday

Ann's been reading the history of the Ottoman empire by a writer born sometime in the 1830s in England we presume. The moral, imperial, and racist attitudes together with the elaborate style amused Ann and she read out several passages to me.

Later we spoke of the differences in opinion about decisions made and recorded historically, that is the dissenting opinions that didn't count when a decision was made. Perhaps, it occurred to me, variations in thought are not remembered unless they bring about change or revolution. Would Diderot be remembered if the French Revolution hadn't happened? The seventeenth century literature asking for the freedom of women disappeared from history, and we know about it only because the modern revolution unearthed it. There's a strong sense of civil rights in American society that continues to force people to consider it; will it disappear as the sense of beauty and generosity in the German people disappeared under Hitler?

Ann also spoke of what she called "terminal boredom." There's nothing that really interests her these days while she's not feeling well.

October 26, 2001, Friday

Dinner time brought frustration and fear, discovering that people like Ann and me are powerless to have any effect on the hysteria that is sweeping the country, making people like Diane willing to forfeit civil rights fought for at great expense by millions of Americans in order to calm her fears. I suspect she wants to trust G. Bush, and if she does, how many more are being swept to tyranny?

But again, at bed time, we played with the words. Turbulence – how I feel – and other tur or tor words: torpid, turgid, turpitude. Is there a turbid? Yes – dark and turbulent. Also turmoil.

October 27, 2001, Saturday

Having worked on the C-bel story, soaked in the hot tub, and had a pleasant shopping excursion with Ann in the mid-afternoon, I looked forward to having dinner with Harvey out – so that he wouldn't have to do dishes, I told him. As soon as I arrived at Benton Way I saw the envelope from the DMV on the television set. Harvey was lying down, later admitting he hadn't read it.

I took the letter back to the computer room to read it carefully and figure out what would happen, all of them the results of Harvey's not being able to remain silent when he's emotionally disturbed. Six pieces of paper, all having to do with his medical condition was covered by a letter saying he had to make an appointment for a reexamination of his right to carry a drivers' license. Before the appointment, he was to ask his doctor to fill out the forms and mail them to the DMV. My reaction: fear that I was going to have to become Harvey's driver. I couldn't seem to calm myself by working out an instant solution. When we went out to dinner, Harvey seemed happy and pleased with life, totally unworried by the letter, or pretending to be. I could hardly eat.

I couldn't help telling Ann how seriously I took this. Harvey is just beginning to feel okay about life again, partly because of his ability to drive around and see friends. He's made this as a project to get himself out of his depression, and it's been working. If he were to be confined to the house or to see his friends only with a taxi ride or a bus ride, I was sure he wouldn't be able to manage. Moreover, I'd have to drive him to many places he needs to go. Ann became excited because of my fears and despairs. She felt sorry for him, as I do, that terrible cross of pity he places on everyone. Then she became terribly angry, expressing anger at how my connection with him has robbed me of much of life already and the thought of his taking away more was impossible not to feel angry with.

I wonder now, if she didn't express the anger I should feel, whether it might not save me from the pity and grief for him that overcomes me.

October 29, 2001, Monday

In the morning Dr. Doyle reviewed his plans for Ann. The cancer is clinically okay and x-rays show stability. He plans to order a chest x-ray after the next infusion and a CT scan if there's any progress visible. A week or two without chemotherapy, then back to another course of taxotere. Generally, he seems pleased with Ann's situation. He doesn't even think blood tests will be necessary every time she gets an infusion.

Taking Harvey's case step by step, I tried to help

him to fill out the papers that must be brought to his doctor's office and mailed from there. He had some trouble believing he had high blood pressure, or a cardiovascular problem and had written his own explanations on a separate sheet of paper.

October 31, 2001, Wednesday

At noon Diane arrived for our regular Wednesday lunch, late for the first time ever, having been waiting for the arrival of a man with new soil for new flower beds in her new mobile home. On the way downtown, I laughed at the news that during this "high alert" period, Cheney was hiding out again. Diane wanted to know why I was laughing.

"Because it's all so unnecessary. Because he seems to be a coward. Because I oppose him politically and don't like his connection with oil companies and energy producers."

"Don't you think it's a good move for national security?" Diane asked.

"Why?" I responded, "Why not hide the Speaker of the House?"

Diane was quite firm that I was thinking irresponsibly, laughing inappropriately, making fun of those who were frightened of the Terror, instead of its effects on the American republic. She said that these were men of good will who were trying to help our country. I said I had many doubts about that.

As we walked down to the restaurant, I asked her how she felt about things, explaining that I was much more incensed about limitations of civil rights just signed into the Patriots' Bill. We would have argued, but I kept asking, telling her I wanted to understand. Which I did, because I've never combined in my mind the personality that lives liberally, yet accepts the often destructive dictates of those in charge. Social conventions, especially sexual, are to be defied; yet we all come home to rest under Daddy's roof. I had to fit my concept into my knowledge of Diane as someone who likes those the society praises, who trusts excessively, who does not know history. She herself spoke as a person who does not want to waste her energy becoming angry at things she can't do anything about – and I didn't point out to her she was wasting her energy becoming frightened of whatever the media said to fear.

November 1, 2001, Thursday

Today Ann forwarded to me an email she'd written teaching peace and reason to some of her friends on the east coast. I read it and was impressed with its care and wisdom – and grinned at its use of Aristotle's rhetorical device of identifying with the audience. I admired it I hope as profusely as I felt it deserved. I am proud she's taking advantage of the time she has to communicate with people who need to hear reason and old-fashioned American values. (Old-fashioned meaning the concepts embedded in our Constitution and Bill of Rights.)

November 5, 2001, Monday

Yesterday I developed a fever, couldn't eat, had to force

myself to drink. The night was difficult, a repeat of the night I'd had on the train – miserably depressed, unable to think of anything but my discomfort.

Ann fussed over me, climbing the stairs at least three times bringing me things. Once she put her hand on me while I was asleep, and I woke up with a start, feeling her hand. I'm reminded now of the time in England when I dreamed I felt her hand on my shoulder and wondered if I'd felt a ghost.

November 8, 2001, Thursday

We spoke briefly about how I become depressed when I'm ill, and she advised me to write this out as a directive to Claire as well as to herself. I mentioned all the thoughts I had when ill – the negative thoughts, the fears of loneliness and pain, the thought that the earth was going to swallow me, distress at the way the nation has changed – and she said she had those thoughts when she was insomniac. I said so do I . . . I hope not too callously because I didn't mean it to be callous – and said that's why I try to get all words of my own out of my brain when I'm not sleeping by listening to book tapes.

November 13, 2001, Tuesday

Not a particularly good day. Harvey brought home the papers from the doctor's. The doctor not only recommended that he have a drivers' test, but he suggested that his arthritis might keep him from having quick enough reflexes for driving and that he had a mild unspecified dementia, with mild memory loss, mild loss of judgment, and mild attention deficit. I can agree with the attention deficit, but I think that's been lifelong, not a result of dementia. I can also agree with loss of judgment, especially since 1980 or so. I don't agree with the memory loss. He's clear about what he remembers, and he doesn't forget much of what happens. He does forget names, but that's all.

An undercurrent always when I'm worried about the difficulties caused by the ticket: how am I going to learn to live with anxiety, especially if/when Ann becomes ill again? I've not been particularly successful recently in calming down, though I have been trying to use the energy tension provides in positive ways – that's all I can say.

November 14, 2001, Wednesday

Harvey didn't want to phone the DMV safety officer this morning, so I said, "Well, this afternoon then." When I walked with Jean, I was somewhat relieved to hear, as she recounted her husband's case, that there is recourse after having your license revoked: you can take a driver education course and then pass a test with the DMV. I wasn't sure when I told Ann this that she thought I should be relieved, but upon questioning her, I learned that she was skeptical Harvey would pay attention to an instructor. My private thought was that if he didn't, then he is responsible for his loss of license and will understand that he is and deal with it.

November 15, 2001, Thursday

Harvey at first refused to make the call to the DMV in the afternoon, pleading nervousness. But then he did it to please me. Unfortunately the person talking to him was hard to hear. He told her so, then realized he was on hold, then said again he couldn't hear. There was some back and forth about the doctor's report. Then Harvey repeated the date December 4th, and where will this be, he asked. "Oxnard?" he said, surprised. "Can't you get me one in San Luis?"

He had to repeat his license number then, so that she could see he lived in San Luis. He started to repeat it, then said he was rattled and had to read it off. He was on hold for a while again, then was asked how far it was to Paso Robles. He answered, that's thirty miles. Finally, he was given the date December 31. He began to object to that, and I went to tell him to explain that he had an old car. He handed the phone to me, and I spoke with the person. His car is old and he shouldn't have to go out on the freeway with it. She said this was not a driving test. I said, this is in response to a notice of reexamination, and she said she knew that.

The appointment is in San Luis at 9:00 in the morning December 31.

I felt a little better. We have time for him to get used to the idea and to practice and study the book, time for him to think more about his driving as he drives around town.

November 16, 2001, Friday

We had a long, thoughtful discussion of the depression we both feel about the Bush administration's seizure of congressional powers. We agreed that his ability to do it without much censure – few express the outrage we feel – is the result of the upswelling of the radical right and the failure of most people to have time to read, the domination television has over our way of thinking and living. So far the organizations that take up single issues have co-opted most of the people who think as we do – the environmentalists, the sustainable economists, labor unions, feminists – but they haven't been unified within the Democrats, who are almost as beholden to the power of corporate money as the Republicans are. We agree we may vote only with the Greens from now on – at the national level, though not locally – and that we must write to our representatives.

November 19, 2001, Monday

This morning Ann received a response from one of her eastern friends to an email she sent about torture being used on United States prisoners, She forwarded it to me, with this remark, "Wow! What can I say?" Here's the note from the friend:

I have no problem with using torture at all in this situation. I have a problem, actually, that we are not using it. A few of these people are refusing to talk (3 I think) and there is a reason why. These people (terrorists) want to kill us. They tell us this and have done it to us over and over and over again and rejoice after the killing has taken place. They dragged our dead soldiers through the streets of Somalia and skinned Russian soldiers alive.

Another member of the group, who has supported liberal Democrats in Massachusetts, emailed "Agreed."

November 22, 2001, Wednesday

By bed time we decided Ann definitely had a cold. This worries me. Makes me fluster, want to do warding off kinds of things, like apply mentholated creams. Ann rejects all of that.

November 22, 2001, Thursday
Thanksgiving

Ann was definitely worse, her throat severely sore, and a wheeze like a whistle I could hear six feet away. This upset me enough so that when Noelle phoned to wish people a happy Thanksgiving before she took off for the desert, I laid it on her that her father had been lonely and that I wish she'd called him – as I'd asked – Tuesday or Wednesday evening. Her voice became tremulous; I felt sorry. That and my concern for Ann made me start to cry. For several hours after speaking with Noelle I felt sad, lonely myself. I had said to Noelle the reason I was concerned is that a serious enough cold could kill Ann. Then this fear blinked off and on for me the rest of the day, fear for Ann, fear for myself alone, fear of asking too much of my children, even fear of making bad decisions, the way I had in my 20s, the way I did in my late 30s.

In the morning I walked with Harvey at Laguna. The lake still, reflecting sky. A loon was standing under some cypress trees at the turn toward the lake, black, its head stretched up and forward the way egrets stand when they stalk. On our return the bird was lying down, black against the early green grass.

Most of the afternoon I spent with Ann, until it was time to pick up Harvey to go out to dinner. I listened to her cough, watched her face. Once, when she was lying back, glasses on, nose up, hair outlined by the window, she looked so like my mother I was shocked. I had to rethink – this is Ann, and wipe my mother's features from my eyes. When I picked up Harvey I was shaking.

Another fear, stronger than all the rest, was concern about Ann's feelings, but she wouldn't let me know whether she had any fears for herself. So I could not ask.

November 23, 2001, Friday

In the middle of the night I got up once. I think it was one-thirty. I crept downstairs, listening for Ann's breathing. No sound. I was relieved that during the period I was awake I heard no coughing. Morning, though, she said she'd had a difficult night, waking every hour and a half or so. She still had a fever. As soon as she'd eaten something, she phoned the doctor, a difficult project because the oncology department was closed, the urgent care facility said it wasn't opening until 5 p.m. At last she sat through numerous "holds" to get the answering service, where a woman listened to her symptoms and took her phone number. Though the answering service told her that Dr. Borda would take her call, she was phoned back by Dr. Doyle. He prescribed a new form of erythromycin and albuterol for the wheezes she was experiencing.

November 24, 2001, Saturday

Ann's fever abated this morning, and she was feeling better, though not well. She was still coughing. I worked at both the journal and the c-bell story until shortly after eleven. In the afternoon I continued reading *The Western Coast* by Paula Fox, once or twice bringing Ann a glass of water. Both of us felt reassured by the quick action of the antibiotic. Her back and neck were painful because of her coughing, though, so I heated two of the moist heat packs she keeps and helped her place them, one under her back and the other at her neck.

November 25, 2001, Sunday

In the afternoon when I returned to Ann, her fever was mounting toward 102. I felt frightened. Still, I knew I had to convince her to phone the doctor without seeming more than sensibly concerned. It didn't take much persuasion. She phoned. Dr. Doyle phoned right back. He heard her wheeze on the phone, prescribed cipro, prednisone, and discussed a new way of using her inhaler. Then he checked with me to discover whether she was worse off than she seemed to say on the phone.

I said she looked all right – except for the wheeze. Or should I say whistle, for at times I could hear her across the room, just as I had on Friday.

November 26, 2001, Monday

Ann's fever had dropped to below normal in the morning. We discussed whether she should keep an appointment she had for a general physical and to establish herself with Dr. Borda as her primary care physician. She decided that even though she wasn't sure she was better that she should go because of the amount of time set aside for her on the doctor's schedule, a typically generous and thoughtful decision. All this time she's felt sick and been in pain she has sat quietly, without complaint, except when it's necessary to tell me what she's feeling.

She kept the appointment, and I went with her. Dr. Borda is tall, thin, youngish, with dark waving hair that he wears just below his ears. He's pleasant and he listens carefully. At one point he said "You've beaten the odds on this one."

In the afternoon, she had an appointment with Dr. Doyle. This is the first time she's seen him since the x-ray that showed the cancer hadn't progressed since April. He's encouraging – a little – even voiced the possibility that the root-like projections from the place where the cancer was biopsied might be scar tissue or inflammation. He wanted a PET scan, a picture showing where cells in the body are inflamed, and possibly therefore cancerous. Glucose is injected, then the machine catches its glow. Or something. I felt great relief as we left his office. I'm beginning to think maybe this period of remission is going to last. He and Ann had discussed the possibility that her age may be slowing the growth down. He said studies have shown that breast cancer and non-small cell adenocarcinoma may not grow so fast in the elderly. Perhaps she may not need any more treatments for a while.

November 29, 2001, Thursday

On my way to bed, Ann said she was still depressed. On other days she's said it's about the national situation, the closing down of the left. This time I asked, "About anything but what we're both concerned about?" meaning her health. The dark canyons that will still open up? I told her I was full of hope for her, for us. She didn't seem impressed.

December 3, 2001, Monday

Ann had an appointment at 11:30 a.m. She was feeling well, and we were both able to giggle at the funereal music threading wistfully through the waiting room. (I guessed it was an orchestral version of what's generally called Chopin's funeral march) Dr. Doyle thought her chest sounded all right – at least he didn't say it didn't – and then Ann and he talked about malpractice suits and the topic of abandonment. Ann had become angry the day before when she heard that Kay had lost a suit because of "abandonment."

December 6, 2001, Thursday

The day of the PET scan: We started for Santa Barbara at 7:15, Ann quiet in the seat beside me. She had been told not to take anything by mouth after midnight, and her empty stomach was hurting. She's been bothered by gastritis for several days, worrying me about the possibility of pancreatitis or liver disease. Our arrival at the Cancer Center in Santa Barbara was timely and smooth, but once Ann had been taken in, signed up, and injected, we had a wait while the technician who was to guide us to the nuclear medicine office across the street took care of other tasks. Ann became impatient, not understanding that the injection had to work its way through her body. The technician was kind when she came, however, and walked us over slowly enough for us to recognize she was sensitive to lung cancer and arthritis both. In the office, Ann was given a comfortable chair. I was allowed to sit with her, and the technician brought her water, explaining that she should have been told to drink water. Clearing the bladder just before the scan is important.

When the scan began I went out to sit in the waiting room, one shared by social services and a room where yoga is taught. The chairs were Santa Barbara mission chairs, with uncomfortable straight seats and thin cushions. I read about the Turks, their constant incursions upon Europeans in the Balkans and Hungary. An older couple sat across from me, both grey haired and red-cheeked, the man with short cropped hair and a red head and forehead under its greyness. The woman wore a long-sleeved suit of denim and a windbreaker jacket; she looked comfortable and well-dressed to me. The man wore jeans. They came from south county San Luis Obispo, probably retirees from a city suburb. I wondered if they were as uncomfortable as I.

Before Ann had pulled herself together after the scan, the technician, a thin blonde woman with conventionally curled shoulder-length hair, a tight face, came out to ask me questions about Ann. What is the diagnosis? Lung cancer. She knew that. How long has she had it? It was diagnosed in January this year. When was the last CT scan? In September or August. She's had chemotherapy? Yes.

After a while I heard Ann's voice. Then the technician told me she was ready. We left. As soon as we arrived at the car, Ann told me she was angry. The tech had asked her some of the same questions she'd asked me. She'd asked them while Ann was uncomfortable, lying flat on her back near the scanner. She asked Ann how many infusions she had. Ann couldn't remember. She offered to get her notebook, if only she could sit up. The tech said it wouldn't be necessary. Ann also needed a drink of water to soothe her dry mouth.

For a moment, sitting in the parking lot, we worked through the map of Santa Barbara and directions to Samarkand, the retirement community. We were going to meet Ann's Aunt Marge there, while visiting her friend Jack. We didn't have any trouble finding the community, but drove back and forth among Mediterranean style villas, creamy behind shrubbery, tile-roofed, dark trimmed. We had to find the administration building first, then use it for our bearings.

At last we found a directory, followed it, asked a man where to get into the convalescent hospital, asked help at the desk, and were led to Jack's room.

He was skeletally thin, long arms down to the bone, face gaunt. He waved the long arms about, gesturing as he talked. Later as he told stories he lifted one hand behind his head, used the other to emphasize points. It was holding a magnifier for reading and he brought it down again and again on the papers.

He spoke with great love of Marge, her morning calls what make his life happy. "We do this because we love each other," he said, simply. When Marge arrived, we left Jack to eat lunch in the dining room as his guests.

I thought of Harvey. How necessary it is for old men to have women to love them. Old women – I wonder, if they ailed, would men care for them, would they feel it necessary to have women to love them? I sometimes believe the most truly loving old couples are women.

December 7, 2001, Friday

One recent evening, perhaps this one, (there's been a delay in writing this journal entry) Ann told me she was concerned about her angry feelings. On her way to sleep, she begins to imagine a beautiful scene, a peaceful one, but something happens to turn it into ugliness and violence. She's feeling angry more easily.

"With me?" I asked. "No," she said.

But I couldn't help thinking of the times she's been irritable lately. We talked then about how anger at her situation might be rising up now. We agreed that at first we'd both been so stunned by her cancer and she'd been so sick from the chemo that there was no chance for the angry feelings to rise. I reminded her that we were together on this journey.

December 8, 2001, Saturday

We set out at ten o'clock for Noelle's in Solana Beach, on our way to attend Ellen's music recital on Sunday. I drove to Ventura. Traffic through LA on 101was thick. Not coming down on 101 again through LA, either, we told each other.

Ellen was getting ready for her cotillion when we arrived. Ann settled down with the newspaper while I went off with Noelle and Ellen. We drove down to the old Del Mar race track – county fairgrounds now – steered in and out through parking lot after parking lot. A festival of lights was going on. I could see the outlines of Christmas scenes through the windshield. At last, we found a parking place where adults and children, girls in fancy dresses, boys in jackets and ties, were running, shivering, laughing, into a building that had a glass walled room. Dozens of white chairs were lined up in the room. In the hall children of eleven and twelve stood in writhing, clumping, jumping imitations of lines, boys to the left of the door, girls on the right, all of them talking at once. That is, until they went through the door, a boy and a girl side by side. They turned away from each other toward tables where each gave his, her name, then went through a reception line. I watched Ellen look up into the eyes of each of the people in line, smile, say hello, and even bob a little curtsy. Then Noelle and I walked out to look in through the glass wall to see Ellen sitting in a line in one of the dozens of chairs, a rather tall and good looking boy next to her.

Noelle and I went back home then. Erwin picked Ellen up, and she was thrilled because she'd won third place in the "box waltz" and had a box of fudge.

I like the way her eyes shine.

December 9, 2001, Sunday

Ann felt well enough to sit at the kitchen counter and polish silver while Ellen, Noelle and I went to the Unitarian gathering, which is held in an amphitheater dug out of a sand cliff (I kept examining the cliff and wondering about erosion). The community has built comfortable benches in half circles rising up above the central platform. Umbrellas shade everyone from the sun, even the organist and the speaker. The ceremony followed the pattern I've observed at the San Luis Fellowship. When the time to share "joys and sorrows" arrived, Ellen surprised both me and Noelle by standing up and walking over to stand in line behind a microphone, waiting her turn. A few other children, accompanied by their parents, were in the line, but most speakers were adults. Ellen came at the end, following a man who spoke of the 9/11 catastrophe. She was wearing a red and white Santa Claus hat on her head. She stepped up to the microphone and spoke clearly, firmly, about the concert she was to be in that afternoon and how she was going to announce and how excited she was. I believe everyone was charmed – they applauded, softly, smiling.

At Noelle's house we ate a quick lunch, then got

ready for the concert in the afternoon. Ann had felt well enough to polish all the silver trays and bowls, was still working on it happily when we returned. Since Noelle and Ellen had left at one, we drove over with Erwin just before the time when it was to begin. Noelle had saved seats for us, right behind the children who were to play in the string ensemble.

Just as it had at the Fellowship gathering, Ellen's voice came through the microphone strong, clear. She sounded excited about the program and willing to excite the audience. The first piece was a choral, violin, and piano rendition of "America." Next, Ellen announced her favorite song, Joy to the World, explaining that she was to accompany the violin ensemble. She'd hardly finished speaking when Barbara, the teacher, stood up, gave the downbeat, and started the orchestra off. Ellen had to run for the piano, across the stage, place her music on the stand, and catch up. All this she managed – and more, for the ensemble itself sounded ragged, but as soon as she began playing, she pulled it together. I was impressed she'd been able to find the place in the song by listening, and then beginning to play exactly on the beat with them. After the performance others praised her too.

December 11, 2001, Tuesday

The report from the PET scan confirmed the tumors in her left lung and suggested that the spots seen on ex-ray in the right lung may be nodes resulting from her autoimmune disease. Dr. Doyle believes that now is the time to swing Ann into the ongoing trial of the new drug called Iressa which has been particularly effective on the form of lung cancer she has. If it doesn't work, she can return to one of several forms of chemotherapy.

December 20, 2001, Thursday

Ann felt tired, resting this morning. Linna's arrival for our lunch date boosted her energy, and it got another boost when Janet phoned from Dr. Doyle's office to say her Iressa had arrived and to make an appointment to take her first dose. Then when we sat at the table at 1865 Ann talked so much I had to say "I'm just trying to get a word in edgewise." In a strange way her life on the surface is more shareable than mine because she has a wide circle of internet friends and their problems to talk about. I have to wait until there's a chance to begin a more general conversation. Which I did, after a while.

Linna also created a time for us to talk about how I feel about Ann's situation. She pulled out her pack of cigarettes and stood with me in the garage – it was pouring rain outside – and asked.

Linna is thin, almost frail looking now that she's over 50. She was wearing a multi-colored top and dark pants, not really tights, but almost. Her outwardly loving and generous manner, no matter how used to it I become, doesn't make me suspicious, as Diane's does. But then I've never allowed myself to become close to Linna, liking her enormously, but remaining always peripheral. I don't know how I'd manage if I needed her.

5
Another Kind of Balance

December 21, 2001, Friday

The first day of Iressa.

A man preceding us into the doctor's office was in a motorized wheel chair. He was tall, thin, his head drooped, and he was wearing a cap to hide his chemo-baldness. The wheel chair was his birthday present his wife told us. I wondered whether he'd had to have his nerves cut so he could bear the pain, or whether his cancer was in his bones, thus making it impossible for him to walk.

In comparison with other patients, Ann has been cheerful and seemed to enjoy her visits. She accepted her loss of hair with dignity, and once her hair grew back, took compliments with dignity. When Dr. Doyle came into the office this day, she received him with a big smile and her typed-out list of medications. They joked about the length of the list, and she told a story about being asked whether she was compulsive and how she answered, "No, are you?" Dr. Doyle enjoyed her, and turned to me with a big smile often to make sure I was enjoying her too. As they joked about her being well-organized, he suggested that her house must be terribly neat, and she said, "Oh, no." He then volunteered to "make a house call," and she invited him to drop by for a drink any time.

December 22-27, 2001, Saturday–Thursday

On Christmas day, Ann and I went to Harvey's to share a buffet breakfast while the children played with their toys. I watched Annie learn to ride her bike. At one point, Claire, wanting Annie to teach herself, refused to push her off, and Annie threw the bike down and cried. "You're being too harsh with her," Ian said. Pete then pushed her off several times and she was soon balancing. Ellen waxed her new surfboard. While she and everyone else took it to Avila to try it out, Ann and I dropped by Anne C's tamale party.

Christmas dinner passed well, without incident. Annie wore her blue velveteen dress. Ann and I wore cloth corsages Pete had bought for us – he wanted us to graduate to the corsage wearing level, he said, and took pictures of us.

On Wednesday Ann and I drove to Prunedale, where Beth and Chris met us graciously with a tour of the baby's blue and white room (clothes hanging in the closet on tiny hangers), drinks before lunch in a pleasant restaurant. Beth seemed happy and well.

December 29, 2001, Saturday

A quiet day spent at home while Claire, Pete and the children took Harvey out to Montana de Oro. In the evening, I cooked dinner at Harvey's. Ann came, the children came. We pulled the table out for ten people. Before dinner, Claire told Ann about her new music therapy, spoke of how she's trying it out on Ian. Ann listened, trying to hear the differences in the tapes and headphones, with about as little success as I had. Noelle came to the table with a copy of a chapter she'd written for a conference book, with only a few copy editors' remarks on it, to show Ann and me how well we'd done for her as editors.

December 31, 2001, Monday

Chris woke me at 7, saying first, "Happy Birthday," adding that he and Beth were in the hospital in Santa Cruz, awaiting the baby's birth. I said, "You're teasing," but of course, he wasn't.

The rest of the day was tense, waiting to hear from Beth, wondering what to do about driving up to welcome the baby. Finally I made plans to do so the next day. Claire generously offered to drive Harvey up there and keep him at her house for a few days, relieving my tension considerably.

Most of the day I rested, while the children drove out to Montana de Oro with Pete's plane. I did have a walk with Noelle and Claire, where I confessed I was uncomfortable about the holidays with Ann – are these the last? Will she be here, will she be sick next year? At five, all ten of us had dinner at the Galley – good conversation sitting across from Pete and Erwin, allowing Ann to talk with Noelle and Claire. Civil rights were on everyone's mind.

On the way home Erwin told me about the period

of despair, then the periods of hope in the illness of his stepfather.

January 1, 2002, Tuesday

Beth's baby must have been born last night, I told myself several times throughout the night, rolling over in bed, noticing the ache in my knee, then my hip. At seven, I phoned Harvey's house and Pete answered that Chris had called about two that a baby boy had been born at 12:49 a.m., the first baby of the new year in Santa Cruz County. Later I learned Claire had been up most of the night with Annie vomiting. She'd been keeping her stomach upset hidden from her mother all day yesterday for fear she might not be allowed to play.

Ann and I set out for Santa Cruz close to ten, Ann driving, because I'm too tired, too nervous, too tense. We listened to the Messiah, stopping the tape only for the time when we zipped through the maze leading to highway 183 in Salinas. No matter how many times we've taken it, it's difficult. This time Ann made a mistake, followed too carefully the signs, wound up going down Sherwood and we had to turn around. Rain began, heavily misting, dripping low at the coast.

We had no trouble finding the hospital, and after admiring the baby and eating lunch in the cafeteria, we settled down into Beth's room while Chris made a run for home and a shower. Beth talked almost the entire time; mostly I remember her describing her delivery, but surely we spoke of other things. I held the baby for a couple of hours. Claire, Ian, and Harvey came in, and later, Pete. Harvey sat in a chair and looked from the baby to Beth, but said little. He claimed to have a cold, but I believe it was an allergy.

On the way home, over indifferent sandwiches in King City, I tried to articulate for Ann what has been distressing me for the last week: my girls give me so much time and love, and I feel uncomfortable. I don't know why, except I can't seem to give back as much as I want to, either in material things or time. Ann assured me I do indeed give it back.

"Maybe I feel I don't deserve their gifts of love and attention; maybe I give, but not wholeheartedly," I said. I reminded myself then of what my old friend Mary Gail once said: "But you give. That's what's important."

January 3, 2002, Thursday

Before dinner we discussed what to do with the days we may have while Harvey is away. We couldn't decide about Sunday, because Ann had to talk with Kay about something, but only if I'm not available. She didn't really want to see her but just get it out of the way.

We decided to tell Kay to wait and find out, just as we were doing. Then after dinner Claire and Harvey phoned to say he's coming home tomorrow. We felt terribly deprived, enough to comfort each other after the call.

"We're greedy," I said. "We have so much more than before, and we complain about this."

"But we don't seem to have time together," she replied, "because I'm tired and can't go places some days."

January 6, 2002, Sunday

Ann drove me down to Harvey's on her way to find breakfast goodies to serve Kay at their breakfast/tea this morning. I told Harvey we were going out driving to practice for the exam he's soon going to have to pass and suggested he get dressed.

We did get out on the road at about ten before there's much traffic. At first I was pleased with his driving. But after a while I noticed glitches: telling me who used to live where, meaning he wasn't focusing, and he didn't keep two hands on the wheel. Worse, sometimes he wobbled in and out of lanes. I kept an eye on the rear view mirror, observing that he was usually just a few inches away from the line. Sometimes I heard the wheels going over the bumps. In addition, he didn't always cooperate with my asking him to try certain maneuvers again when he's missed performing well the first time, I returned to his house very tense.

That evening Ann and I were enjoying dinner, the food, the conversation, the music – and then suddenly, just as we were about to get up, I felt nauseated. I got to the bathroom, lost my dinner. Ann said go to bed and I did. At 10:40, she was upstairs, worrying about me. She'd heard me drop my tape deck. Then I woke up at 2, my stomach raw. I took zantac and water, ibuprofen for my headache. My stomach became worse. After a while I went downstairs and asked Ann for Ativan. I threw this up very soon, and Ann came upstairs again with another. I took it, went to bed and to sleep.

January 11, 2002, Friday

Both of us had a difficult day. On my "training ride" with Harvey, he turned into a left hand turn lane, then turned out, swiftly, without looking back or attending to whether other cars were coming. The rest of the day I fretted about whether he'd pass the drivers' test to be administered on the 15th, feeling tension in my stomach, inability to get to work, inability to want to make any plans. I talked to Ann about the fears, just to let her know, then felt sorry that I'd added to her burden because she's had a bladder infection and the new medicine doesn't seem to help the burning she experiences.

Late in the afternoon I suddenly decided I had to have a plan that would work if Harvey lost his license. First I'll see what he suggests as a way of managing without a license. Then I can suggest he take the drivers' course offered for seniors that Jean told me about.

Ann and I read through the evening, nothing important – newspapers, magazines. At bedtime we became close, talking about how Ann was feeling, then about birthdays. We've already decided we'd go out for brunch on her birthday – Sunday the 20th – I'll trade Harvey's Sunday for Friday.

"Your birthday has to be a good one this year."

She turned to me, "Because it may be my last?"

Yes, I said inwardly, but to her I said, "No! Because last year's was so shitty."

We were quiet then, just being with each other for a few minutes.

Before I went upstairs to bed, I fetched a hot pack

for Ann's throat. A pair of glands at the base of her jaw were swollen and slightly painful.

January 14, 2002, Monday

While lying together on Ann's bed, just before I went upstairs, we talked about how I've curled up into a ball, spiritually speaking, the last couple of months, how I'm afraid of breaking routine, because only in routine is there peace, places where I can find an emotional corner. Outside routine, I just shut down. Knowledge that I'm doing this is breaking the curl, though, I think.

January 15, 2002, Tuesday

At 7:30 went to Harvey's to check on his clothes and his state of mind before he went to the DMV for his driving test. Wallet. Insurance. Proof you've had brakes checked. He set off neat and trim – except for the car. He had washed the windows, though, and they gleamed. For a moment we both panicked. He was trying unsuccessfully to shove the station wagon gate closed before adjusting the window but finally his key worked in the window and all was well.

I wasn't as easy about his departure as I wanted to be. I couldn't work. My hands were clammy. All the images of him as he goes to pieces, scenes I've seen as well as those I haven't seen rushed past. I played several games on the computer, touched the story I was supposed to be working on, then decided to phone him. The line was busy until after lunch, when I reached him to hear that he'd failed the vision test and must wait until his ophthalmologist examines him this coming Friday. The question was – and I didn't ask it – was his license suspended until he'd been checked by the opthalmologist.

Beth and Chris called about that time on the way home from the pediatrician. Their baby (whom they've named Julian) weighs over 9 pounds. I told them it was hard to talk because I was upset about Harvey. They promised to phone later.

The rest of the day I fought my tension, or tried to accept it, but the struggle kept me distant from Ann. Distant from myself, too.

January 17, 2002, Thursday

After visiting Harvey I was exhausted and depressed. I decided the only way to cure myself was to work – and I was immensely cheered by deciding to fix up a book of poems from my efforts of the 70s for Ann's birthday. I imagined myself surprising her with it Sunday morning. I worked hard for an hour and a half, setting up the pages and the cover. Then I cooked dinner, washed dishes, and read.

January 18, 2002, Friday

Ann was just as tired today as she was yesterday. Dr. Doyle noticed her loss of vigor, and thought he sensed a bit more of something in her left chest. He planned to order an x-ray and lab tests, but we began to talk about medical money problems, and he forgot. We had to remind him. (For the record, Ann did tell him about the swollen glands in her throat, her bladder infection, her yeast infection, her diarrhea. We discussed her tiredness as possibly a result of her Sjogren's Syndrome.)

At lunch the two of us returned to the topic of why older people feel more and more helpless. Problems with driving are an example of what happens: younger people, wanting speed and precedence, take what they can, pushing older drivers out of the way, making the older drivers seem unable because they can't compete with the speed and fast reaction time of the young.

Later I found out that Harvey's eyes are okay if corrected with new glasses. He does have a cataract that needs treatment in a year, possibly. Later I read the report: also macular degeneration, mild in one eye, moderate in the other. This means that eventually he may lose much of his sight.

January 19, 2002, Saturday

Today Ann was working in her office, taking care of filing she had neglected for six months. For my sake, she told me.

"Why for me?"

"Then you'd have to do it."

Is she fearing, as I do, that the x-ray Dr. Doyle ordered is going to show growth? I can't bear to think of that possibility. I'm settled down into her being here with me, an eternal present.

When I went to bed I was looking forward to bringing Ann her birthday present in the morning.

January 20, 2002, Sunday

All day I reminded myself to remember this, possibly Ann's last good birthday. She loved the present, and we read it together, side by side.

It was a clear, cold, bright blue day when we went out for brunch. Bay calm. Lee, the waiter who served us in October, remembered us. Restaurant quiet. Our conversation riffed back and forth. I drank too much champagne, but it didn't bother me. Read all afternoon. Anne C came over at 5:30 and we drank more champagne. Discussed Mardi Gras, families, illnesses, etc. Read some more, and to bed. Easy day. Quiet day. No responsibilities day.

January 21, 2002, Monday

Today Ann had even more energy than yesterday. It was pleasing to see, especially since she must go for an x-ray and a repeat blood test today and I didn't especially want to go with her.

So I was able to work most of the day, from catching up with my journals to the c-bell story. Even though I'd walked with Jean in the morning, I bicycled at noon. Then I soaked in the spa, thinking of the first principle of Pema Chodron's tape on facing difficulties: focus on the love you feel for someone close to you. I did, focusing on opening myself to love of Ann, something I close down, protectively, for much of any day.

Maybe the meditation made me too open. When I visited Harvey at 4, I was hit with empathy for the pain of his loneliness and had to fight the anxiety this caused me for an hour or more.

Before sleep I shared with Ann Diane's remarks about her conversation with Linna. They agreed we are admirable in the way we take Ann's illness without public tears or fears and I have been good at adapting and surviving. Then I described my response to Diane: I'm tired of surviving and adjusting, and would prefer living. Then I told Ann I subtly pointed this out by saying in response to Diane's reading books about China that I'd once wanted to go to China. This was a mistake. Ann's response: "Well, you can, after I'm gone."

I can't bear to hear her say that kind of thing. I want us to rest squarely in the present. "No," I protested. "No, don't say that kind of thing."

Then I was troubled because she may need to say them and I'm shutting her off. I asked that question, she responded, "No."

January 24, 2002, Thursday

Talk with Diane – who has had a chest x-ray taken – and Beth, who is feeling better and better. I am beginning to want to go north to see the baby again. But I don't want to leave until the DMV problem is sorted out.

January 27, 2002, Sunday

Ann and I hardly ever discuss current affairs any more, at least not in depth. We are both angry about the Enron scandal, but the reporters and columnists in the paper are also angry and give us hope that our concern is shared by millions. Not so the incipient Bush military dictatorship: a field poll shows that most Californians think the American boy caught with the Taliban should be harshly punished, but we don't agree.

February 3, 2002, Sunday

The cold spell we've been having for several days was breaking this morning. I rode out with Harvey to see how he'll do with the driving test. He is learning to concentrate better, at least when I remind him to. Signals are still a little iffy, and I'm not sure he looks over his shoulder. Still, he was happy today, preparing for a superbowl party with his friends. Beth has talked him out of having ice cream and cake. I helped him by setting up chairs, bowls, tables, slicing ham and cheese.

In the afternoon I spoke with Noelle about her friend Deborah's response to my Manzanita ms; pacing and Crossman's character and more of the mental hospital are the criticisms Noelle remembers. It's okay – I can see what Deborah is seeing/disliking/critiquing about the book. Nevertheless it's left me with some troubled feelings. I really can't change that book anymore. I think of myself as not being able to tell a story. I should have stayed an essayist or poet.

February 4, 2002, Monday

We had lunch with Diane, agreed to emphatically by Ann after we delivered my car to Los Osos for repairs. It was Ann who kept the conversation going. I didn't have much to say, and if I'd been alone with Diane would have asked questions instead of talking.

Diane always seems thrilled with time spent with Ann. I consider how she's worked for hospice, playing her harp for the dying. I remember the books about death she's told me about and her professed fear of death at the hands of terrorists right after 9/11. She is afraid, I think, in ways I'm not. I've had to tell her there are worse things than death when she reported her friend Dorothy was having an operation to reduce, sew up – whatever – a brain aneurysm – an operation that could kill her. Perhaps I myself deny my fear.

February 6, 2002, Wednesday

In the evening, the living room became too stuffy for me. I was sleepy, and thought of going upstairs. Ann opened doors and windows, saying, "If you have to go upstairs every evening, we would never be together."

February 8, 2002, Friday

At seven in the morning my nephew Steve Beck, Jean's son, called. His father, Kenneth, died last night. I surprised myself with tears – it's not that I don't feel, but that I usually feel without tears, except when overwhelmed by self-pity. Jean then came to the phone to tell me she had fallen asleep in the chair while they were watching television. Kenneth had said, "Wake up, it's time for bed."

She replied, "I wish you wouldn't wake me up that way." But she'd arisen, gone in to the bathroom, washed her face, brushed her teeth, pulled the sheets down. When she returned to the living room, she found the oxygen/humidifier by the door. She pulled it into the bedroom, plugged it in, and returned to the living room. There she found Kenneth lying on the floor. No pulse, not breathing.

The morning was a flurry of phone calls and activities. I had to tell Harvey, who had known Kenneth from childhood. Later I picked up a quiche at New Frontiers, dropped it off at Jean's house, then decided I should stay for a while.

I cried with Jean a bit, sitting next to her on the couch. Then I tried to be helpful, providing a phone number for Greg [Jean's son], putting out food with Joni and Deb [daughter and daughter-in-law, respectively], encouraging Greg to fill in the details for a good obituary. I stayed until after Bernadette and her husband arrived. Dettes looked and sounds completely recovered, except for her cane.

All day I thought about Jean's coming empty days, resolving to help her fill them, but not on a regular basis. I also couldn't help thinking of the possibility of my own empty days.

At bedtime, Ann asked for special healing blessings. The area above where her tumor is had ached the night before. This night it felt warm. I wasn't sure what she meant by that. I said, "Maybe the tumor is shrinking and pulling away from the healthy places it's clinging to."

February 11, 2002, Monday

Again I took it easy, trying to stem tension, which I believe contributes to the weary aches I've been experiencing. I went over to Jean's at around 9:30, talked with her as she folded Kenneth's laundry and placed it in bags to be given away. "I'm not going to put it back in the drawer," she said.

We were standing in the bedroom, Joni on her right, I on the left, when she told me she'd baptized him in response to my saying I was pleased for her sake about having arranged burial in the church.

"I always knew you would, you said you would"

"Before I let them carry him out the door I ran for the Lourdes water and did it," she said.

"I thought you would have before you called 911."

February 12, 2002, Tuesday

Beth arrived with Julian early in the morning, soon enough to accompany me and Harvey to Kenneth's funeral. Beth in a long dress, a dark top, looks well, not at all overweight for someone who's just had a baby. Julian was plump and happy, stretching his mouth in grimaces. He's dressed up, wearing a jacket and fancy trousers, matching socks on. Beth carried him in the car seat, which attaches – we found out – to the stroller.

We gathered with relatives at the side of the church, where I found Jean, embraced her, told her that Ann wasn't well.

Of course Julian fussed in church, and Beth had to leave. But not until after the coffin, covered with a white cloth got through the door. After that I saw Beth as a shadow, now and then, at the door.

February 15, 2002, Friday

At the doctor's today we met Liz and Hank A. We talked in ordinary voices, which sounded a little harsh in the deliberately muted atmosphere of the waiting room. Liz wanted to get our situations straight, took down our phone numbers. Joking about the chemotherapy, Liz laughed about her bald head – she's lost more hair than Ann ever did. Someone in the room with the window curtains lifted the curtain – perhaps we were disturbing them, I suggested after Liz and Hank left. Another person in the waiting room said, "No, it does people good to hear the support, the humor, the good spirits of those threatened with early death."

February 18, 2002, Monday

Now and then Ann has been forgetting details of who and what, but nothing important, we've agreed. Today, though, we'd planned that I was to drive down to the Mission Medical lab after dropping her off at her ophthalmologist's office, then come back and accompany her to the x-ray. She forgot I was going to the Mission Medical lab, and waited for me half an hour in a cold wind. The consequence was that she didn't feel well waiting for the x-ray, an hour's wait, and then didn't want to wait to see Dr. Doyle so they could look at the x-ray together.

She's utterly confident that the x-ray will show no

change or positive shrinking. I'm not. I'm trying to visualize our receiving the good news, though.

I'm having a hard time not allowing the gloom I feel to overcome me. For several nights, coming from being with Claire or Beth or, on Monday, the vigil and rosary for Kenneth, I've been unable to talk with Ann, wanting only to curl in upon myself, read, listen to tapes. Conversation makes me too aware, too tense. I don't think Ann feels happy about this. At least last night she didn't.

One constant cause of my distress is – as ever – Harvey's refusal to cooperate. Now he's faced with losing his driving license, he often resists my attempts to get him to prepare, not all the time, but often enough that dealing with the problem is like pushing a heavy stone up hill.

February 19, 2001, Tuesday

I scheduled my visit to Harvey at 10 o'clock, in order to see him off to his driving test at the DMV. Before I left I couldn't write much but the few lines of poetry I've been working on for days. He was almost ready when I arrived, wearing his new trousers and a green shirt. He helped me make Ellen's bed. I straightened up a few things, preparing for Beth's arrival, thinking of Beth's sadness when she says goodbye to Chris [who will be at sea off and on for the next two years].

Harvey asked me which sweater to wear, and I suggested one, fixed his collar out. He looked respectable and the car was as handsome as it could be with rust on the hood and fading on the drivers' side. I reminded him not to talk and to keep two hands on the wheel. I assured him he'd pass. I watched him leave. He said he was nervous, but it showed only in the revving up he gave the engine before he headed off down the street. I returned home, reminding myself not to expect an answer soon. But he called by one o'clock, "The little lady says I passed. I had only two minus points." He sounded calm ("Little lady" for him means literally, someone small and possibly youngish, but not young and pretty.) I congratulated him. I told Ann and went upstairs to rest. She was still waiting for a call from the doctor.

Beth phoned early in the afternoon to say she'd been delayed because of stopping to let the dogs run in a park. She wasn't expected until five or later, so I have the afternoon to wait with Ann for a call from the doctor. When I got to Benton Way after Beth arrived, Ellen was changing Julian. We rocked the baby, fed him, I fixed dinner, and helped clean up the dishes before I left.

Ann and I chatted: "How's the prince of Paradise Road?" she asked

We considered his need to suck. Wasn't he sucking his thumb in the ultrasound picture? "He's like a little stuffed goose," I said. "I don't think he's hungry so much as he wants to suck, but every time he sucks he gets more milk." I remembered how he liked to lie against my shoulder, his hands in his mouth, the way he purses his mouth as if he's trying to suck his tongue. Or is sucking his tongue.

Going to sleep, I told myself that if Ann's okay, we could settle into a calm life for a while. I tried to release myself from the worry that's plagued me with Harvey, but I couldn't feel a good sense of relief.

February 21, 2002, Thursday

Worry flew in anyway, early morning. I attached it to my fears for Beth's loneliness, then told myself to attend to me. Harvey too had worried – he hadn't slept all night, he claimed. On Wednesday he was angry with the highway patrolwoman who gave him the ticket and put him through three-and-a-half months of anxiety.

Yesterday on the way to buy sandwiches, Diane asked me how I was feeling. I admitted to depression.

"How are you when you're depressed?"

"I withdraw. I want to do nothing but read. I don't talk much to anyone." I described for her the night – last Saturday I think – when Ann had been lonely, and I couldn't talk, didn't want to talk. I described our days as solitary. I said I wished Ann felt less fatigue and discomfort.

At my suggestion, we drove up to Montana de Oro to eat our sandwiches, to watch the waves, then walk into the wildflower garden. Then we drove, slowly, in the balmy sunshine, along the road, looking for birds and wildflowers. Nightshade, buttercups, vervain, and many Indian paintbrushes, scattered here and there in the fields to the east. Towhees and wren tits and white crowned sparrows ... we agreed that it was a wonderful return to our old habits. I pointed out the hillside where she took me two days before my surgery in 1998. Back at her house we talked about poetry until it was time for me to go, analyzing the two poems I brought from my internet collection.

Ann had put together a stew for dinner, one of the best I've ever had. The conversation was pleasant, like old times too. Later, while I was reading the paper and trying to discuss pieces of it, she told me she didn't want to talk. When she went to bed early, I followed, somewhat discontented. Just before saying goodnight, I'd been discussing the navy surplus pullover windbreaker I acquired at age fifteen that I loved with all my heart. It reminded me of other clothes, like levis I also loved. Eventually, though she'd been telling me about recollections of hers, she remarked that she didn't want discussions of fashion. After a while I pointed out I'd hardly been talking about fashion, but about things I'd loved but forgotten about. She accused herself of being careless, and I agreed – care – less.

Later, in bed, I was sorry for having been harsh. What am I to do about feeling angry or insulted – yet tender because of her situation?

February 22, 2002, Friday

All morning I fretted about Ann's not feeling well, her confessed depression, blaming myself for being harsh, even, in the early afternoon, thinking of the time she became upset with me for – she thought, incorrectly – not remembering a birthday party she'd given me one time. Should we talk this over, I asked myself? No. Let's ride it out, let it pass.

February 23, 2002, Saturday

I thought about the many ways I've been separate from intellectuals of the era, both because of having lived in California, because of spending most of my college time on a failed and stupid love affair, then becoming overwhelmed by work and children. Most women my age I've been in touch with have had similar experiences – a life that went by without ever coming to a place where you felt in command of your mind, felt you could work with it as well as extend it and then work with it again. Or, again, a life that went by knowing you were missing something, but not knowing quite what because you didn't have the time to find out.

February 25, 2002, Monday

All day Saturday I wondered about Beth by herself, imagining her as lonely and overwhelmed with work now that Chris has gone to sea. I'm allowing her my fears and worries, my past; and I have to tell myself that I survived that past and am here, now. I do the same thing with Harvey – maybe it's allowing myself to feel my future – or, in another way, the only way I can allow myself to fear the loneliness that will come to me – if I don't die before Ann. Every day I imagine myself living alone in this house, then tell myself I can't imagine it, or the steps that are going to lead up to it. Not every day, but often, I feel sorry for Harvey because he is living by himself. I can hear the empty house around me/him. I can feel the helplessness of legs not working as well as they should. I recall the times when I stayed alone in my parents' house on the campus, with no job, nothing to do but feel helpless. The smoking, the books and papers on the bed . . . leaving the house, rationing the times when I did.

Late afternoon Sunday I notice the flakiness of Ann's facial skin – tiny white pieces, like dandruff of the face, but without the oily lumps.

On Saturday I finished a book that is a journal kept by a Jewish man married to a German woman from the beginning of Hitler's regime until the end of the war in Europe. Ever since, I've been living with it in my head, trying to apply the long but slow changes he records to my life. How could I write about the insidious changes that take place as you move in a direction you haven't chosen?

February 26, 2002, Tuesday

Three phone calls during the day formed the subject of our talk until 10:30. Jean, first, in the morning during my working hours. She's back in town, sounding strong, busy, and we arranged for walking on Wednesday. She's much concerned about Bernadette, who is having trouble with short term memory – she couldn't recall which of her daughters was going to visit Cathy in Europe, or when, and her forgetfulness upsets her. I believe Jean agreed that she might feel better about things if she wrote them down as she hears them. When I hung up, I felt first, troubled about not being able to do anything for Bernadette, then bothered by not having asked Jean to come over, to eat dinner with me, and finally, by my not wanting to become so deeply involved that I become a daily necessity to her. I can't do that, can't add another lonely person, a dependent one, to my already full set of responsibilities. I'm afraid I can be present for Jean only a little bit more than I've been before. Nothing regular. Then, at noon, Mary LaSalle Rickert, Helen's daughter, phoned to "update me on Helen's condition." We spoke about her new doctor, her new appointments. How Mary keeps tab on her by calling three times a day when her husband has travelled to their property in the valley, leaving her behind. How she's trying to find some help to come into the house, maybe drive Helen to doctor appointments, so that Emile [Helen's husband], who needs to keep moving, can keep moving and not be irritable and overly energetic around Helen. I felt I should be volunteering for something, but as with Jean, I couldn't – except to find the name of the agency that provided good care for Harvey when he broke his hip. Mary told me "Dad is afraid of death. He won't admit Mom is in as bad shape as she is."

News from another sister, Julie, was also bad: Monica [a daughter] in the hospital, probably going to have her baby prematurely; Deirdre [a daughter] with a possible ruptured disc; Brian [a son] with pneumonia; Bill [her husband] having had three car accidents in the last several weeks, and her doctor said he's not going to get any better.

Ann and I discussed the last situation. I'd told Julie to be careful about who takes care of her when she's ill. I'd suggested she needs to have a power of attorney for health care naming one of her children. I used as examples how Helen and Bernadette have wound up with eighty-three-year-old husbands who aren't emotionally capable of caregiving, yet these men have power over their well-being. At what point, Ann and I wondered, had both Julie and I the opportunity to fade away from our husbands. Ann claimed she would have behaved badly, have left. I said I had opportunities, but gave them up so I could write. Now, only a piddling success as a writer, I wonder what I should have done.

February 27, 2002, Wednesday

The other day I had an hour-long panic because I imagined I had a symptom of a return of my 1998 breast cancer. It was a strange reaction, especially in comparison with the physical courage I'm not usually aware of that surfaced yesterday. I've always thought I was rather cautious. Yet on a drive with Diane to Tassajara Canyon, the brakes on her car suddenly gave out – floorboarded – and when she expressed grave fears of driving home, back down the canyon and then down the grade, I suggested, "Just put it in second gear." She asked me to drive then, down the grade, and though I felt slightly tense, I took over the car and we made it safely to where the car could be taken care of.

This is what I told Ann when I returned: "I wasn't worried about myself, but I did think of you, and that made me worry a bit more than I usually would have."

She frowned, shook her head, then smiled. "I do worry about what might happen to you."

February 28, 2002, Thursday

This morning Ann was pale, light in the living room shining through her hair and outlining her skull. Her left side has been hurting for several days she told me and she believed it had become worse.

"Are you spooked," I asked.

"Yes."

"For some reason, I'm not. I don't know whether the reason's denial, though."

"I don't dwell on it."

Meanwhile, I've been reading more Turkish history, as background to the coming war in the Middle East. Late in the evening I speculated about how it would have been to have been an Ottoman sultan, knowing that his life was likely to end violently one day. Then I thought of women in preceding centuries getting married, knowing about the dangers of childbirth. I would become a nun rather than face the horrors of childbirth I told Ann. She thought she might have found some way to avoid marriage. Not if you're middle class, or in poverty, I thought, but stayed silent, recognizing I'd been callous, not understanding that Ann may have taken my speculations about fearing death to heart.

March 5, 2002, Tuesday

Monday was a Beth and baby day, while Ann went to lunch with Judy C, a former Stanford classmate. Beth and I went to visit Diane, who lifted Julian up, tried to hold him, but he wasn't being placid. To lunch, home from lunch, nap, then Beth came up to Ann's.

As far as Ann's health is concerned: she's been experiencing severe muscle cramps, all over, which wake her up at night and make her tired and tense during the day. Medication isn't helping for more than a couple of hours at a time.

March 7, 2002, Thursday

Before bed Ann was almost crying because of the fear of muscle cramps coming on in the night. They'd frightened her the night before, waking her up in terrible pain and not stopping when she used the usual tactics. We talked about the half-life of Valium. Then about her position in bed. We spent some time arranging pillows in a precise position so that the leg that cramps can be elevated. Then she went to bed, snuggly, with the neck warming pad behind her head. I had a hard time going to sleep, worried for her.

I also worry for myself. How am I going to behave when Ann is suffering what I can't stop or bring comfort for? How can I bear to leave her by herself in the night with fear of pain?

March 12, 2002, Tuesday

Monday afternoon I drove with Jean and Bernadette to Helen's, having been more or less dragooned by Jean into going. I'm glad I went. All three older sisters seem suddenly lost – Jean, because of her hearing and her arthritis problems, Bernadette because she has problems remembering family facts and telling stories, Helen, because she's weak and has lost so much weight that her facial muscles seem unable to bear the weight of her skin. I watched Bernadette weep for her lost self, and hoped I'd never have to go through that as the result of medication or a stroke. Helen is coming back to herself again – but for how long will we have her? Jean – I would like to rely on her as I did when I was young. But such reliance is dangerous because of her social, conventional self. I may find myself pressured by her disapproval of my living apart from Harvey.

March 13, 2002, Wednesday

Ann had no cramps yesterday, none last night. She believes it's the result of drinking V-8 juice, providing her body with just enough more potassium. This morning she went to Santa Maria to a new podiatrist, reluctantly, because she hates to begin with a new doctor, one who will suggest surgery. "I wonder if I play the lung cancer card – just make me comfortable for my remaining months, if it would save explanations."

Last night, after I read how our federal government has acceded more and more to the military, to the war industry, and has been responsible for massacres in central America and Korea and Indonesia through its support and training and secret funding of oppressive regimes, I said I would advise my grandchildren to go to live in Scotland or Sweden – small countries with liberal governments and with little to tempt global greed.

Ann became upset, "We should stay here."

"But we're helpless here, so why stay? Why not vote with our feet?"

March 14, 2002, Thursday

I can't keep all of my life on hold, as I'm keeping the marketing of my finished novels. I must get my mammogram, but more important, call for the date for the colonoscopy, since I hear people must wait a long time to see the gastroenterologist.

Yesterday morning a blue jay, wings hunched, legs and claws in the gutter, perched between two of Ann's roof tiles. She was pecking fiercely at something I couldn't see – I could hear the banging, see her beak come down fiercely as a woodpecker's into the gutter. Or maybe it was between her feet, and she was trying to shred the wood. Success, after a while – a two inch piece of shred, a leaf? A twig? Part of Ann's roof?. She moved on down to a position between two more tiles and picked up a similar piece. This she took over to the pine tree, placed it in what looked like a basket strung among the highest branches, slightly hidden by needles.

March 16, 2002, Saturday

Jean phoned at seven this morning. She wasn't feeling well–rapid heart beat last night, this morning dizzy, erratic heart beat. I offered to take her to the hospital, but she said her daughter-in-law was on her way. I asked her to have them let me know what was going on. Steve [her son] called about eight to say it was atrial fibrillation, now controlled by medication, but they were going to put her through several tests. I offered to go down and let the house cleaner into the house.

White shoes beside the chair. Tissues on the floor by her bed. Tears, I wondered. I thought, my heart sinking, about how she's held everything in, trying to get her balance after Kenneth's death. How frightened she must have been!

In the evening Ann and I disagreed about how to handle saying good night when one of us – Ann, usually – needs to stay up. I confessed I liked the idea of both of us leaving the common living rooms at the same time, and that it was almost a necessary ritual for me to spend some time lying side by side trying to focus on keeping Ann well – a kind of prayer.

I feel this is a stricture on Ann's life, however, so we'll have to leave it that I will just go upstairs without waiting for her when she wants to stay up.

March 18, 2002, Monday

Rain on the way to Morro Bay with Harvey, yesterday. A barbecue in the county park, people huddled under an awning and over the smoky pits, many in bright yellow slickers. Bright light in the Galley, for it was one o'clock, and because of the rain no need to pull the blue shades down. The restaurant was hushed, everyone subdued because of rain? Some time during lunch the rain slanted in from the southwest. A family group behind Harvey was difficult to figure out. I'm caught because of the good looking boy about fourteen. At first I think of

Ian that way, then wonder about Julian and know that I may never see Julian at that age. The boy had dark brown eyes, wavy blonde hair, a pink complexion that turned pinker when he laughed. The woman sitting next to him was his sister, I think. Was the woman next to his father his mother? But as time went on, I saw that it couldn't be a family who always are together, for they were having long conversations and the boy was listening avidly to whatever the women said, laughing, blushing, laughing again.

I told Ann about this before bed time. She was enthralled, happy I had something to occupy my attention during the long time Harvey took to eat his crab louie. She herself had been spending the day editing something for the Sjogren's Syndome list. She didn't quite know how to deal with a badly written piece by a man who had been requested to make a scientific article available to lay people. She was energetic in her discussion, yet this morning (Monday) she said she had had to take a pill in order to sleep. I commented that perhaps she does really need something to occupy her mind – that some of the fatigue she complains of is depression and boredom.

March 20, 2002, Wednesday

This morning was unhappy all around. Ann had had a fierce siege of muscle cramps so bad she had to walk up and down for a time, keeping her leg straight and waiting for the medicine she'd taken to work. She appeared frightened and desperate.

March 21, 2002, Thursday

Another seriously bad night for Ann. She didn't sleep until two, when she took Halcion, then was up by nine. We went to Dr. Doyle at eleven. He ordered another blood test to check electrolytes, discussed whether or not she'd seen Dr. Trace [the neurologist] yet. (Not until mid April.) Suggested paraneoplastic symptoms, felt her leg and ankle.

March 23, 2002, Saturday

Off and on during the night wind blew, rain pounded. This morning the sky was grey, with patches of clouds here and there.

Ann's spirits flag as she must stave off the assault of muscle cramps. She's losing sleep, and taking sleeping pills, whether to relax away from the fear of muscle spasm or because of the spasms themselves. It's hard to tell. She's grim, mornings, but in the afternoons seems less distressed. Yesterday she felt unable to grocery shop with me, but marinated and cooked lamb and potatoes for our dinner.

Meanwhile, another national move by the president, this one hitting close to home for the elderly: change of the privacy rules requiring a patient's signature before medical records are released to insurance companies, other doctors, and hospitals. I see this as a step to benefit the insurance companies, making use of the excuse that doctors and hospitals sometimes need the records before a signature can be obtained.

I'm also troubled by the way the federal government

is using Bush as a campaigner. Today he's telling us that we're going to save the poor throughout the world. Yet the global trade treaties he's backing will simply make it easier to keep the poor enslaved.

March 24, 2002, Sunday

Last night Ann and I, lying side by side on her bed, discussed the difference between cramps, spasm, and charlie horses so that I could understand her symptoms, and maybe, I hoped, make intelligent suggestions about them. Nothing came to me, but Ann thought of increasing her dose of anti-depressant to half a tab every day, instead of every other day. What else can you do when you're on your own and the medical profession has no suggestions?

This morning she said she'd slept until, at around 7:30 or so, two big cramps hit her thighs and she had to jump up to walk them off, straighten them out.

March 28, 2002, Thursday

The clamp down on civil rights continues, with the legislative branch barely able to keep track of the executive branch – or rarely interested, rare meaning just a few outspoken ones. Senators running in states that voted for Bush last election are conceding on issues they ought not – like most Americans, I push them out of my mind. It's easier to believe in the legends, rather like the isolated tribe, my ancestors, who believed they could put a king on the throne of England. It's an untried belief at first, then when you need to put it into practice, it fails. Like civil rights – as long as they're untried, you believe you have a frontier freedom. Bookstores are being asked for lists of books people read. Libraries are going to have these lists – are they private? Tom Ridge, national head of security won't answer Congress's call to testify.

March 29, 2002, Friday

Ann slept late this morning. I guess it means she had another difficult, cramp-wracked night. I tried to soothe her, hoping that some of the cramps come because she's tense. I'm also concerned lest the extra anti-depressant she's taking may be adding to the potential for cramping.

Yesterday was a routine day, and I'm thankful for that. Yet ordinariness gives me time to notice how I feel – not quite here, meaning not quite settled into my place. Someone's going to come and take me home – that's the feeling. Why?

I read about, think about, humans in unsettled parts of the world. How is it they live? The way I thought yesterday, according to myths and legends. One long day of peace gives peace?

I am really not in a settled or peaceful existence, yet moment by moment seems calm.

April 5, 2002, Friday

This morning I can't focus on any of the continuing tasks I've set myself – this journal, the c-bel story, writing another poem. Oh, I know I could start on the

Another Kind of Balance   183

poem and become involved. But I'm not sure I'd be doing anything but word puzzles; I don't know what I want to say about anything. And that's why working has been hard.

One reason I don't know what I want to say: I have too much to say. Too much to recapture from the last week. Too many moments of pleasure, joy, concern.

Claire came last Saturday, arriving in the early afternoon. The next morning, Easter, Harvey, Claire, the children, Ann and I went to the Elks' club brunch. Claire found us a table in the sun. Annie ate nothing but bacon and a muffin or two. Ian worked on his cartoons. (Ian has returned to making full page art, Claire says. He worked hard on a geodesic kind of dome picture, multicolored dots connected with dark stripes for my guest book.) Annie planned to go on the Easter egg hunt, and gleefully captured two plastic cups for her eggs when she saw that other children had brought baskets. She's an independent, carefree spirit – I hope she retains this – full of feeling, yet trusting and practical. Ian hadn't planned and was a little troubled about not having a basket, but at the last minute decided to go, and I was pleased. Claire tells me he has asked the drama coach permission to write and appear in his own skits for this year's performance: two boys telling jokes Ian has made up to be used as the entr'acte. In the afternoon we walked up Dairy Creek in El Chorro campground, the children as interested in wildflowers as they were in blue belly lizards. The slopes of the hills were covered with filaree, buttercups and California violets sprinkled here and there. Over the hill between us and the prison, a kite and a hawk in the sky. A Western bluebird, orange breasted, blue back and head on a fence post. Later, vultures sailing overhead.

Ann had a seriously difficult night with cramping Saturday night, and she was tired, and grim during the breakfast. When I returned to the house after saying goodnight to Claire, we spoke of how she was close to panic. She described some of the contortions her hands, feet, and legs went into and how her torso also knotted up, her neck too: "I'm telling you this because you may have to tell someone else about it. In the emergency room, for instance."

I tried soothing her fears, which had some effect, because she slept a little better that night. She's been taking Halcion, which seems to help her sleep.

The next day we met Dr. Doyle at a regular appointment. Before we went I advised Ann to give him a thesis sentence, e.g., I'm having a difficult time with the cramps and spasms and I need some help. He was ready to help, having spoken with Dr. Trace, who advised an ionized calcium test. He also prescribed baclofen and neurontin, either taken together or separately, testing at a low dose to see what helps. I picked up the prescriptions for Ann Thursday afternoon. She began, as instructed, with the baclofen. Thursday night was a good night and she slept late. Friday she felt that she might be getting some relief. We even spoke of making plans to go down to Noelle's for Claire's birthday party. When she went to bed, the muscles in her hands and legs weren't jumping, the way they have been much of the time for the last several weeks. This morning when I looked in at 9 o'clock, she had just roused herself to take her baclofen. "I didn't sleep until five o'clock," she said. She went back to sleep, with me promising to answer her phone.

April 9, 2002, Tuesday

Last night Ann didn't sleep well. Again. I suggested trying Robaxin with the baclofen. She spoke with Dr. Doyle in the early afternoon. He suggested more baclofen, especially after she expressed concern about adding the Neurontin to the batch.

I am continuing to give more thought to Harvey than I'd like. I spoke with Diane at lunch yesterday about this: I don't want to take full time care of him after I lose Ann. I don't know what I want to do, but I don't want to continue with that. I can't imagine having to spend all my time in ways that are already painful for me. She advised that I think through right now what it is I will do if I lose Ann while things with Harvey are status quo. Last evening Ann and I spoke about it. Laughingly she said I'd be so busy lining up her business affairs that I wouldn't have time for him. If I didn't think her affairs were messy enough, she'd mess them up some more. Beth arrived yesterday, and in response to her probing I revealed Harvey and I never had shared values and interests. When I married him, I thought like the stupid child I was that I could get him to change, but that wasn't possible. I laugh now to think that with Harvey especially that wasn't possible. He hates change. He's afraid of it, and his living here in San Luis all his life has enabled him to ignore it. Why should he change? He wasn't made unhappy by the marriage.

As far as Beth is concerned, I ought to say that I decided long ago not to care much what people thought of my behavior here in San Luis, or elsewhere. Let them think what they like. It's not going to be altogether good. But if those people who know me like me, that's all that matters.

April 13, 2002, Saturday

At noon, Friday, we drove up 101 to Tassajara Canyon. This was to be the first stop on a wildflower excursion. Having Ann drive Tassajara Canyon road for wildflowers wasn't satisfactory. Cars behind her trouble her, and she's too aware of the possibility of cars coming around corners behind or in front, to make her feel comfortable about stopping where a good view of flowers spreads out before you. But in spite of her growing irritation – she denied it, but I was aware she wasn't comfortable – we saw almost my entire repertoire of coastal valley wild flowers. These I've recorded in the record book Diane gave me a couple of years ago. (Missing, of course, phlox and Indian warrior, Indian paintbrush, the silver bush lupine, and beach primrose.) When I finally gave permission to Ann to turn around it was at least two miles further than she'd wanted to drive.

This morning Noelle phoned. "What is a liberal arts education?" she asked. I discussed traditions, culture, society and helping students to examine their lives and think about themselves as human beings, sharing a human culture. Well, I did better than that, really. I put Ann on the phone to answer the same question. I could hear her wheeze, and so could Noelle. When I got back on the line, she said at first she was worried, then started to reassure me. I reassured Noelle by telling her Ann hadn't had her medications yet.

April 15, 2002, Monday

This evening Ann told me I irritated her by telling her what to do as if she were a child. I asked for examples. She gave as an example my questioning her about whether she was going to mail her income tax without getting a post office record of having mailed it. I replied that I asked her, but when she said she wasn't going to do so, I said no more. This morning when she was on her way to mail the quarterly payment, tax that counted for next year, I asked her where the big envelopes were – not because I was checking up on her, but because I was curious about how she could get away with just the slim envelopes. I assume she saw this as an invasion of her privacy and jumped to a criticism she sometimes makes of people: they are ordering her around, they want to control her.

I also think she is/was being affected by the drugs she's taking. Tonight when we began to think about it she was also affected by alcohol.

Her emotional aberrations scare me. What position am I going to be in if she loses her ability to think? What if she goes full course ahead with this kind of misunderstanding of what I say or do? Being with her will become untenable.

When I asked her to give examples, she went back to my telling her what to say on the telephone, something she always objects to when I appear to do it.

Angered by this reversion to ancient history – we haven't spoken to enough people on the telephone for a year to make this a reasonable objection or irritation – I said "how does this connect with your telling me how to fill ice cube trays?"

When she didn't see the point, or at least didn't seem to, I became angry and reminded her that she tells me what do to in several ways having to do with her house and – frankly – my children. That this is every day. That I am almost afraid of the way I walk down the hall, concerned lest I be asked to do it another way.

All of this argument or dismal discussion then moved into my telling her I felt bad. What did I mean, she wanted to know.

"Generally alone," I responded. "Generally depressed." Who wouldn't, I was thinking, in our circumstances? It's there all the time. It just came to the surface tonight.

She wanted to know what made me depressed – and I spelled out the events of the day. Her pain. Her frantic work in the office. "You're seriously ill," I said, "What else do you expect me to be?"

At another point in the conversation, she brought up another old difficulty: we can't have a give and take conversation. I agreed that I do withdraw.

At present, as I write, I don't want to see anyone. I feel deeply hurt by the accusations.

The pattern: I'm depressed, unhappy, not my usual

"ebullient" self. Ann feels attacked, and then finds fault with me. Big help.

I might as well accept that I'm going to go to my grave failing people. I can't hold up the world for everyone. I can't I can't I cant. It's at this point that the Buddhist here and now practice is important

April 16, 2002, Tuesday

After I completed the entry above, I went upstairs, first asking Ann whether she wanted me to come down to say good night. She did. I went upstairs and began to cry, and couldn't stop, great wrenching sobs, then fast breathing, to try to stop the tears, then another set of sobs. Ann came up, and we both cried together.

I felt ashamed of myself for having distressed Ann with my depression, when hers is much more serious: fear of pain, fear of a painful death, fear of not being able to breath, all soon to come. I slept not too well. When I came downstairs at eight, Ann was sitting in her chair in her pajamas, holding a hot pack to her leg. She'd had another terrible cramp and was afraid to move, but her spirits were up. I reheated the pack, helped her get robe, warm socks on, and fetched her medicine, water, and later, tea. Later still, toast. I feel better for being able to help her.

One source of my tears last night: the homeless feeling I sometimes get came on sharply because of Ann's irritation with me. Together we analyzed it, discovering that it's that I don't have friends to support me in my new home. There's been no ritual recognition. And we have few people coming in.

April 17, 2002, Wednesday

Yesterday evening I asked Ann to read my C-bel story, shifting the ending just slightly. It was exciting to see her laugh, sometimes out loud. She liked the story, finding two problems. One, she thought Stander would have told Doris about Christabel's background if he'd known it, especially if that was the story he wanted her to write. The second problem was that she thought Doris was smart, sharp, on her way, and when I said no, she suggested I was ambivalent. Otherwise, she thought the structure of the story was fine. She laughed at Jessie and at Bomland and at the whole tea party.

Then at bedtime, she grew panicky, worried about the cramping she'd been experiencing early in the morning. I suggested she take pills in the middle of the night if necessary and lower the head of her bed when she wakes up. Maybe it's caused by her position, I thought, because the seriously bad cramps have come on mostly in the morning when she's been lying in bed in rather rigid positions all night long. This morning I peeked in to see she'd followed my advice about the bed. Later she told me she'd had no cramps. Maybe this will work, maybe.

April 18, 2002, Thursday

Again this morning no cramp for Ann. Lurking, she said, but nothing happened. She thinks that perhaps flattening the bed early in the morning helps.

We went to see Dr. Doyle today. When he came in, he sat on a stool, backing it up so he could see both of us. Another patient of his knows us, he announced. I guessed the A's, so we gossiped about them a little bit – how intelligent, that we'd dedicated a book to her, her work on Mothers for Peace. I was a little surprised when Ann recited the scene in front of the AEC in the early 70s, claiming she'd been there as a reporter. I don't believe that's true, but I'll not correct Ann at this point. What difference does it make? As for Ann's condition, he didn't think her lungs sounded any different. He suggested more baclofen, going up to 15 mg. He also suggested that seeing Dr. Trace would help . He'd been to a meeting where he heard that other drugs in the class Iressa's in can cause muscle cramps.

April 19, 2002, Friday

Last night Ann and I discussed our differing reactions to the visit to Dr. Doyle. Ann expressed surprise that I'd felt comforted by his discovery that Iressa may be causing the muscle spasm. I told her I'd been cheered because I'd considered several worse possibilities. She, on the other hand, felt trapped for life with having to ward off the muscle cramps.

"As long as the baclofen and other meds work, I don't see why," I said.

Ann had also felt discouraged that Dr. Trace told Dr. Doyle she didn't think she could help. I reminded her that she seemed to have more energy on the baclofen than she's had for a couple of years.

On the other hand, I've been surprised that Ann's spirits, her sense of being lucky and indestructible, have so thoroughly revived. I'm glad, but somewhat worried.

The more hope, the harder it is to let it go. Having to go through last January again without even seeing the possibility of medical assistance, may be horrible.

April 22, 2002, Monday

At seven this morning Ann called me downstairs, and I ran to find her leaning on the bathroom sink. She'd had a spasm and couldn't put her foot on the ground. I tried rubbing it. That didn't seem to help. What she wanted was a hot pad. I suggested she put the rub-on medicine the pharmacist had given her. We rubbed that in and while I was in the kitchen heating the hot pad, the muscle relaxed. I noticed her face was white.

When I returned from walking with Jean, I suggested and Ann concurred instantly that she ought not to drive the grade tomorrow to her physical therapist with the possibility of spasm. I postponed my mammogram to 4:15 tomorrow instead of 11:30 so I could drive her.

Last night we watched the Ansel Adams biography on PBS and at the end, thinking of the pictures of Yosemite when it was still wilderness, thinking of the great loss we've sustained here in the US over the last century, Ann began to cry. We talked about her tears, which didn't stop, identifying not only the loss of the wilderness but the loss of honor in our government since 1960 (it happened at the end of the last century, too, I reminded her) as causes for her despair. After she'd stopped crying, she said "Given my condition, if I knew how to organize it, or whom to aim it at, I'd sacrifice myself in order to get rid of the criminals who've seized power in this country." I proposed non-violent thinking, and then we parted, each trying to think of some form of non-violent direct action to use.

April 24, 2002, Wednesday

I was impressed by Dr. Trace at Monday's visit. She's tall, thin, young, blonde, serious, crisp and appears to be extremely efficient and intelligent. Her take on Ann is that she has an hereditary or congenital predisposition toward cramping and the Iressa probably has exacerbated it. She's asking Ann to experiment with both salt and potassium trying them each for three days and checking blood level after the three days.

Yesterday Ann felt relieved and happy after Patrice [the massage therapist] worked with her, energetic enough to go to Barnes and Noble to get some of the books she'd recommended. These books were about mind and body working together to heal, and Ann was reminded of Betty K's [an old friend] approach to cancer. After dinner, on the way to bed, Ann commented on how wonderful it was to start this new approach. I said something about my attempts to do this, night after night. We'd even been pretending it was working for her. I'm not sure what Ann's exact response was, but it made me want to withdraw, to not talk, to not be cheerful and companionable. She noticed my reaction and asked its cause, but I didn't answer. I'm glad I didn't, because I wouldn't have wanted to make Ann unhappy with my feeling she hadn't given enough credit to me for trying. This morning it doesn't make any difference.

May 8, 2002, Wednesday

Again Ann and I had the discussion about society's expectations that the family of sick people provide all care. People are made heroes for giving extreme care – the woman whose husband became a paraplegic and who thereafter took over his total care, who wrote columns about it, and then a book. Those who don't provide the care are made to seem cruel or simply callous or selfish by the culture. Ann sometimes makes remarks about men who leave their sick wives, men whose wives belong to the list online Ann belongs to. I pointed out again that she applauds my sister for leaving her husband, who is ill with bipolar disorder. I could point out, but don't, that I've refused to be the caregiver to an old man of 87.

I think Ann has been touched because I'm willing to care for her to the best of my ability until the end – if hers comes first. And she, willing to care for me, if that's the way it goes. But we'd had 25 years of thinking together, supporting each other, loving each other, without bowing to any of the forces against us.

The solution lies in society, I reminded Ann yesterday. (We were sitting at a table in the Atascadero gourmet sandwich shop, and Ann was teasing the pastry away from an excellent pasty. Outside wild pink checkermallows growing.) More help and less responsibility. A sense that all of us need help – as infants, as sick people, as old – and a means found to provide it from the society at large.

May 15, 2002, Wednesday

Ann's recovered her energy today, and I'm not bumbling around, making stupid mistakes the way I was yesterday. At lunch time, the Webers came so we went to the trattoria on Higuera for lunch where we discussed how Ann would help the nuns Ginny and Elizabeth write the chapter on administration for the SHJC history. After a discussion of how the nuns organize themselves, how religious orders were a good example of women's methods of administering a corporation – not that we think of them as different from men's but wondered whether there was less competition for top positions, more retreat into refusal of responsibility – we came up with a couple of ideas for thesis sentences. When we got home, Ann asked me to write them down. I'd warned her I never remember what isn't written on paper, but she insisted, so I sketched out an idea and handed it to her. She worked most of the afternoon on a paragraph or two, and not long ago I helped her with the first two sentences. I think she's sending it off to Ginny now. Point is – she worked hard all afternoon, suffering frustration with the computer, and still felt okay.

May 16, 2002, Thursday

Last night, after we'd watched a movie, I asked Ann how soon before she could go to bed. I don't like to go to bed without having time to talk with her about healing, time to be peaceful together, to draw upon spiritual values, a sense of unity. My question, however, made her feel pushed and she raised her voice to say not yet. I was offended, and told her so. Later she said she knows I need my sleep, but thought I didn't understand that she hates to go to bed because of the cramping that comes in the morning. I said I did understand, then listened to her frustration about having to spread the pills out over the day, how she wants to wait until the last minute at night before she takes the last one. I, however, noticed, but didn't say, that staying up late allows her to have a second drink of whiskey. In a way I can't blame her for wanting to drink more because it helps her deal with fear of bed. At the end, though, I told her that I felt pushed all the time, trying to fit into every day the responsibilities and activities required of me – or I require of myself

Meanwhile, I feel we're getting closer and closer to the edge. More than last year at this time, I feel set in the way we live here and more fearful of Ann's absence. Then I guess I was stunned. Now, I'm seeing what's real. I'm seeing her long-term suffering.

May 17, 2002, Friday

Yesterday she felt well enough to shop for dinner and cook most of it, a roast chicken with rice and asparagus. After dinner while talking about two elderly couples where the wife took care of a demented spouse in a nursing home, I tried to point out to her that if you really loved a person, it might be possible to live in a place like the Village. I mentioned some couples I see walking hand-in-hand. I thought, I might be able to manage that, if Ann were to become demented. She said she hoped I'd allow her to put herself out of her misery. I said that wouldn't happen for her, since any dementia she got now would present the possibility of a swift ending anyway, meaning the cancer. The conversation became mixed up after that, and we began telling each other how alone who ever survives the two of us will feel, how I worry about being alone and ill every day, how grateful she is for me. After an hour she wanted to end the conversation, and I was willing, but denied it had been an empty and depressing exercise.

Then at bed time we tried to remember the "tomorrow" speech from MacBeth. Ann got to laughing, saying she always enjoyed my attempts at reconstituting half-forgotten speeches. We disagreed about whether yesterday went with tomorrow, I insisting that it did.

May 25, 2002, Saturday

Friday night at bed time, we heard the thick motor sounds of a truck. Made curious by its continuation for more than a couple of minutes, I went outside to see that the EMT truck had drawn up outside the next door neighbor's house. Ann came out then, went over to see what was going on, then crossed the street to inform another neighbor before she came back, not even out of breath.

We spoke then about the neighbor, Ann beginning the conversation with her hope that someone would stay with her that night. I instantly thought of how people would expect me to stay with Harvey if he became mildly ill, and thought how I would hate to do so, and said, "You mean if Harvey were to fall, I should spend the night at Benton way?"

Ann paused then, and after a while agreed she was thinking selfishly of how glad she was that I was with her and that if she fell she'd have someone. I said – I have to look forward myself to being by myself, probably, and that's scary, and so I have to think of people in places like the neighbor or my sister Jean or Harvey as brave, strong, able to manage what life's going to throw at us; I don't like to think of them as needing support. I added: "I want this to be clear. I'm not here because you need taking care of. I'm here because these may be our last days and I don't want to miss any."

June 7, 2002, Friday

This morning I'd just begun to work when Ann answered her phone. I must have had my ear cocked toward the living room, because I heard the word "progress," and thinking of the MRI Ann had done on Wednesday morning, I left my desk to go sit in the living room while Ann finished the conversation. She was frowning, but she didn't look shaken. But then it's not like Ann to reflect her upset while she's talking to someone. She did say that the results should be sent to Dr. Doyle, however. After she hung up, she told me the call had been from Dr. Trace. The MRI showed progressive arthritis in her cervical spine. More important, there was something showing on the left rib, near the navel, and this is what Ann suggested she inform Dr. Doyle about. I'd just heard from Jean about Joni's father-in-law, whose lung cancer was in his ribs and his hip. He's in great pain. I watched Ann to make sure she was taking this news okay, at the same time telling myself I'll wait until it seems serious. It might simply be something that was there before, and is, like the lung cancer, controlled by Iressa because Ann hasn't had an MRI of her body this time round. Though there was the PET scan.

I asked Ann if she felt okay. She said yes. I told her I'd learned to wait and find out what's going on before becoming upset. Yet all morning my undervoice chanted warnings and worries.

Yesterday when we saw Dr. Doyle, he thought he heard more wheezing in her chest and ordered an x-ray and lab reports on liver, kidney, and pancreas. He believes that even if the cancer is progressing, if it's only a little bit, he may keep her on Iressa because it may be holding it back or slowing it down considerably.

June 11, 2002, Tuesday

This afternoon when I came downstairs from my nap, I found Ann on the phone. Dr. Doyle had called. He thought the tumor looked a little bigger, and we needed to do something. He and Ann decided on a CT scan to begin with. Then he has a whole bag of chemicals he can use, infusing her about once a week so the side effects won't be too bad.

We just looked at each other for a while. I didn't want to break, for fear she would see the news as more serious than she already did. We said a few things about seeing what the new drugs might be and how it will be good to get rid of the flaky skin from Iressa. Still, I thought she looked upset. She kept saying she'd expected this. I wanted to put my arms around her, comfort her, but if I comforted her, I'd have been saying there's something to be comforted about.

June 17, 2002, Monday

Last night Ann had taken three anti-cramping pills at nine o'clock, so we had some time together. I rubbed oil on her back, which was scaling badly. Big peels of skin covered the rest of her body. She said she feels prickly, but mildly numb on the surface of her skin.

"I'll be glad when I'm not taking Iressa anymore," she said, and then that old song, "There is a tavern in the town," came to her mind, and she began to sing "Adieu, adieu kind friends, adieu."

Was she saying, 'I know what's happening, I know the Iressa's failure is my last chance?' I didn't ask, but began to sing the song with her, and we examined its origin, trying to remember some lost lines. She believed they were "I'll drink my wine midst laughter free – and never, never think of thee."

June 18, 2002, Tuesday

Yesterday I became so tired that by dinner time I wasn't functioning well. I went walking through the oak preserve with Ian, Annie and Claire, as we'd planned to do. Ian, wasn't feeling well, off and on, with headache and dizziness, caused, we all believed by sinusitis: this created tension for me. I so want him and Annie to enjoy themselves visiting. Then I helped Claire to take them out to play tennis and go swimming. When I came back home in the afternoon, I was so tense I couldn't nap. At four when I returned to Benton Way, a talk with Claire suggested that Ian was really sick and should be checked. The insurance company said he must go to "emergency," so while Claire and Ian went there, I brought Annie home. Claire finally picked Annie up – Ian has a virus, not a sinus infection – at around 6:30. Then I had a drink, and then I couldn't function. Drinking water helped – but meanwhile, Ann had fixed dinner. During dinner, Ann bit her tongue, and began to cry, great gulping sobs. I held her. She was blaming her tears on her sore tongue. "I want to be brave," she said.

June 24, 2002, Monday

Meanwhile, Beth began a series of phone calls describing Julian's cold, which developed into a kind of flu. The only kind of help I've been able to give is reassurance . . . I worry more about her flu than Julian's, because she doesn't feel well enough to go out and go shopping.

Friday Ann and I went to the doctor, where the news was – as we expected – not good. She has developed more lumps in her lungs, and Doyle is pretty certain they're cancer. And the ones in the right lung have been cancer. There's evidence of it in the hilar and mediastinal areas, also, and possibly her lymph system is beginning to be involved. He suggested, after a careful analysis, courses of chemo in light doses, given for four weeks. After walking her up and down the hall and checking the level of oxygen in her blood (only 91) he ordered oxygen for night time use, promising that it will make her feel better.

We lunched at 1865, feeling a traditional pull there after hearing bad news. It's one of our ways to brace up and think through what's here and what's ahead.

Later in the afternoon, Noelle and Ellen arrived at Harvey's. I visited with them until five before I returned to wait with Ann for the man bringing the oxygen tank. He finally got there with the oxygenator at about seven. After showing us how to use it, discussing his other patients and how angry they get with him, he sat down with us in the living room, where he drank a soda while telling story after story about people who have had terrible accidents and people who fought the war in Germany, patients of his when he was a massage therapist. He left, at last, close to nine.

Friday night Ann began to use the oxygen. Saturday morning was the first day she hadn't taken Iressa since December. On Saturday morning, when I returned from seeing what the children's plans were for the day, she was asleep in her chair. She was asleep in her chair when I left to spend a day with the children and grandchildren at Lopez Lake.

Sunday in the evening, as a possibly last shot at Windows, Ann spent two hours, enjoying everything we were tempted by. A long, slow, marvelous sunset. Our own summer solstice. Loons black against the sky, a lone pelican, the mirror water.

6
A Steeper Path

June 25, 2002, Tuesday

Today at 9:30, chemo began again. I checked in last year's journal to see how severe carboplatin might be; its main effect seems to have been weakening the platelet count, so we might expect Ann's energy level to be low. She became cold on the ride home and has been wrapped up in a blanket all day and sleeping for most of it.

I'm much more afraid this time.

June 26, 2002, Wednesday

Yesterday Ann had phone calls from several relatives and on Monday three friends.

I have a sense we've reached the last battle. In fact, Dr. Doyle has said so: "Let me know when you want to stop."

Beth phoned last night because Noelle told her I was upset about Ann. "Of course I am," I said. She talked about fighting it. I spoke of quality of life.

I can't become interested in any novel project. Last week, I just coasted along in conversations with Noelle and Claire, bringing up nothing about what really occupies my thoughts.

At the same time I'm dreadfully bitter about the state of the nation, more than I've ever been before, partly because I'm not willing, nor do I have time, to start or participate in a movement. I've given up hope of changing the Democrats. All I can do is read and become more upset – hardly deliverance from despair. When Helen phoned me last week to chat in the morning, I couldn't think of anything to say. I was bored with relating the visits of children, the parties and family exercises. I did blurt out the news that I was going with Ann to the doctor's to discover what could be done about the recurrence of her cancer, and Helen's response didn't tell me she was concerned for me. "Oh that's too bad," she said. But what else can I expect her to say? I think maybe more emotion in her voice? Surely there'd be more if I said Harvey was sick – the relationship to husbands is all she can identify with. But I don't know – have I found the right words when she's told me about dear friends of hers?

Then last night, when Julie called, I had a similar experience – and that convinced me I was depressed. Walking around in a depression. Like walking pneumonia. I felt nothing except hollowness when talking with Julie, couldn't think of anything to say, as if nothing I could say would be interesting to her.

Cure: some mental activity? Maybe now's the time to get back to writing the poems in minor keys that I started, to see what comes out. I feel I'm not able to express myself. I have to pretty much keep from Ann my undercurrent of thought: fear of not being able to cope with serious illness; fear of what my own future is.

June 28, 2002, Friday

I answered Diane's questions about how Ann was reacting – our talk about not being able to be depressed. She took exception to that – "Why shouldn't you be?" And I tried to explain the difference between depressed and sad, finally with some success when she recognized that we can't lose courage. I mentioned Ann's reaction to what either Claire or Noelle had asked her at dinner Saturday night about what she feels: that she'd answered she was in a position where there aren't any options.

Diane cried, and for a moment I regretted telling her. She said, "I'm not needy and I don't want comforting, but . . . I love you so and I don't want you to have to go through this."

My unspoken response was: all of us have to go through something.

She also suggested something I think I shall have to work on: Ann and I should not go on as we have been doing. The truth is that this morning we both said we wished we weren't having to have separate days today. I said I wanted to cling, that I hated to have to spend any time doing anything else these days except be with her, and she said she felt the same way. What Diane suggested was that I plan special days, doing something that pleases both of us.

June 29, 2002, Saturday

Last night Ann's breath came fast after she'd simply dressed herself for bed and brushed her teeth. My reaction – fearfulness, imaging (imagining?) the future, when her breath may come much faster. Empathy, or rather, wondering what it feels like not to be able to catch my breath. Maybe half way remembering what it was like when I had pneumonia – having to sleep, because nothing else would leave my body at peace.

I found it hard to go to sleep after that.

June 30, 2002, Sunday

I went early to talk with Harvey and see him off to the Old Timers' barbecue, returning to Ann at about 10:30. We planned to go to the movies at 1:30 to see "Monsoon Wedding," but as we sat reading the paper, Ann said she hoped I wouldn't be too disappointed: she didn't feel well enough to go. I wasn't, and we planned to watch a movie video in the evening instead. It wasn't so much that her stomach was upset, but she just didn't feel well.

Before I went upstairs for my lunch (and nap) she said, "I don't like feeling this way." Except for the annoyance of the itching and desperation over the spasm – the only real complaint she's made this whole time.

Later in the afternoon she felt well enough to drive me around on the errands we had to run. She had one drink before dinner, the one Dr. Doyle suggested she might have. I don't know whether the drink helped her or the rest she'd had all day, but she seemed better. We considered whether she'd been tired from two days of visits and phone calls from relatives and friends. We considered whether she'd better tell people to limit the visit to an hour or so, because she and I lose out when she gets too tired. Some of them say they plan to make spur of the moment visits – I hope they telephone first so we can tell them how she feels.

Then, just before bed, as I have for the last three nights, I heard Ann breathing hard and remembered my fear. This time it came clothed in questions of "what will I do when?" How am I going to deal with death? I imagine scenes, hard scenes, similar to what Jean experienced, and I have a hard time calming myself. Same in the morning, this morning.

July 2, 2002, Tuesday

This morning, infusion day, Ann told Dr. Doyle about some sharp pains she's been having on her left side, about where the cancer is. She had them last Friday, when Casey [Ann's cousin] was here, and two other times, not quite so severe. It lasted about five minutes, I think she said, then went away after she'd stopped walking around. He suggested it was the cancer, either inflaming or rubbing against the pleura. Nerve endings in the chest are nonspecific, so that heart pains go down the arm, and so forth, he explained. He said she could have narcotics right away, if she thought she needed them. She said no, not yet. They discussed Oxycontin – hillbilly heroin, he said, because the pills can be ground up and sniffed or injected. Ann laughed and said "Wow, let's have a party."

Dr. Doyle kept looking over at me, checking, I guess, to see how worried I was, or to see whether Ann was just pretending for his sake. I smiled back, in agreement with Ann.

My dream last night, long and involved: Several people, including me and possibly classmates from Mission School or possibly my children and possibly Ann were hiking along a wooded and hilly trail. I see yellow and beige in the rocks, possibly orange, dark green woods, sandstone cliffs. It was supposed to be just a short distance, but it was turning out to be a long hike. I was leading us down a long slope, a smooth trail, with sandy yellow gravel on it, when I realized we weren't coming to where we'd intended to go. One of us is frightened, feeling she can't go on. I discover it's twenty miles more on a trail, since I'd led them past the quick way home. We start out on that trail. Below us, at the foot of cliffs, is a wide river. Suddenly, Ann and I are in the river, deep and blue, and I urge us to hold onto a snag. From the snag we look back at the high sandstone cliffs. I wonder if I can persuade Ann to hold on.

July 3, 2002, Wednesday

I'm concerned about my procrastination, my wishing that my obligation to Harvey would just go away, that I wouldn't have to deal with it. But the reality is, that I'm going to have to. There's a lot I'm going to have to cope with, a lot I don't want to have to cope with or that I don't know how and don't want to have to learn. I'm troubled about my inability to set things in motion that Ann would ordinarily and easily set in motion.

July 6, 2002, Saturday

Friday morning Ann told me she hadn't slept until six in

the morning, and then only for an hour. We tentatively cancelled the plans we'd had to go to Santa Maria to buy pads for the outdoor furniture. Instead, I took my ease, reading the paper in the living room with Ann instead of rushing to the computer. At eleven we took the Bose upstairs and relaxed, listening to operatic arias we rarely play. The first, Lucia Popp: light, loving, lyrical songs, included Dvorak's "Hymn to the Moon," from *Rosalka*. I noticed Ann wiping tears from her eyes, and had to wipe my own. I hope I never forget this – and the general feeling, which I did express to Ann, of the atmosphere in the room, of the day, as if I were a child in summer vacation again, no urgency, nothing I had to do or felt strongly I wanted to do, except just lie and look at the sky – at that time nicely varied with white clouds. Some time later, Schumann arias with Natalie Stutzman, contralto. Rich and dark, smooth as velvet. I had a strong feeling of my mother in the room with me – another way of saying this – I returned in feeling to the day my mother sat near my crib up stairs in the back bedroom, singing to me "Sweet and Low." I couldn't remember her face, simply her smock, a sense of dark hair, but I felt her love, my love, strongly then.

July 12, 2002, Friday

Last night fear again as I listened to Ann breathe heavily after getting ready for bed. Is she at peace? I ask myself. What kind of thinking goes on? – Hope for day after day? Hope that one gets better, not worse? The same thinking I do?

Right before dinner yesterday, after we'd been

talking about the amusing obituaries that appeared in the paper – A.L.'s mother, and the charge of the Light Brigade in her ancestry, and the three marriages, and recollections of somebody's wit – Ann told me to be sure to have her obituary published in the *LA Times* and in the Stanford magazine. Of course, I said, thinking – and what shall I do about your funeral, but I couldn't speak to that.

July 15, 2002, Monday

Sunday evening Diane came to dinner. I'd been planning to have a simple steak dinner, with salad and baked potato, but Ann suggested a shrimp salad, and considering the hot days we were having last week I consented. I bought much of the food Saturday morning, but Ann went out to Trader Joe's on Saturday afternoon and bought shrimp, dip, potato chips and crackers, and Stilton for dessert. Then on Sunday, though I asked her what I should do, all she asked me to do was to cut up and wash carrots and celery, set the table, prepare the fruit. Everything else she did, even to preparing the salad after Diane was here. I was concerned I'd regret the invitation to Diane, but Ann didn't get too tired. Although Diane noticed her breathlessness, I did not – something I should consider a bit – and we enjoyed the conversation with Diane, the laughing and joking with her. She displayed more of her many talents as she remembered old songs, old comedy routines. Ann laughed as hard as I've heard her in many months. I shall have to tell Diane, she provided one of the memorable occasions she recommended I set up these days.

This morning Ann feels mildly tired only.

July 16, 2002, Tuesday

This morning Ann went for her last in the first series of carboplatin. We'll discover this week, I hope, how it's working. I'm more aware of her shortness of breath these days. But whether this means she's worse I don't know.

At the doctor's office, Ann seemed duller than I've ever seen her – the fatigue, of course. Dr. Doyle looked to me for confirmation when she said she felt all right. I didn't shake my head yes or no – then he listened to her chest. He didn't smile, and his eyes narrowed a bit, losing their sparkle. At first he said he'd have the chest x-ray done today. Then he decided, not. He'll have it next week instead and asked Ann to schedule an appointment.

July 17, 2002, Wednesday

Ann was stirred yesterday by a report on CNN that the new homeland security department, if created, might deploy troops against domestic targets, might standardize drivers' licenses, might give the President power to move money without authorization from Congress. And a lot more without Congress's authorization. I am a shirker not to gather my articulateness together and write to my senators. I shall do it this week. I swear.

July 18, 2002, Thursday

Foggy this morning, again. Wet and damp when I went to see Harvey. When I returned, Ann was up, getting ready to drive out to Los Osos with me so I could leave my car at Smitty's. She answered, when I asked, that she'd had a troublesome night, especially early, when her left shoulder began to bother her. She'd taken pills (Valium and Tylenol, I think, or maybe a sleeping pill) and slept more or less well. Her shoulder was "better" she said – but by better I gathered that the pain was still there, just not as bad as it had been last night. She's pale – grey – my mother's coloring when she was eighty years old.

By the time we'd dropped my car off and shopped at the grocery store, her shoulder hurt so much she needed some heat on her shoulder. Since then the pain has not diminished significantly, though she's taken, now, Valium and baclofen.

I want to hover and make the pain go away. I can't bear the thought of her having the pain. I can't bear the thought of her worrying about the pain the way I am – I keep thinking about referred pain from the cancer. I go about the work I'm trying to do, and I wonder if we're moving into another phase of this illness. More than wonder. I know we're in another phase, I just don't want us to be there. Certainly not where there's pain. I'm already beginning to look back on yesterday as a last day of the old phase – and hope it's not, hope there's another, and another, and another. I think about what we had for dinner last night, and wish I was back there.

I think about breakfast this morning, and wish I was back there.

This is different from last year's series of blows, as we discovered first the cancer and then how far it had gone. We figured out a way to live with the illness as chronic. That was the hope, that we could keep it chronic. Now that there's a threat it may slide into sliding – descend into descent, I want to hold it back.

Written at 5 pm: Around two, Ann thought of lidocaine patches that Kay had given her for the pain caused by the spasms she was having a couple of months ago. She tried one, and it brought her relief – this, after heat, Valium, and Baclofen just barely diminished the pain. Now, though there's still discomfort, she's sitting up at her computer, reading her email. She's offered to start the meat and the potatoes – if we have them – for dinner.

I feel we've swayed back into the life we want to lead, rather than the life we're going to be forced to lead. Balancing, teeter-totter.

July 19, 2002, Friday

After dinner I suggested Ann was spending more time than she should cosseting one of her internet friends – a woman who's going to have an operation next Monday and writes as if she's never been sick before and therefore doesn't know what to do. I've wanted her to go on with her notes on girls' education she'd been making for a woman preparing a book on the topic. She agreed she should, excused herself, and wrote until it was time to go to bed.

We talked about her illness after I'd placed the lidocaine patches carefully on her back, fetched her heated neck pad. "I can't help getting a little tearful," she said. "All these things I have to do . . ." I thought she meant things she has to do to keep going, but didn't finish her sentence, because she was tearful. I started to comment on how brave she was, then thought better of it, because sometimes I think it's harder to be told how brave you are than just to be brave. But she knew what I was going to say, and finished the sentence, ironically. Then she said, "But that's the way you have to be. That's the way to keep going."

I talked about being with her, how I wanted to be with her always, and together we promised each other eternal companionship – though not in so many words. I'm reminded now of arias when lovers come together – beginning or ending an opera – and think, this is an aria not of coming together, but of separation. She spoke of how she wished for me the night before, almost called me, but didn't. I said she could have, I said I wanted her to. She doesn't want me performing the attendant care tasks, and I said when that time comes, we'll get someone to take care of you that way, so I can be present for the important things.

July 20, 2002, Saturday

In the afternoon, Ann went out to talk with John [the gardener] about things bothering her in the garden – the roses needed cutting, for example. Then, because the front door had received its yearly varnishing, she went to her room and rested with the oxygen tubing in her nose. At four or so she rose, went to her computer, and finished the discussion of PE in Catholic girls' schools that she'd started the night before. (Pleasing me, because I want her to finish the entire assessment, including comments on what kind of person she believes this education encouraged her to become.) Some time in between, she found a bird had flown in through the door – left open to dry and also to keep the room clear of varnish fumes. She called me. It was a tiny grey and brown backed bird with a yellow front – a small, perhaps immature female goldfinch. It was fluttering against the window, beating the glass with its wings, feeling it with its claws. I moved it down one window pane, while Ann went to get a dust mop. I put the dust mop next to the bird and tried to move it gently on, but it was too frightened to move anywhere. So I put my hand around it – it was smaller than my palm – and let it loose outside.

Then I noticed she was breathless. She told me she'd been short of breath all day. She was also quite tense, distressed about the stock market dive, distressed about a bill for insurances she'd received. I reassured her, and we sat talking about her distress for quite a while. When she went to bed, cramping was beginning to bother her, and her neck hurt enough that I went to fetch the hot pack for her before I went to bed.

I went to bed extremely sad and tense. This morning I phoned Noelle from Benton Way in order to talk with her about how I'm feeling, but Harvey came into the room and I couldn't talk. All I could say was how Ann was.

Death becomes a familiar, a household companion, something that will never happen, but will.

July 22, 2002, Monday

Ann seems to be suffering a little more pain each day. Last night after we returned from a dinner at the Galley with Anne C we watched a KCET program about the sinking of the Hood and the Bismarck in WWII. Sometime during the program her shoulder began to hurt and when she went to bed her ear was bothering her.

I thought the cancer was causing the pain, though I didn't tell her so. She's been trying to believe in other reasons; I desperately wish I could. I put the lidocaine patches on her back, and then she took Vicodan, in desperation, I guess, because it causes nightmares she says. Later, she told me, she took more Vicodan, and managed to get through the night all right. But this morning her ear was beginning to hurt again soon after she got up. She feels depressed about it.

So am I, because I don't know how to help. I did say, take the pain medication, take it. But she doesn't want to take it. Fearful of being dopey?

I'm also concerned because her heart might be causing the pain. The cancer is, after all, very near her heart.

I'm glad we went out last evening, though. Morro Bay had no fog, and the water was calm, reflecting sun, water, orange, rose, brilliant sunset.

July 23, 2002, Tuesday

Death – the greatest fear of nightmares and futures. Present now, waiting, its time not chosen yet, but near. When I found I had cancer, I woke up every morning into fear that I had to struggle up out of. Now, with enormous changes in my life, with Ann's death stalking us, I wake in the morning to the ordinary. What time is it? Sun. Birds. Time to get going? Then I think of the day – the doctor's appointment, what we'll learn, and then my great fear – that Ann will die suddenly, from heart failure. Next, I think, but that would be best for her; the jump from the window to escape the flames. Then I wonder, am I going to be able to get through this with grace. Then I think of the routine, how the day will go, and I'm back into comfort again, just hoping that this one more day will go as the last two hundred have gone, with consciousness of the illness, not of the changes to come.

All of this is not what I want to say. I want to say – it's a chessboard, strait and restricted, and I move from dark to light to dark to light, no matter whether I go across the board or simply take one step. Sometimes I'm tearful, but I hide that from Ann these days. Sometimes I'm denying that anything's wrong. One constant: I want to ask Ann minute by minute how she's feeling.

July 24, 2002, Wednesday

My morning's difficulties illuminated the repression of fear and other feelings I've been experiencing. First, having put my keys down in front of me, I thought

I'd lost them and went all over the house looking for them. Then, on climbing into the car, I accidentally touched the lock button on the keys and the car began beeping. I drove to the doctor's office, forgetting to use the California right turn, not changing my lanes in time, and so forth, just barely safely. Once parked, I went upstairs to fetch the wheelchair for Ann, who had stopped in Radiology to get her x-ray. She was at the elevator, ready to come up when I arrived on the first floor with the elevator. I managed to get her to the door of the doctors' suite, when I forgot how to open a door and get a wheelchair through, and we got stuck. Ann couldn't help because her hands were full of papers. I went to grab the papers and dropped them all over. People waiting to see the doctor came to help, and did, and I got to laughing so hard tears were running down my face. I think it was the tears that told me I was reacting to strain.

Wonderfully, the x-rays taken yesterday show the cancer is stable again, much to my relief. As for the pain, Dr. Doyle doesn't think it's her heart; he has ordered an x-ray of her jaw; he wrote some very reassuring prescriptions; and for today, at least, the pain has disappeared.

I want to say the relief was palpable, but I don't know what I mean, physically, by palpable. A desire to celebrate, to break out of routine. Loss of focus on Ann's every move. There was no elation – the kind of elation I've felt when I've worried about losing something beneficial and then haven't. More – a return to an even keel, a sense that an imminent disaster hasn't happened. Shoulders less tense, maybe. Expanded thinking – meaning, less narrow.

Ann felt relief, too, she said. She claimed, however, not to have been as distressed over the week as I had been. She didn't think the pain was caused by the cancer, but by an exacerbation of her old problems, something that her PT could relieve.

July 27, 2002, Thursday

Ann returned from having her jaw x-rayed. It was difficult, she said, because of the several positions she had to arrange herself in. Worse, the tech who's been doing all the work for her since the initial CT scan said the next step would be a bone scan, signaling to both of us that he sees something in the jaw. I'm horrified. I think Ann is frightened, but puts the fear out of her mind and projects many of her feelings towards relief of others.

July 29, 2002, Monday

This morning when I woke I felt as if I'd been clenched, gripped – or, rather, that I was gripping sleep. For dear life. Oblivion, safe and soft oblivion. For the first few moments of consciousness I relished the hold sleep had on me, thinking about the life crisis I'm in, and feeling only the sweetness of sleep. I find myself moving in and out of stark terror, gloom, satisfaction, peace, worry every day all day, depending on whether I'm in the routine I've set forth for myself and everything is going as it has for the last week or so. That's the point, I adjust, the way you do when a baby has come into the family. Certain activities become routine, change slightly, become routine, change slightly. You only notice the big shifts in awareness.

Gradually, in the last two weeks, things with Ann have changed. She's taking pain medication, oxycontin and oxycodone (for breakthrough) every day and night. She's paler, her hair is straightening, and her face looks strained. She is getting less sleep, yet doesn't seem to have the long days of not being able to move from her chair because of fatigue.

She's been irritable because of the pain, possibly because she's worried and depressed, and because of a generalized itch she's been suffering. When she's irritable she sometimes lashes out at me – mostly about things I'm trying to tell her. The old story: "I already know that. I read it yesterday" – when it's really breaking news. This tells me she's listening less and less to distinctions, more and more to generalities, is in fact not interested in details.

Saturday afternoon we went to see John Sayles "Sunshine State" a wonderfully apt political satire, focusing on all sides of a development problem in such a way that it presents grassroots struggle for and against development, small town ugliness, new civil rights laws, and complex human beings torn by responses to complex issues, as well as corruption. And it was funny, after all that. I enjoyed it, but was concerned lest she not be enjoying it, and kept looking to see if she was. This is not good! But her illness and irritation put me in that mode – I want her to enjoy it and if she doesn't it bothers me. Shouldn't do that to myself.

July 31, 2002, Wednesday

Before dinner on Monday evening Ann stopped me from talking about a book I'd read, suggesting I might tell her more than she wanted to know before she read it. I felt insulted, answering I knew how to write a review and I knew she still read book reviews. She became upset about my response and went outside saying she needed quiet time. After a while we confronted each other: she said she couldn't put up with an upset every twenty-four hours. Apparently yesterday she'd become angry when she burned herself, creating a "shock to her system."

"Angry at what?'

"At the situation."

What was I to think? What about the situation? My being present? My trying to be part of her life as she is dying?

What should I do?

Leave, is my first response.

But is she being rational?

We settled down, forgave each other and said goodnight in our usual manner on Monday. I slept well that night, but Tuesday morning I kept feeling sadness – a wrenching of my gut, tears rolling down my face. I couldn't pull myself up into normal feeling. Ann too felt sad, even sadder because I was unable to hide grief from her. It was the whole sense of our life diminishing, her life diminishing.

The visit to the doctor didn't brighten the day. My feelings of sadness or grief continued, increasing Ann's inability to keep herself steady. I kept seeing her standing in her black costume in the garden, near the gate I love to look at, to look through out into the hills. Or her room, with the big French doors open. Sundown. The way we were Monday night, at the height of our misunderstanding of each other. Tears rolled down my face all the way home, and in the kitchen we hugged, both of us tearful then. "What can I do to make you feel better?" Ann asked.

"Nothing," I said, "Just hug me, that's all."

But I can't do anything to make her feel better.

I went on doing chores, shopping, and so forth. Calming. Routine.

August 1, 2002, Thursday

I enjoyed the time with Diane, telling her my fears and difficulties. Summarized: I don't know how Ann will be on any one day. She might collapse. She might be in pain. She might be depressed and become irrational because of the depression. I have no sense of an ideal end, I told Diane, in answer to her question. I've seen deaths from cancer before. We talked about that, and my knowledge of how lung cancer might go.

In answer to the trouble about interruptions, feeling cut off, and so forth, partly owing to Ann's depression and her irritation with loss of hearing, Diane suggested something I should keep in mind. "Maybe as we come toward the end, Ann may want to isolate herself and/or no longer feel responsible for you."

August 5, 2002, Monday

Saturday continued a quiet day until I returned from cooking Harvey's dinner. Soon after I'd settled myself with a book, Noelle phoned. I went down the hall to the office to hear Noelle's news and gossip for the last time until September: she, Erwin, and Ellen are flying to Princeton to visit friends. They plan an extensive trip through New England and Prince Edward Island before going to Noelle's political science conference in Boston.

Ann was deeply upset because I'd spent so much time on the phone with Noelle. She had wanted to talk with me and hadn't had a chance all day, she said. I could see tears in her eyes and she was wiping her cheeks. I admitted that my girls had called me this week more than usual because they were worried about both her and me. That yes, Julie had phoned and kept me talking another night, but I needed to keep in touch with the people I loved. When I asked her what she wanted to talk about – herself or others, she said others. Finally, after she'd calmed down, recognizing that I do indeed need to talk with my children and sisters, she told me about the way she felt about her internet group. Basically, she feels they're accusing her of being the kind of person who would try to proselytize a woman newly diagnosed with cancer and persuade her to get chemotherapy. One of them called the woman brave – and, I thought, possibly they are calling her brave for not taking chemotherapy when Ann feels she herself is brave for taking it. But for the most part I believe Ann was overreacting to the letters on the internet, becoming upset and angry about what isn't intended to hurt or alarm her, so I tried to put new interpretations on what the women have written and this seemed to help her.

August 6, 2002, Tuesday

Monday night Ann's irritability stretched into dinner time. She wanted to know why I "persisted" in serving her too much food. Didn't I know that she didn't have much appetite? and that people without appetite become even more turned off by having too much food heaped on their plates? I pointed out that she usually served the meat and the starch and often the vegetables and salad – not I – and that when I was serving, I usually asked her how much she wanted. I said, "You must be feeling a great deal of irritation."

This morning she informed the doctor about her irritation. After talking it over, they decided she would take Valium in low doses three times a day. After he left she commented on the way they always say Valium is for anxiety.

"I'm not anxious, I'm irritable," she said.

I agreed. "You frighten me when you are." I don't want to start avoiding her because she's irritable and I'm worried she'll lash out at me again. I don't want to go through her last days feeling tentative. Censoring myself.

August 7, 2002, Wednesday

Tuesday evening Ann began to feel ill around four,

possibly earlier. I fixed chicken noodle soup for her dinner. At 9:30 she wanted to go to bed, but felt she couldn't until she'd downed the potassium she's still taking. She complained of chilling, and when she finally got into bed, around ten, she was shaking all over. I heated the "bed bunny" in the microwave for her neck and a hot water bottle for her abdomen, which hurt – constipation, she believed. Her right hand seemed bloodless to her. She asked me to get close to her in the bed to see if this would stop the chills, and I did, and after half an hour her hand was warm and she wasn't shaking any more. I was frightened and at the same time having moments of feeling I was immersed in the greatest drama of my life, and what did it mean, what did life mean, what did Ann's seventy-two years mean, my seventy years mean. I would have stayed and warmed Ann all night, if I had to. I offered to sleep across the hall from her in the guest bed, but she didn't want that.

About midnight, after reheating the hot water bottle and the moist heat pack, I went upstairs, promising to check back when I woke up to go to the bathroom. I checked back around 12:30 and she was asleep. I tried counting her breaths – I thought over 20 a minute. When I woke at two or so, and went downstairs, she was up, having gone to the bathroom. She was warm then, and didn't need any more heat. When I woke again at 4:30, she'd turned the light out, so I didn't go downstairs.

Today is our anniversary. At this time, 11:45, I'm not sure Ann is going to be able to go out to the dinner we'd planned. After reading the paper this morning while I drank coffee and read too, she seemed to have decided to take her morning nap but then I saw she was starting to cry – her chin was trembling, her hands were over her eyes. I went over, hugged her. Brought Kleenex. Cried myself. She didn't know, she said, whether it was the cancer or the medicine. She's never felt so awful for so long. I said, "You don't have to be brave for me."

She was sure her hemoglobin count was way down and she won't therefore receive chemo on Tuesday. We talked about whether she would go on with navelbine, since it makes her so sick. I suggested that if she improves Saturday she give it a second week. I also asked her about her neck and jaw pain. The jaw pain seems to have been relieved somewhat; at least it's not bothering her all the time. Her neck pain is sometimes bad, sometimes not. Yesterday she went without either of the opiates all day, because of her stomach, and the pain wasn't too bad.

I told her I wasn't clear about when she has it or when she doesn't. Or how severe it is. We agreed we didn't know whether the neck pain was cancer or arthritis.

This morning she said her stomach was better. I haven't asked her about the rest.

After much discussion, we decided that I should pick up good champagne and cheese and frozen shrimp at Trader Joe's so we could celebrate our anniversary with a light supper for Ann. We did, and in some ways it was as much fun as Windows would have been. We spoke of going to Windows on Sunday, but I don't feel we have to. Not if it will make Ann feel ill.

August 10, 2002, Saturday

When I told her I was going upstairs for lunch at 12, she said, "I've missed you all morning."

"Should I take my nap here then?"

"Yes," she said. So I promised to come down and nap on the couch. I did, with my tape deck, as I had on Friday afternoon.

In the evening after taking care of Harvey's dinner, she heard me come in and moved out of the kitchen. I saw immediately something was wrong and she wanted me to hold her and let her cry like a child. She was crying, she told me, because she could hardly bear what was happening to her internet friend, who has fallopian tube and ovarian cancer which has metastasized. She's been corresponding with her internet group during the evening, and had become so distraught she almost phoned me to ask me to come home. She kept saying, "I haven't sobbed like this for forever." And "Why?" she kept asking. After a while I said "Because we're human beings, and this is what happens to us."

Even though I had tears, even though I despair of the human condition some time, I was crying because Ann was experiencing agony. As far as believing that she was dying, I was still incredulous, emotionally. I go through light and shadow: enjoyment of the day, then terrible fear of what's to come and grief.

August 11, 2002, Sunday

When I returned from Benton Way at 4, Ann looked

awfully pale and confessed to being tired. She'd continued with her commentary on Mayfield as a girls' school and its effect upon her life and she'd also corresponded with her circle of friends. But not too tired to go out. And we went, Morro Rock was catching the fog, creating darkness before real sunset, bringing me a sense of peace, an escape from the dreariness of summer.

The dinner was interesting, the conversation pleasant. On the way home we listened to Fassbaender and Fischer-Diskau sing Brahms "Liebeslieder," and drove through the Los Osos Valley. The moon was a reddish thumbnail. In the living room we sat for some time discussing Ann's Mayfield/Stanford/Youth recollections. I recollected my own notion: fear of or distrust of intelligent women; or conversely, only men made good conversational companions. Ann not only respected women's abilities, she also received help from them. We also discussed the changeover at Stanford from the old guard and her counselor Anastasia Doyle (who was encouraging women in the sciences) to the 1950s types of counselor for women.

August 14, 2002, Wednesday

The visit to Dr. Doyle also brought relief, of a sort. Ann described for him her severe symptoms from last week, and he decided it wasn't worth it to go on with navelbine. He said theoretically, the severe reaction might mean that the cancer was breaking down and revving up the immune system against it, but it was only theoretical, and he thought we'd try other things rather than go on with it. He is going to read up on two drugs used for small cell cancer but which have been tried on NSCAC. They are irinotecan and topotecan; the first is harder on the stomach than the second – which may cause diarrhea. Another drawback to the first is that it may have to be injected five days in a row. He asked whether we remembered other drugs he'd mentioned – I said only taxol. Well, yes. He'll try the others first though. Meanwhile, he gave her a shot of B12, procrit, and suggested she take folic acid, at least 1 mg per day.

When he was out of the room I confessed I was a little disappointed, because like him I thought maybe the navalbine was working. But I assured Ann it was her body, she was undergoing the suffering, not I, and I respected what she wanted, and I respected his decision also. I reminded her of how I'd been disappointed she hadn't had surgery, but that I knew now it would have been absolutely the wrong thing for her.

August 15, 2002, Thursday

I like watching her hands cut the vegetables. I like listening to her voice as she talks about the latest civil rights horror – that Ashcroft has suggested internment camps for American citizens who are suspected of terrorist activities or sympathies, but against whom there is no real evidence. I feel proud of her ability to write instantly about the issues that I struggle to express myself on or even to remember details about.

August 16, 2002, Friday

Some time ago I stopped telling Ann at night, when I was working hard at wishing her better, that I was trying to make her better. It now seems phony to me. I just can't say it. Unless I add, I've been a failure in that respect

Diane and I ate at Hobie's in a booth near the window. I told her what's been happening here, and added, thinking about the night Ann cried for a couple of hours, thinking of how I blot out feeling, or try to blot it out. I cried with Ann because of her distress, but not because of what I'm going through. I blotted that out. "Anyway," I said to Diane, "here I am going through the most important event of my life (except my own death, we both agreed) and I don't know what exactly I'm feeling."

She said, "We just go through things, and it doesn't make any difference if we feel it all the way through or not. We just take it as it comes."

I don't know whether I agree with this.

August 20, 2002, Tuesday

Last night I was tired and achy from arthritis. While opening a can of soup for Ann – tired, stomach bothering her – my hand slipped, and my left forefinger, right at the knuckle was pinched. I swore, put it under cold water. Ann came rushing in, got out a couple of towels to wrap ice in. We settled down, and I tried to go on fixing dinner. Ann refused to let me. She was an old self I see rarely these days, the care-giving Ann, who takes over your life and won't stand for any protests. I tried to protest – she wouldn't hear of it, and fixed the whole dinner. Out of breath though. She gets out of breath walking down the hall these days.

This morning, when I returned from walking with Jean, she asked how my hand was before I could get a word out to ask how she was.

"Would you like me to sit in the living room and read with you?" I asked.

"No, do what you feel like doing."

I teased, "You mean you're not going to ask me to sit with you? Hold your hand?"

"That day will come soon enough."

Right now she's working in her office, putting things away, she said.

The depression I felt yesterday has settled in my stomach. I don't want to do anything but be with Ann. All summer I've been putting that feeling away. Now, it's like a tide riding in and I listen to the roar of the breakers.

August 21, 2002, Wednesday

Yesterday (Tuesday) Ann worked most of the morning in her office. She was organizing business affairs, worried, I think, that she'll not be able to work on them for much longer. She told me that we'll have to work together on some things, and I agreed that I'm ready any time, she doesn't even have to let me know beforehand.

In the afternoon she rested and then felt well enough to go on the internet in the early evening. At one point, she told me I should know where information about her mother's estate was, where tax records are.

Another thing we talked about: she asked me not to interfere with her performing whatever tasks she can do. I've been saying, "I'll do this, I'll do that," and she doesn't feel it's helpful. When she needs help she'll ask. 'You'll be doing it all soon enough': she didn't say this, but the words lay unspoken between us.

August 22, 2002, Thursday

A thought from yesterday: Ann now needs to lecture me when she speaks about something important to her, partly I think because she's short of breath and she doesn't want to expend much energy. We were talking about what Dr. Doyle might plan, and we admitted to being a bit nervous. I said, "I guess the navelbine scared us." I got a fiercely stated lecture on the topic of chemotherapy, none of it addressing my questions. Anyway, as a result, I saw us no longer together, but each of us alone, and this enabled us to talk again about how lonely Ann feels too. In the end I was able to say that when she hurts I hurt and want to make it better. It bothers me that I can't.

We've both been concerned that Dr. Doyle is just throwing things at her. We talked over what she was going to say to him on the next visit. I said the navelbine experience bothered me in that I was concerned that when she said ouch, he stopped treatment. That he was so sensitive to her reactions that he backed down. She listened to me, and I believe agreed that we should know what he's intending to do. She also wondered whether he was treating the cancer aggressively. He had explained the principles by which he worked. He said there were several drugs that have not been tried yet, which he plans to try as others fail, and the purpose was to prolong her life as comfortably as possible. He thought she was doing well. She wasn't suffering too much from the chemotherapy, she hadn't lost much weight, her blood levels returned easily to where they should be. He said he tries to balance the suffering induced by the drug against living a reasonably comfortable life; that eventually you reach a point of diminishing returns; and often the patient tells him when she's had enough.

He's starting with Taxol – paclitaxel – and then possibly trying topetecan. He mentioned etoposide – or is it atoposide? – which can be taken orally. Cytoxin, an older drug, used before he started practicing, and several others which are all in the notes I took and gave to Ann.

I think both of us felt relieved after talking with him, in spite of the fact he's hearing more fluid in her chest than he did last week. Which means going without treatment is dangerous at this time.

August 24, 2002, Saturday

Today I made myself aware of Ann's way of doing things precisely, how she makes note of every pill she takes, every time she wakes in pain and the place of the pain and the level of the pain. She maintains control of her body this way and control of the way others are dealing with it. I wondered at it today, because we seem to be coming closer to death. In the kitchen when I noticed where she wanted her dishes, how she wanted her oatmeal, how high up the glass the water should be so she won't spill; all during the day when I noticed her saying to herself and to me that she has to do something for herself, she can't let me do it: I see the strength that's kept her on her own for years. I love and admire that strength. Enormously.

It would have helped yesterday if I had some of that precision when the doctor told her to get in to the emergency, and I, having forgotten where I left first, the key to her car, then my purse – if I had ever disciplined myself to keep things in one place – well, I do try – I do keep the keys on top of the dresser or in my pocket, but if I absent-mindedly set them down, then I'm lost. And that's what happened about the purse.

I didn't really believe Ann was in serious danger; it crossed my mind, but hit my wall of thinking this couldn't really be happening. I was terribly concerned about her pain, I wanted her to see the doctor, I wanted her to make sure it wasn't a heart attack. I looked up the drug on the internet and discovered that chest pain could be a side effect, perhaps even an allergic reaction. I did suggest benedryl. But I just didn't see, at a moment of real danger, that this is a serious event and I have to shift my priorities. That is, I could have done without the purse – and I would have, if it hadn't shown up where it did – but I should have made that decision earlier. I don't have that reaction when I'm in danger or when I'm prepared for the danger. I remember reacting very swiftly when a man came up to me in a dark parking lot outside a grocery store – I backed away and told him

I didn't want any help. I remember reacting swiftly to large waves and near falls. But when someone I love and wish to care for is in trouble, I just can't seem to believe there's any danger. Denial and optimism.

It was Ann who dialed 911.

At the hospital, once they checked Ann with an EKG, the doctor suggested a pulmonary embolism had to be ruled out as the cause of the chest pain. So we waited. A pleasant nurse, sensitive, reassuring, capable, a woman about fifty, blonde scraggly hair, glasses, directive voice, dressed in blue pants, flowered blue shirt, gave Ann morphine, then again, again, again.

They had to watch to make sure it didn't affect her ability to breathe, but what was affecting her ability to breathe was the pain in her chest. Once, while we waited for the CT scan, she had to get up to go to the bathroom. They wheeled her there, but when she returned, she was shaking from the pain, which she said had gone from a 5 to an 8. Pain as she breathed.

I couldn't bear the thought of her having to put up with pain. I think we were both scared this may be the end of a comfortable life for her – not just fear, but terror – and I wanted to see the morphine work without putting her out. It didn't, not really, and she went through the CT scan in agony, returned in agony, in spite of Valium and morphine. They did give her more morphine, and it eased slightly, but she still had pain with each breath. Around 4 o'clock, they got the results of the CT scan – her cancer had grown since June. No pulmonary embolism.

They gave her a patch of fentanyl that will last the weekend, if necessary and released her.

I brought her home at five, grey, in great pain when she had to take deep breaths. I pulled the oxygen compressor out into the living room – it's clumsy, and heavy, and doesn't want to roll on the carpet. Ann told me we had to have the surge protector, and so I fetched that, got her sitting down, got the oxygen going for her. She leaned back in the chair, eyes closed.

Later I heated some pea soup for her. We sputtered a bit about how she should be served. At last I got her to take it in a cup – I didn't think she should sit up at the table. At night I fetched a pillow and blanket for myself, put on my sweats, tried to get all the necessary equipment for getting to the hospital in a hurry together. I collected Ann's pills, at her direction, and put them and other things she needed in a small box. Speaking tired her because of having to project air. When she went to the bathroom, she returned shaking all over from the pain, from the effort of trying to breathe against the pain.

I went to sleep on the couch, comforted by being near her, but deeply worried: is this the way it's going to be from now on? How are we going to deal with the pain? I told her that if she wasn't better by noon tomorrow we'd call the doctor and ask for help.

This morning, Ann still felt great pain, though it lessened as the day went on and the oxycontin/oxycodone pills began to help and to work with fentanyl. At night she decided to return to her bed. I slept with my door open, so I could hear her if she were in trouble or see if her light went on. Sunday morning she believed she could go without the oxygen compressor. I fixed oatmeal for her, as I'd done on Saturday morning, and that evening I cooked a lamb chop for her, and she ate almost all of it.

August 31, 2002, Saturday

Last evening we had the time to talk over the clash we'd had Wednesday night, both of us understanding the other, I knowing how rotten Ann may feel, how irritable when taking opiates and she realizing she criticizes personally, instead of just expressing her irritability. There'll never be another loving friend like Ann, partly because of the years we've put in trying to understand and work with each other's weaknesses.

When we are calm and thoughtful of each other, as we were last night, there's nothing better in the world. I don't think I'd trade it for any other moment in our lives.

This morning because I didn't have to rush off: quiet, long moments side by side.

September 3, 2002, Tuesday

Sensation of playing peekaboo as if I were a child watching mother hide herself, come back, hide herself, come back from Ann well to Ann in pain. I don't shriek with glee at the reappearance of love and comfort – but I do peer to the side of the blanket that hides her face, searching for the real, and I'm aware of the blanket held up, ready to take her away again.

Yesterday she slept most of the morning, then in the afternoon worked while I fooled with birds on the internet and typed notes for Jean's books. I didn't know what she was working on, though I was aware she had been preparing food for dinner. Around five, she came into my office with the statement she'd worked out for her relatives and close Catholic friends, declaring that it was her wish not to have a public memorial or mass, not to have any priests at her bedside when she lay dying. I didn't read it immediately, but picked it up after she'd left, then went out to the kitchen, where we stood discussing its diplomacy and efficacy. I said it would be hard for anyone to receive in the mail as the first news of Ann's death; she believed I should go ahead with the plan before notifying anyone. I don't/didn't know whether that would be possible. I thought of Irish families, people on the phones. I was going to suggest I call Clare W, when she said one of her biggest fears is Clare's brother-in-law, a priest, who has intruded where she felt he ought not. So I finally said I'd call her Aunt Marge myself.

I asked one thing more – a letter, signed and folded now, possibly even addressed, to be sent out saying this first letter to be sent out was being sent out at her request.

September 4, 2002, Wednesday

Another evening last night of old style life – that is life like what we were living last year – Carol and Ann working on bills, then political commentary on internet, then reading Carol's attempts at short fiction, then dinner, with figs and pears and blue cheese for salad, then talk about this and that. This morning when I came downstairs at 7:30 ready to go walk with Jean, see Harvey, help him get papers and bins out, Ann asked me to stand by: she had a severe pain in her left side, what Dr. Doyle has described as a pleural pain, which hurt to breathe. She wanted me near, she said.

September 5, 2002, Thursday

Yesterday Dr. Doyle told Ann that the pain from pulmonary embolism would come on very quickly, but he believed the pain she was experiencing, because of its position and because her ankles and feet weren't swollen, was the cancer irritating or rubbing against the pleura. Or it could be the pleural effusion causing pain as it increases. He said the pleural effusion could be drained, or eventually, the lung could be collapsed upon itself – though that would be painful in itself. Ann thought she could deal with it for the time being with the oxycontin/oxycodone combination, and we went on with the infusion of topotecan or hycamtin, a drug for ovarian cancer that might be helpful in small cell lung cancer.

Later, alone, my tears began to roll as I thought of her physical struggle; I don't know how I could bear what she's bearing. I've thought of not going on myself, before. This morning, for the first time, I wondered if maybe it is a real possibility for me. Why live to go through by yourself the illnesses that precede death? Maybe I should consider a method, and keep it in reserve.

September 6, 2002, Friday

Ann was short of breath, she told me, and very tense. I didn't ask her how she felt; the night before I'd said I hate to keep asking her, that asking her was a form of anxiety in me, fear that she's not telling me she's suffering. I should just assume she is, and suffer with her. As I'm doing right now. At this minute she's lying in her chair, asleep, having pulled the curtains to. I've begun to worry about her taking her own life.

September 9, 2002, Monday

In general, I'm worried all the time now. I don't know how that differs from last year. Except now I know that routine is what keeps me (and Ann) sane during this time. Last year I didn't know that – I think I hated routine. Routine allows you to pretend life is forever. Nothing is ever over – until it's over and as we discovered yesterday, Ann isn't strong enough to go out for breakfast and follow her old Sunday routine. So you build a new one.

Maybe my continuing with my normal life helps Ann too.

September 10, 2002, Tuesday

Ann showed me what she'd been doing all day: making a sign on the nicknames of the people in her address book who would need notification at the time of her death. I went into her office, taking my usual place in the rolling chair, and sat down to watch her move the computer to her address book, and then said yes, I understood. We talked a little about writing notes to a list of people, the list she will put in her "Instructions" folder; she suggested having something printed, a card, perhaps, and then follow it with a letter. I tried to hide the tears in my eyes by gripping her hands and looking down at them. I saw the tears in hers.

I agreed she should get this done, so we can get back to routine.

September 11, 2002, Wednesday

The chemo went well this morning. Some discussion of Ann's shortness of breath. Doyle recommends O2 pack – some unobtrusive device. On the way home we went past the plaza, where the Women in Black were standing silently, facing outwards, away from the non-denominational services which were in the center. Many faced Chorro Street, and it would have been easy to let Ann out so she could join them. Then I could park the car and come be with her. I suggested this, but somehow, Ann didn't understand that it was just a suggestion, not an attempt to urge her to do something she wasn't physically able to do. She started to cry, putting her face down, hand over her eyes. She said she would love to participate, but couldn't. I said I was just trying to make it easy for her, if she wanted to.

September 13, 2002, Friday

Yesterday Ann asked me to drive with her past Staples, where she stopped to go in and get a pocket calendar.

"A highly optimistic move," she characterized the errand.

I said, stupidly – I am slow – "Do you think they're in stock yet?" She didn't answer, and it was only after she'd gone into the store that I knew what she meant.

September 18, 2002, Wednesday

Dr. Doyle said he can hear no air in her left lung at all. After trying to make up his mind whether to send her down for a chest x-ray, and ultra sound and a thoracentesis right away, he decided – with her prompting because she had other appointments – to have it done next week. Her platelet count might be up by then. So, after a shot of procrit, she went off to radiology to make an appointment for next week.

She decided to walk to radiology, believing it would be just as far to walk from the emergency entrance down the hall as to walk from the entrance from the building we were in. Down the elevator, around the corner, through the doors, through the covered passage, down the hall. Wait at radiology breathing hard.

"You have to go back to the Women's Center," the man at the desk told us.

Ann was almost crying when she said: "This system doesn't work well."

We walked back. She was groaning with her inhalations by the time we came into the room. The young woman looked at the papers, then disappeared. When she came back she made a fuss about the papers; they didn't tell her much. "Usually, we get a call from upstairs."

Ann said, "This time they gave them to me."

Back and forth about chest x-rays, what comes first, blood tests: it became apparent that the young woman couldn't contain her irritation or emotions or – I'm not certain what. Ann turned to me and said, "What did I do, what did I say?"

"Nothing," I replied.

The young woman had gotten up from her chair and gone into another room as if so angry she had to leave.

In the end we straightened it out, Ann explaining that her platelet count was down; that the doctor wanted it next week; that she had oxygen; that she wanted the chest x-ray right before to save energy; that the chest x-ray may not show the pockets that are filling up. Finally, the young woman calmed down, said she'd been worried she wasn't going to be able to help Ann. We left, amicably.

September 19, 2002, Thursday

Ann went to bed with pain last night; I went to bed trying to live with Ann's pain. What did I do when I went to bed? I read, carefully, twenty more pages in *Swann's Way*.

This morning I came downstairs just as Ann was leaving her room: "Good morning," she said.

I asked how she'd slept. Offered to make breakfast for her. Then went into the kitchen and announced I was going to try to scrape the crud from the spaghetti pan. I scrubbed away, dropped the pan, then noticed silence. I went into the living room where I found

Ann holding her mouth the way she does when she's trying to keep back tears – sobs maybe. I knelt beside her, took her hand, cried too. She thought, somehow, I'd been brusque with her. This may have been a carryover from the evening before, when we'd had a sort of non-understanding over a program of ethics I'd been watching. I was trying to share a little of what I'd learned – the concept of ethical decisions requiring confidence in the society, its fairness, its equally ethical behavior, together with a feeling of belonging to it on an egalitarian basis – and I thought she was challenging me and became tense and told her so. (I think she was challenging me because she didn't understand what I was saying, or didn't quite hear it.) Anyway, this morning I said I hadn't been brusque, had wanted to help her with breakfast. She wondered if she was beginning to give way. I said it was okay to cry. I said I was with her. I said maybe she was reacting to the potentiation of the opiates by the ativan, and that when she'd first started the opiates she'd been easily irritated and tense.

I made her breakfast, then went down the hall to look at the paper. I was overwhelmed by the news that Bush is pushing for congressional approval of a unilateral attack on Iraq.

September 20, 2002, Friday

National news was altogether discouraging today. The Democrats for the most part are allowing themselves to be pulled along toward a war with Iraq without the blessing of the UN. Bush says that cooperation will follow when we're in control: the words of an emperor.

Yesterday I wrote to Capps, Feinstein, and Boxer, pleading with them not to support Bush's resolution. Today I suggested Claire do the same. She believes we have to work to get the people from 20-40 who don't read the papers to understand just what's happening to our country.

Last night (Thursday) at dinner I told Ann: If you were well, we could move to another country. Words I regretted immediately, because she said, we have to stay here and resist. How awful to have this nasty change in the country happen when you haven't much time left to live!

September 21, 2002, Saturday

In this journal, who am I? Where am I? I don't think I'm ever going to be able to read it again, correct it, unless I begin now. So I had better think who I am here. I see myself as an observer of Ann, yes, and a somewhat sloppy note taker, recording mostly her illness. My focus has been there, rather than on the person she is, still. That's not quite fair. My record of my emotional states has not been fair to Ann, either, because though I note the calm, the necessity of routine, I tend to describe my stress, and sometimes that stress is with Ann. I don't record how often she demonstrates her courage: the methodical note taking she does, pill after pill, reaction after reaction; the upright and friendly response to the people in the doctor's office; how she calls the doctor Brother John from time to time, how he grins, his center upper lip lifting, the ends curling, ever so slightly at her insisting she do what she's able to do. The other evening she asked me if I thought she could have a drink – I said I didn't see why not – and the next thing I knew she was on her way out the door.

"Where are you going?" I asked.

She was already in the car with the garage door up. "I was out of whiskey."

"Why didn't you ask me?"

"Didn't want to impose my evil doing on you."

Her attempt, still, to take care of me by not asking me to go on simple errands, this hurts me the most, because she has to try so hard to overturn my efforts to care for her when she needs it most.

September 24, 2002, Tuesday

All weekend I was worried about the thoracentesis that was to take place Monday morning if the ultrasound demonstrated Ann had another pleural effusion. Friday telling Claire about it, my voice broke. I apologized and then I let her know how hard it was for me to handle any extra tension these days without tears starting. I asked her to let her sisters know that I'm having a hard time dealing with ordinary out of step events, like car problems, plumbing problems, mail problems. Smooth, smooth, one predictable and recurrent event after another is what I wish for.

Ann, for her part, has been gobbling up mysteries. She keeps a pile in the living room, and I suppose living in those ever recurrent forests of semi-events is a way of holding off the inevitable next day, when she's going to feel worse.

I keep thinking of writing poetry, but don't, because

I fear reaching for form will force me to reach for more than I can bear. I think we bear things by staying absent from the future. I need to be totally present – or totally absent – when I write poetry.

As for the thoracentesis, turns out they didn't do it. Whatever they saw wasn't fluid enough. Sounds like that lung's gone??? I'm postponing this reality for a while. I don't believe it. I fear the visit to the doctor tomorrow afternoon, though.

Before it was time to go to sleep last night, I said, "You seemed more energetic today."

She became mildly upset with me. I had to explain that I wasn't saying she seemed better – her difficulty breathing certainly told me she wasn't – but that I'd been trying to point out the moments of light in the shadow. I said that energy to me meant the ability to force yourself to do things. I often am not feeling full of energy, but I feel I'm energetic when I can force myself to do what I should do. She wanted me to describe why she seemed more energetic.

"You didn't sleep today, and you worked on dinner and spent time at your computer."

Her response: she had to do some things, and she was forcing herself.

I didn't reply, not wanting to get us into a hair-splitting semantics discussion, and we settled down with I hope her understanding that I hadn't been saying she seemed well. Long experience has taught me she hates it if I think she's better than she is or suggest it or seem to urge it – probably some old resistance to her parents pushing her on or even to her own desire to participate as a child when she couldn't keep up. Just before I went upstairs her face had softened, a signal to me that she's about to cry, and she said, "This is a bad business."

"Yes it is," I said, and before I left I told her I'd be there with her – in spirit anyway.

This morning she told me it hurts to breathe in. I said she'd tried to do too much yesterday, and that I'd warned her – not that she'd hurt herself – what I'd really done is to tell her to go rest. She said that yesterday she'd had to keep going. Whatever that means, I thought. Then as I went down the hall to work, I said, "I love you," and she said the same, followed by "That's what keeps me going."

I said, "Me too." Then, after a little, I added, "but you don't have to – to keep going, I mean"

She said, "I know."

September 26, 2002, Thursday

Yesterday: Wednesday.

A respiratory therapist was supposed to arrive at 10. She arrived shortly after 11. She had with her a cylinder weighing six pounds or more and a halter to carry it with. It was obviously not the small pack advertised in the ad we'd seen. Ann asked her about it, and she said she knew nothing about the ad. She didn't know about any liquid O2.

Ann, upset, because it wasn't what she'd ordered, asked several questions. The woman knew nothing about anything, apparently, and Ann became more and more upset, finally, saying she didn't want the heavy pack, she wanted liquid O2. She took the O2 saturation level measurer from her finger, almost throwing it down. The woman packed up, leaving in a huff. I asked her as she left, does your company know anything about liquid O2, and she said no.

Ann then phoned Art, the man she'd spoken to before. He said she'd not talked with him about liquid O2 or any kind of light pack. They began to argue, so I took the phone, listened to the man's arguments, and eventually said, "How are we going to solve this problem?" He wanted to talk about appointments, emergencies, etc. and I told him this was almost an emergency, that last week the doctor said he heard no air in Ann's left lung, that Monday they couldn't do a thoracentesis and that she was out of breath walking around the house.

He offered to come up to the house today, so I told him he needed to make this appointment with Ann, handing the phone to her. He began to argue again, apparently, instead of promising to come to the house, and Ann argued back. Eventually it was decided that he'd come at noon

Art arrived at noon, bringing with him a short, plump, blonde young man with a tiny goatee. They were both pleasant and careful with Ann, who settled down.

September 28, 2002, Saturday

Chris from the oxygen equipment company arrived yesterday (Friday) about two in the afternoon. He's a big man, in his thirties, dark-haired, olive skin, large hook nose, small mouth. Last time he came to the house he said his father was a chiropractor and he'd learned massage from him, had worked at massage for several years. Probably as a result of hands-on rub downs, he's friendly and though he talks too much, personable. He explained how to work the portable tank, how to fill it, how often to fill it – every seven hours, or so – and what to watch out for. From previous experience with the concentrator, I knew I wasn't going to remember everything: he explains very rapidly. So I took notes while Ann watched – I tried to watch too.

After Chris left, Ann and I worked together to adjust the belt so she could wear the pack easily. In the few excursions she took around the house, she was still getting out of breath. I felt discouraged, but didn't let on. And, as we listened to the little breathing sound the machine makes – a hiss with each inspiration – Ann said, "I guess I'll make myself really popular wearing this in to the movies." We laughed together. Then she said, "But I'd just use it to get in there; I wouldn't need it sitting down."

Later in the day she said that she still got short of breath walking around. She said the same this morning.

I feel we've begun a new phase, one where I must help more, one where I must be on hand more. I've been more worried. Routine, I tell myself, has to change more rapidly now. When Noelle phoned last night to ask whether I objected to her coming to San Luis at the same time Claire came in October, I thought: by then I may not be able to leave Ann at all.

Ann has said it was emotionally disturbing to see the kids – I think because she's afraid it's the last time. I noticed she'd been upset writing the little note to Annie.

September 30, 2002, Monday

Both of us have learned how to fill the oxygen pack. Sunday morning Ann planned to eat breakfast out, as she likes to do. At the foot of the stairs she called goodbye. I continued getting dressed, then heard the door to the garage close again. I went downstairs to find that the battery on the Volvo had died. When I left the house, Ann was smiling, lips held together, the brave smile, the go ahead, I'll be all right smile.

When I returned at four she was feeling just fair and wanted a scotch, but her bottle was almost empty. I sighed deeply at the thought of having to go out again. I'd been looking forward to having a quiet time before I had to fix dinner, and I said so, feeling guilty. But I started to stand up, to get ready to go. Ann said she could drink gin and tonic instead. I felt as if I'd let her down, but rationally I knew it would be wrong for me to go after the scotch when she could drink gin.

"I feel guilty," I said.

She said she did too. We were both close to tears, Ann at the thought she'd got me upset because I really didn't want to perform that task for her. Me, feeling I'd let her down.

I worked at being rational, telling myself I had to stop thinking I could fix every little thing for her. Fixed dinner, ate, did dishes. Ann chose mashed potatoes because she felt they'd "go down more easily." I worried but said nothing about the possibility the cancer is impinging on her esophagus.

October 2, 2002, Wednesday

Ann is letting her lack of patience show, a sign she doesn't feel well. She said this morning she was depressed, and we rode in the car for miles without speaking. We thought to go out to lunch in Los Osos because the Webers were coming, but all the cafes where we might eat were crowded and the menus didn't sound particularly interesting to Ann. I didn't try to speak, because I'm depressed too, and I don't know what to say when she's depressed. I'm trying to have patience for both of us, but doing so leaves me with a feeling of being trapped. I suppose it's work for me, trying hard to please, to keep her happy, to make her feel good. Since I can't, I keep trying, and keep failing, and that does indeed rob me of myself.

October 3, 2002, Thursday

Courage and clarity – two characteristics I admire in Ann. She had written a note requesting to see her x-rays and to read the last report of the radiologist before we went to the doctor's office. Dr. Doyle took us from room to room in that office warren, looking for an x-ray screen that worked on both sides. Then he put them up, not exactly in order because they weren't in order from the lab, but enough to show that in August and September, taken a month apart, there are two big round cancers in the left lung, one above the other, maybe four or five inches below and two or three above just about where it hurts. The right lung has scattered flecks of cancer and so does what's left of the left lung.

Ann asked him to show on her body where the cancer would be, especially about her shoulder, and he was able to say it might be the bone, and radiation could help to cut the cancer there and the pain. She asked and received information all without tears or noticeable fears. This helped me. It also helped Dr. Doyle who could be forthright.

I still can't.

Later, going over the session while she got chemo, she said, "It didn't look as if the chemo did much good."

"It certainly slowed things down." I added, "You haven't had much since Iressa stopped working – the carboplatin and taxol probably didn't count, and this new chemotherapy takes a while to work even when used at full strength, and it isn't being used at full strength."

At some point, I don't remember when, we began to laugh at a joke, not remembered either.

October 5, 2002, Saturday

Today I explained to Claire on the phone that Ann is trying terribly hard to remain herself, to retain her dignity, in spite of not having enough air, in spite of being more and more limited in what she can do. I didn't add, she wants to continue to look after things for me in the way she's always done. I suspect she's deeply worried about thinking precisely too, and this must be hard when you feel overwhelmed by drugs.

Claire told me Annie read Ann's letter and put it under her pillow.

At five o'clock, just as we were settling down for

a comfortable, non-rushed evening, Ann filled her "escort," the light-weight liquid O2 carrier. The valve shutting off the escape of O2 from the place where you fill it wouldn't shut, and all the frozen O2 began to pour out of the bottom. Ann tried to phone the company that provided it, but no one answered the phone. She tried her drug store and then the pharmacist's home number. All of this she did apparently calmly, except for saying "bastards" at the failure of the company to answer the phone. But after a while she sat down in her chair, breathless, breathing with a croaking sound. I raced down the hall to pull the night-time O2 concentrator out for her, attach it to the electricity, and provide her the cannula. Around 6:30 she dialed 911, explaining to the dispatcher quite clearly that she didn't have a serious emergency, but had a problem she couldn't solve. She said she had a concentrator, but that the equipment that allowed her to move about had failed and that, though the company promised 24-hour service she'd been unable to get anyone to answer the phone. She gave the dispatcher numbers and names. Within twenty minutes Sean from the company phoned and after much discussion decided to bring her the portable that can be wheeled around.

At bed time I said to Ann, "I wish we could have a few days without exciting adventures."

We both laughed.

October 7, 2002, Monday

On Sunday because Harvey was going to a barbecue, I'd planned to drive out to Morro Bay, pick up dungeness crab for dinner, then drink with it the Adelaide wine Noelle gave Ann – was it two years ago? Ann thought so. Gloriously hot morning, pleasant and relieving breeze off the bay, thoughts that it breaks my heart to see Ann struggle to stay strong enough and clear enough to do most of the caretaking of herself.

After dinner, just before bed, Ann wanted to talk about plans for getting help when we need it, about how panicky she got last week when I seemed to be terribly tired – I was, but it was because of lack of sleep. "What if your back goes out?" she asked, thinking of hiring someone or asking for help in running errands.

"Aside from groceries, there aren't any errands, particularly. We can have all the stuff from the drug store delivered from now on. If my back goes out, if I become ill, we use Alice's nice service and hire someone in for help in the house. We can both sit, you in your chair, I in mine, while someone else does the work."

This seemed to satisfy her. We did discuss ways of getting to bed earlier. I made it plain that 9:30 was the time I should start for bed so that I could be asleep by 10:30.

I just hope that Harvey stays in one piece this year. We had real fear last year because of the drivers' license problem.

The girls have been kind, all of them asking after Ann, asking for details. I give them, usually with my fears on top, rather than my hopes. That seems to be the most realistic. They're coming on the 18th (maybe not Beth) to try to weatherproof the Benton Way house for winter, to protect stuff that's been left out in the garage and to check the basement to make sure it's not likely to send the house up in smoke. Maybe I'll have them move my green recliner up here so that Ann can sit up in it in her bedroom when she needs to read late at night.

I hope last night's occasion, the wine, the crab we love, isn't the last time. If this chemo really works, it won't be. I think the events of last Friday frightened us. I wonder if we can change the company/provider.

October 8, 2002, Tuesday

When I returned from Benton Way, we began to check out the sprinkler system. I was to stand at the west and call out to Ann through opened doors, when the water came on. No water came on. I went to check Ann. She was becoming upset because she didn't understand, or couldn't operate the system any more. Her voice broke explaining it to me, and she bent into the computer set up, leaning her head against it as she began to cry. I tried to comfort her, but she sent me away. After several failed attempts, we began to water where there were dry spots made needy by the heat we've been having (over 100 probably on Monday as well as Sunday). All this time, Ann didn't seem to need extra O2. In spite of her emotional distress, I was elated. Have her lungs cleared up because of the prednisone? Or is the chemo working?

When she came inside, we spoke of her feeling she can't give way emotionally or she'll give way completely. This troubles me, because it tells me she's absolutely holding back the idea of death – the total fear we humans have – and is aware of it. I imagine what it would be like if she gave way completely: refusal to live right now, refusal to do anything because what's the point, rejection of everything, distance from everything, total anger? What then would come after? Is she holding herself together for me? Perhaps, the idea of community, of being part of something more than self. The last generous act.

October 11, 2002, Friday

Ann continues to feel better than she did last week. She was up early, writing material for Dr. Borda and reading the paper. We've both avoided talking about the failure of any filibuster in the Senate to stop the Bush war juggernaut. Feinstein voted for the resolution in spite of receiving mail and phone calls 50-1 against the war. I'll never vote for Feinstein again.

October 12, 2002, Saturday

A point Ann made once again in our discussion last night: I'm not to rush in and offer to do things for her. She believes this causes extra stress for her. She's right. In the last couple of weeks I've occasionally become frightened by what we're going through. The fear makes me over-solicitous. It's not just fear that she's in pain, but fear that she's going to be upset, that she's going to suffer psychologically. I suppose I'm troubled because I can't even dare to try to make her feel better. Just comfortable.

October 15, 2002, Tuesday

Last evening on my way down the hall past my office I walked for a moment in the non-present. I didn't belong in the time and place I knew it was. I understood that if I allowed myself, I would be present in another period in my life and dreaming about the real present, dreaming that it was real. Ann's week of comparatively good health (if you compare it to last month) seduces me into the past, into which, once I am descending, I can't stop myself. So I was a child in my parents' house waiting for dinner, secure and loved, just dreaming of living in Ann's house, while she's dying, and having a (comparatively) comfortable week.

Whether this experience, which is not uncommon for me nowadays, develops from my dissatisfaction with the directionless moves I make as I try to create stories and poems or from my refusal to meet the chores, duties, obligations of the present, is hard to determine. I yearn for a sense of having more years than I can realistically expect in order to establish what my vision is beyond this: attending to the fallen and unsung in our society, the import and the importance of their lives. I constantly tell myself that I want to write essays, work through my thoughts; that I don't know what my thinking is because I don't nourish it or see it grow and branch. I'm content to allow just one or two topic thoughts or paragraphs take me into nothing, a blankness, and I fool myself into thinking that if I could go back I'd find what I wanted to say. Then and now.

October 17, 2002, Thursday

Wednesday morning I felt close to tears, a sluggish or heavy sensation at my heart. I was quiet with Ann as we went to the doctor's – where we received good news – Ann's chest is clearing a little. She herself told him that she'd had less pain in the lower left side. This was the first time I knew about it, but I do understand why she hasn't told me – superstitious feeling we ought not say you're better until you're sure.

Maybe this news gave me permission for what I did, because I don't think I would have let myself do it if she'd been worse. On leaving the doctor's office, we decided to go to lunch. We tried the Spirit at the airport, but they were too crowded. We'd decided to go to Morro Bay, and I was driving down Broad, thinking to pull over to go down Santa Barbara, when Ann pointed out that I was going too slowly. I felt irritated. I began to make an explanation – I was pulling over and I wasn't sure about the car beside me. Then as we approached Osos Street I slowed momentarily to look at fraternity houses – and she asked me why I was slowing down again. I became angry, shouted at her, "I don't have to explain anything to you."

Within seconds I apologized, saying I'd been made tense by the earlier criticism. We then began to go over criticism in general and of course earlier episodes that I remembered. I explained that I was doing all I could temperamentally and physically, and that the criticism made me feel confined. Her response was that I was blowing the whole thing out of proportion.

Reaching the door of the restaurant in Morro Bay, I dropped her off then parked. In the silence as I walked in, I understood myself a little better. I'm feeling so inept all the time in everything right now that any criticism seems extreme to me. I want to make her well and I can't. I want to make her stop hurting, and I can't.

She'd chosen a small table at the window. Her black shirt, her grey hair were between me and the Rock. We arranged my drink and I told Ann what I'd thought, walking in. Her face was white in the noontime glare; in the corner of my eye I saw birds flying past, about a hundred feet up. A pelican dived, surfaced. Far off there were kayakers, six of them, one far out ahead. We smiled at each other. She understood what I was saying, and reminded herself: "You're so fragile."

October 21, 2002, Monday

Last night Ann was concerned when I told her I had to get up very early to take Jean to the Amtrak bus in the morning. She added that she wondered whether I should take some kind of medication to calm me down. I said no, fiercely, thinking that I couldn't even think about trying to work on my short stories and the Myra novella if I did. Then she said I needed to let go of some of the things I do or plan ahead better.

I couldn't help thinking this: she needs me around more, she's more insecure, and so for the first time in our long relationship, she's wishing I could concentrate entirely on her. Breaks my heart to see this happen, and she's troubled about it herself.

October 26, 2002, Saturday

Every morning I rejoice in Ann's life. I do live every day for itself; I do live every day just as it is in this string of days. Assuming that Ann is passing through our life with the same attitude, I hesitate to speak with her about it these days. Maybe it's easier not to be conscious of it.

Last night we spoke of early training the nuns gave Ann, for which she is still grateful, and around which she still centers her personality. As long as she's in control, performing precisely, as she was trained to do when very young, she's all right, she's spiritually content. The world will care for her. And so it has, though it's the combination, the generous spirit together with the precision of action that carries her through. The doctors, for example, grin, then begin to appreciate her careful day by day, hour by hour notes on her condition. There's an innocence that's hard to resist in her presentation of herself as really knowing how to perform.

Then we spoke of me: I learned early on what it was necessary to do in order to please others, both in the family and in school, but I performed precisely – put my name on the paper just so, organized my books in my desk just so – only as long as people were observing. When I thought no one cared, I tried to find my own way. In simple things, like headings on papers and book marks and places in line, I succeeded. But with complex and life-controlling decisions – what to say to people I didn't know, for example, I froze, trying to make up my mind. I lost my self in chaos, never knowing just what it was I wanted to do, just what it was I wanted to mean or understand with my life.

After a while, trying to describe my half-baked minor rebellions, I got to laughing like a child with the giggles, and she laughed, and we both seemed happy when we went to bed. This morning, she got up about 10, saying she'd been awake for a couple of hours during the night and felt very tired this morning. She was upset because she'd wanted to have the energy to work today: "I'd feel much better if I could get some filing done."

"I can do it," I said.

"No, you can't. One reason I want to do it is so you won't be faced with a mess when I can't do it any longer."

October 28, 2002, Monday

For the last two days Ann has been better able to breathe. On Saturday she ordered new clothes from a mail order company, the first time she's paid attention to getting new clothes since my attempts early this year. This activity of hers comforts me. I think: she'll get these clothes and she'll live into next year, and then there'll be a new chemo she can take that will keep her alive. Right now I also consider this: perhaps I should change my decision about writing projects. Perhaps I should try to market "Manzanita" now.

October 30, 2002, Wednesday

We didn't have to wait long for Dr. Doyle, but he had only an x-ray report, not the x-rays. He sat down next to Ann, listened to her chest. He repeated what he's said the last two times, that he can't hear anything on the left side, possibly because the cancer is up against the chest wall. (He leaned in, his dark and closely cropped curly hair against the dark brown shirt he was wearing. I've never looked at his hands, specifically, but I expect they're fairly small, because he gives the impression of a slender, small man who works out a great deal, has built up muscles.) Then he commented on the x-ray report, which wasn't satisfactory, because it made a comparison with one taken in June, and we already knew the cancer had been growing since then. We just didn't know whether the treatment with topotecan was working and so needed a comparison with September. He dithered about walking down there with us, "Can you get down there?"

"I can," Ann said, "I have my O2." She volunteered that maybe he kept the x-ray himself, which sent him off to his office to look. When he returned without it, Ann asked about how long would the cancer continue to grow? In other words, how long would she live?

He then told her that she'd outlived the statistics by a long shot. Then he described what was going to happen, eventually: the cancer would fill up the lungs, and then she might develop pneumonia, for which he may give her antibiotics. They began to discuss that: "Why bother?" Ann asked.

He answered that it might help, but if not they wouldn't do anything to cause more distress.

What I found important about what he said: the brain as you get sicker doesn't recognize air hunger, especially with morphine and atavin, and that what she'll do is just gradually sleep more and more.

"If it comes to going to the hospital, I don't want to go," Ann said, "not unless my not going causes difficulty for others."

In response he spoke of Hospice and a nurse who would come in with IVs of morphine, of gradually becoming comatose, and then just slipping, sleeping away. "Calmly," he said, his eyes picking up mine as well as Ann's, as if it's normal, the usual, the expected, what happens to all living things.

Good Irish boy, used to priests.

Finally, he decided to walk down himself to get the x-ray. He came back without it, but said he'd looked and there probably was a little growth since September. So, since the topotecan isn't working, he was going to start carboplatin again next week. Agreed, agreed,

In the car, we didn't say much of anything. I waited for Ann. Finally, at a stop light, I said, "I'm glad we're going back to carboplatin." I thought it just might work.

November 1, 2002, Friday

Yesterday, Thursday, a calm, quiet day that ended in one of my explosions of "I'm doing all I can." I fail Ann when this happens to me. I should notice the steps I take toward it. First of all I have to recognize that I'm desperate, feeling desperate about Ann. Her pallor, her nearness to tears, the sight of the O2 pack, her occasional irritability . . . I can't make her well. I've been hoping for a long time, wishing for anything to hold back the flood of darkness that looms over both of us. Yesterday I went shopping for groceries after getting my hair cut. Hoping to be able to get some variety in our meals, I lingered over a decision to buy pork chops as well as lamb, thus covering our needs for two nights in one shopping expedition. I bought the pork chops, deciding to have them Friday night. Then because string beans would seem to go best with the meal of pork chops, I decided to have them Thursday night. I worried about that. Then I fussed over a recipe, hoping to keep the chops tender for Ann. But somehow, what I did still turned out stiff, not tender, no matter my having sliced them as thin as possible, like pork tenderloin. I felt bad. Ann didn't eat much of it. Then, when I said I'd take the rest of it upstairs to eat for lunches, Ann said there were other things we could do with it, and I sank into tears and reiterated, "I am doing all I can, all I can." Later, Ann asked me if she didn't help, and I said, frankly, "Not much." I named the dishes she'd prepared, but named also where I'd failed her somehow in getting it together – e.g., getting curry simmer sauce instead of curry paste. I didn't stop crying, really, until time for bed, and I'm still near tears this morning. I feel too apologetic all the time and have to stop it. I'm not fair to Ann. I make her burden harder to bear.

November 2, 2002, Saturday

After dinner and dishes we read the paper, I strewing the *Chronicle* at my feet as I finished pages, Ann deciding to entertain herself with the *Tribune* obituaries for a while. She read one out to me, and I commented that these days people are showing off how much money they have or how well they loved the deceased by how long an obit they put in the paper. "Maybe I could write an extremely lengthy one for Harvey, enough to take up a full page with a complete history of the whole family in it – if I live that long – just to show off." I also considered writing false obituaries, sort of like Edgar Lee Masters' tombstones and wondered whether the *Tribune* would take them if you paid for them.

Ann opined that she would have to write what she thought should be sent to the *LA Times* and the Stanford alumni magazine for herself. I suppose this led us into the last conversation, held just before bed, both of us lying side by side on Ann's bed – heads up, of course, and Ann with her oxygen piped in. I started it by repeating this conversation I'd had with Jean:

Carol: "The doctor said Ann is doing remarkably well. Outlived almost all the statistics."

Jean: "It's the nuns praying for her, I'm sure." Pause. "And all the rest of us."

Carol, putting her arm on Jean's shoulder for a minute: "I know."

Ann then got thinking about whether she should be more concerned about her approaching death. "Am I in denial? Should I be going through what the nuns taught me just to see whether maybe they were right? I try to pursue it, but I just don't. Maybe I should be more aware of the bad things I've done."

My response, several times over, is that I believe we're all part of the communion of saints, that the nuns are indeed here with us, and there, over the boundary, that all humans face what she's facing, that it's silly to inspect what myths and legends say about sin, as long as you are truthful with yourself about seeing yourself as good.

She spoke of failure, and I said no, given what we both have had stacked against us.

She cried a little, I did not. Mostly she cried for my sorrow, my loneliness, my having to go on alone. When she spoke of herself, she said that she was not particularly concerned about her approaching death. Sometimes she wonders about it, but she just can't get too excited.

She doesn't want any religious person saying prayers over her in her last extremity, she said.

She thought my constant thinking about writing and how writing can express the human condition has made me understand things more deeply than she. I didn't quite accept that . . .

She said she'd been meaning to have this conversation with me for a long time, but we just have never got around to it.

Then she got up and went to make herself some popcorn, feeling relaxed and comforted, and I went upstairs to bed.

Today she's feeling as well as she did yesterday, which is okay. I think.

November 8, 2002, Friday

When I arrived home, I discovered that Ann had gone out on errands, leaving a note on a letter from J [her friend from Silicon Valley days] at my computer reading "I'm heartbroken for her."

In the letter, J tells how her husband is too weak to move away from his bed for more than a few feet; how he can't really read any more, yet insists on subscribing to several magazines. She has help coming in, but I wonder – and later I learned that Ann did too – how much it's costing their finances for J confesses to taking only a half dose of pills prescribed for her. J does maintain her volunteer work and the work as an accountant winding down the last business she worked for, which went bankrupt a few years ago. When Ann returned, she cried, bent over her knees, hand holding up her head. "Those men," (meaning J's husband G and and her son B) "have sucked her dry." Ann knows that her husband hasn't worked for a long time, and she also knows that her son has been getting money from his parents probably because his father insists he be supported in his artistic endeavors. I agreed. I stayed with Ann. Hugged her. Finally tried to comfort her by reminding her that J seems to feel proud of herself for being able to do what she does, that she doesn't despair.

In the late afternoon, after I returned from seeing Harvey, Ann had written a letter of advice and comfort to another old friend and wanted me to read it. I suggested she add a sentence to soften it, and before dinner she did. But not until she'd cried some more that there was nothing she could do to help these two beloved women in their anguish. A part of her identity and strength given up.

At bedtime she was close to tears again.

November 9, 2002, Saturday

Ann has begun to discuss her problems with writing letters. I denied the problem, by praising the letters she'd written this week and by trying to say (and I admit I did it clumsily) that her more complex reactions and tendencies of thinking have made finding the words more difficult. Then she commented that we were different and I was speaking from my own experience. That I'm a perfectionist with everything I write. I took offense at this, because that's not the reason I write. I write because I'm trying to find the place where my inner self and the world can intersect. But I didn't say then that I took offense. I tried to go on with reasons why she might be experiencing the verbal difficulty she expresses: not keeping the oxygen on when she's moving about, stress. Her answer to that I have to attend to – that she believes I try to minimize her problems, say there are solutions. I don't think that's true, but I have to pay attention.

November 13, 2002, Wednesday

Back from the endoscopy before 10 o'clock. Dr. Henry said Ann's esophagus didn't look bad. He did a few biopsies. In case her problem was caused by stricture – and it didn't look that way to him – he stretched it with a balloon. If her dysphagia didn't improve, he suggested that the tumor could be pressing from time to time on the nerve controlling the sphincter and he could then use botox to stifle the nerve for a while.

The nurse who helped Ann prepare herself – top off, gown on, tied in back, shoes okay – was interested in Ann's portable oxygen carrier. Her mother had one, but isn't happy with it. "She goes to the market with it on and feels people stare at her. I say, yes, well some people are ugly. Some people have eyes in their foreheads. What difference does it make?" Ann agreed.

While Ann underwent the procedure, I sat, reading, looking up now and then as people came into the waiting room. I couldn't stop thinking of Beth in the waiting room upstairs in Stanford Hospital [an acoustic neuroma was growing again], how scared she was, how I wished I could calm her. She was so quiet. Many here, many in the oncologist's office, are scared, and quiet. Is there a point where fear breaks through, makes a scene? Or do we all figure there's no point. If there is no point.

And then Beth's phone call to me. She was crying – her bad luck. She was in the 1 % whose tumor grows back. It's 4 mm, rooted in the balance nerve. I cried a little too. It is bad luck, I have to agree. Next May she said, another MRI, and then the operation, perhaps in June. Sounding stronger, she made plans, not fighting it, but accepting that you've crossed a boundary and now have to go on as if in a foreign land. I felt that way when my breast cancer was diagnosed. Let's just go on, do what we can. And Ann, that's where she is. It's when you have to tell someone that you cry, Beth said, and Ann said so too. You have to look at where you've been and where you're going, then.

So all these people, the ones sitting in the waiting room, they've crossed that boundary, they're in a different world. How many worlds are there? Institutions, I guess; the institution of bad health? Everyone else is outside.

November 16, 2002, Saturday

Ann's unsteadiness lasted all day yesterday. I was late with lunch and my rest because I'd made some of the lime custard for Ann that she liked. At 4:30 when I left for Benton Way, Ann asked me if there was anything she could do, and I suggested she prepare the chicken for dinner with the marinade she liked. When I returned, it was ready. I washed the lettuce, mixed up the left over spaghetti with some new tastes – olive and red pepper – suggested a pear for salad with blue cheese. Then Ann came out and began to take over the salad, partly because I was shaky and needed to sit down and regain . . . what? Is this shakiness from lack of water, or sugar, or too much stress and hurry? Anyway, she made a delicious salad from the pear and the cheese and some nuts ground up, working and fussing for twenty minutes

When we sat down and I began a polite conversation, asking her some questions about her email group, she became upset. She didn't want to talk about this, and she was on the verge of tears. "I don't have any conversation," she said.

"All right," I said, adding I would provide and all she had to do was sit there and listen. She became tearful again and had to work to regain composure, while I talked about this and that. Family Christmas plans among other things, which I'm not entering into, except to ask if someone can take care of Harvey so I don't have to. (And they are, they are, I have such wonderful and loving children.)

The rest of dinner went all right, but after dinner

she became tearful again, saying she didn't know what came over her. "I'm not afraid to die, I don't think so," she said. "I worry so about you though."

I reassured her that I get upset, but that I have a certain positive physical sense that often rescues me from depression. Then she calmed down and we read the rest of the evening. She went to bed early, but not before telling me she'd been questioned by Dr. Borda about how she manages, and she told him how I had come to stay with her. She also told me that he reaffirmed the way in which to take the oxycodone/oxycontin set of pills.

November 21, 2002, Thursday

I am constantly amazed at Ann's strength of will and desire to remain whole, for my sake sometimes. She worked hard to prepare the turkey we had for dinner last night, and when Beth phoned at just the wrong minute and I wasn't able to go ahead getting things on the table, she did it cheerfully. Some time earlier I think I said this was her greatest strength, this ability to do things precisely even as life disintegrates.

Good times have been eluding us this week, and I wish we could have them. Or to put it another way, I am in charge of good times because Ann is so ill. And because she is so ill, there's not much I can suggest. I can entertain her with stories and laughter, and I do, the last time the story of the demon in the crowd at Jean's retreat. But I'm not doing much else that's positive as the entertainment committee. With the birds no longer present while I eat breakfast, I don't even have tales of bird behavior. I did set aside some poems to read to her a week ago. Movies maybe once a week? I've been reading too much, without having much to share from it.

Meanwhile, the national news continues to announce the end of our democratic society. I believe I should relish my privilege now, for who knows how long it will last? Ashcroft's and Bush's "Homeland Security bill" passed in the Senate, in spite of an amendment that allows corporations to hide more from the public than presently allowed. Not only did it pass in the Senate, but California's two senators voted for it. I'm in despair about the virtue of democracy. What good has it done to write either of them?

Ann and I can't even talk about the news of the day anymore – too depressing.

November 22, 2002, Friday

I should no doubt be dating these on the day I write about, not the day on which written. I write in the morning, usually, so that almost everything that happens is yesterday.

Yesterday, Thursday, then: Ann didn't sleep particularly late, but when I asked her, mid morning, whether she planned to go to Cayucos to see Carmelita, she answered with tears in her eyes that she didn't feel well enough. Nothing special – she just didn't feel she could be herself. Or couldn't sustain her public persona well enough or long enough. Maybe she feared becoming tearful, for in the evening, when I was consulting with her about her preferences for dinner, describing what I thought might be better than earlier plans, she burst into tears. "Don't ask me, just don't ask me," she insisted.

I wanted to find out what bothered her, so I could avoid it. "Was it my asking at all?" "No, no, nothing sounded good. I hate sounding fussy."

A reasonable answer, given not feeling well, not feeling confident about ability to swallow, taste buds overcome by queasiness, and inability to control outbursts of anger or impatience or tears. She blames the prednisone she's been taking for this, and maybe she's right. Grief, too, for lost controls.

In the talk we have every night before bed, she asked me how I felt.

"Grief everlasting."

November 23, 2002, Saturday

At bedtime I spoke of my disappointment in the ending of Carol Shields' *Unless*, and we got into a strange discussion first about Shields' works, generally, and then specifically, where Ann said she didn't know why I kept reading things that didn't please me, like Marcel Proust. My response: if Carol Shields had not been stymied by the lack of a heroic tradition for women in novels, she might have been able to carry this off and I was interested in the way she'd failed. Why do you need tradition? I then had to explain about tradition, the need for the sense of an audience willing to hear the story.

Ann has a misunderstanding and I'm not sure what it is, even after a continuation of the personal part of the discussion this morning. She believes I'm unhappy with my work – well, she's got that right. She blames what I've been reading, which doesn't quite make sense. I suspect she yearns for more time with me, and blames my preoccupations. Yet, when I offered to give up my time, as for example, my offering to drive her to Cayucos to see Carmelita, she refused.

Probably more likely: she's terribly upset about her condition and can't hold it in all the time because of the prednisone. She wants to be angry with something, and she can feel protective of me about the books I read.

How can I tell her that my sorrow is for her condition, my tension is about how ill she feels?

And what difference does it make if I'm seventy and won't get done what I want to get done. At least I have a quest – and if I fail, well, then I've tried and failed. Don't we all?

After this discussion, Ann turned to her reaction to – her refusal to read – *Balzac and the Little Chinese Seamstress*. I'd described the book as light, with a fairy tale plot. A pair of Chinese adolescent boys sent to a primitive village during the Cultural Revolution discover a horde of books, do whatever they can think of to earn the books, read them, tell their stories to people, and change the lives of at least one of those who read the books. Ann, however, couldn't enjoy the book and in fact was angry with me for thinking that she could, given her illness. She began to cry as she told me of her horror at the sufferings the boys go through. "What do we learn from this?" she asked.

"That the human spirit can survive even the worst

circumstances. That literature can change people's lives."

"Why do people write this?" she said, not agreeing with my answer.

"To bear witness," I said. "The author, Dai Siejie, experienced the Cultural Revolution."

Ann began to sound angry. I didn't argue, though I wondered how she could bear to read murder mysteries. I decided she'd hit bottom in a fearful depression, and I began to think how I should react to such a depression, what could I do to help her? I suppose I shouldn't show any emotional reaction to what appear to be attacks, but deal with what she says with understanding and honesty.

Later she discussed her depression, without my saying anything like 'I noticed.' She said she'd been unable to come out of it. She had more work she needed to do and refused to do it. She doesn't plan to tell the doctor because she doesn't want to have another drug thrown at her, like paxil. Then she asked me what she could do for me, that she knew I was heading into a difficult time. I asked for praise for things I value in myself, my insights, my writing, my understanding, my little stories. I don't want praise for helping people.

November 26, 2002, Tuesday

Ann's great generosity of spirit always manifests itself when she is able to help me. I've noted here in the journal several times that one of her great losses this year is her inability to take care of others. Whenever she realizes it, she becomes upset, sometimes grieving, sometimes simply frustrated. Monday evening she asked me to read a letter she'd received from an old Stanford friend. This time the woman told her that her neurologist said she had incipient Alzheimer's and was putting her on one of the medications that improves memory. She wanted Ann to look up possibilities for diagnosis (PET scan) and possible treatment on the internet for her – this the reason for the letter, in addition to recognizing the work Ann had done looking up things about macular degeneration for her. Ann found what she could and printed it for her. In her letter she first commiserated, then suggested that she and her husband go to a library to discover what they could online, using a librarian's help. But this just wasn't enough. We both wondered about the diagnosis, wondered if it's small strokes she's having, wondered if her husband is not causing a diagnosis because he demands perfection. Before bed time we spoke of Ann's letter to the newspaper, suggesting that they should stop ignoring the nationwide criticism and FBI investigation of a corporation that owns one of the local hospitals, especially since our local hospital had been upping the prices of drugs 1800%. She'd had comments from Dan Krieger and Mary Moses praising her for writing the letter.

This morning, Tuesday, the *Tribune* responded by printing two articles about the corporation, one about their drug pricing, and the *Chronicle* also had an editorial accusing them of gaming the system. I was proud of her for what she'd written, and I told her so.

November 29, 2002, Friday

Wednesday turned out to be difficult. Ann was unpleasant at lunch with Noelle and Ellen, then became angry with me afterwards because I misunderstood her need for timely assistance in looking information up in a consumer magazine. I became angry with her and then felt terrible for having been angry.

Thanksgiving at Benton Way: Ann pulled herself together, though she didn't feel particularly well. She was angry because the girls had shifted the time of dinner, and probably angry with me because I hadn't controlled the scene a little better. As far as I could determine, the talk before dinner and then the dinner went well. A couple of times Ann spoke sharply to someone, outside the boundaries, and I touched her knee with mine. When everyone had left the table, she turned to me with an angry face and said, "What was I doing wrong that you pushed your knee against mine?" I said I didn't remember, and put my head in my hands, about ready to cry.

I'd thought all was going well, but it wasn't. She left shortly after this, and when I arrived home she was quiet, in pain, she said, and had to sit up until quite late because her pill-taking schedule had been shifted.

Today (Friday) she's been quiet all day, and I haven't felt much like talking with her. It's been difficult enough with Beth needful and my not being able to comfort her. I tried last night, phoning her after her sisters had gone to the show while she stayed home with her baby. Then today she became upset with me because I wouldn't let her interrupt me as I was talking. She was also upset with her sisters again because she's had a lonely week and they were about to leave her again to take the children to the playground.

I've been having a hard time, wondering what's happened to fidelity, loyalty, and love. How can it bear up under the pressure of constant anger and upset? It's still there, just not bearing up, not on the surface, not anywhere.

Upstairs today, after Ann passed me going out to have her blood pulled, hardly speaking, I felt so cut off from love. It's gone. It's died – that's all I could say to myself. And, I'll never be able to love anyone ever again. It's over, because nothing can stay the course of physical disintegration.

December 3, 2002, Tuesday

Monday:

All the way to the doctor's office to Ann's afternoon appointment, I kept silent, remembering the times when we were first going for chemotherapy when I chatted about inconsequential things to keep Ann's spirits up.

Ann's agenda for the doctor emphasized her depression and the destructive emotional volatility she's experiencing, pointing out to him that it was my impression that it began in October about the time she began taking the prednisone. He agreed instantly that it was the prednisone – after teasing her that she couldn't be as she described, 'naturally a volatile and impatient person' and after teasing me that I could never have said she's been volatile. He suggested she cut back the prednisone, very gradually, like about one mg. every two or three days and added in an anti-anxiety, antidepressant medication called Effexor.

The change in Ann's behavior was dramatic. She was her happy, generous and loving self again – and commented to me as I folded clothes and she changed hers that she felt tremendously relieved after Dr. Doyle had agreed her problem had been caused by the prednisone. I suspect that she'd been worried the cancer had spread to her brain. Later she mentioned to me that Rose, a young woman one of her email group knew, who had also taken Iressa, had metastases to brain and spine.

December 5, 2002, Thursday

Wednesday afternoon and evening: after a short nap, I spent the afternoon with Harvey hunting for computer games for the children. When I came in the door at home, Ann was reclining in her chair, eyes closed. She'd been suffering pain and nausea most of the afternoon. I fixed soup for her supper, and she went to bed fairly early, still hurting. In spite of the pain, she was her steady, generous self, not complaining, optimistic that she'd feel better the next day.

But she didn't. She was up by the time I left the house, this morning (Thursday). The pain had become sharp, near her shoulder blades and down on the side where the original cancer grows. Oxycodone didn't touch it. She called the doctor, who called back fairly quickly, to tell her to increase the oxycontin and stop the Effexor.

I hope the emotional volatility doesn't return. Perhaps it won't now that she knows what causes it.

December 6, 2002, Friday

Because Ann and I agreed I should talk over the problems of Ann's emotional volatility with Diane – perceiving Diane as a former minister and as a hospice worker – not for Ann's sake, Ann made clear, but for mine – I brought the topic up at the lunch table yesterday in the Garden Cafe, somewhat distracted by conventional, amateurish watercolors on the wall above us.

I wish now I hadn't, because Diane jumped to judgment where she ought not. I would have been seriously upset if she'd jumped against Ann, but still feel we were friends. I think I could have felt strong and loyal, defending Ann. However, I'm afraid she didn't understand me or give me time to say just what it was I was trying to express. Or, another way to say this: she doesn't have a clue about the relationship between Ann and me, but she spoke as if she did.

The comfortable and comforting ideas she expressed came close to what I believe in and try to act upon. Let things be, she suggested, when Ann is emotionally upset. Just be there, be with her. And yes, this is right, what I try to do. She suggested, from her observation of a couple where the husband is dying, that the woman is not ready "to let him go," but that she must come to a decision to do so. What she might mean – what the psychologists must mean – with this jargon – is that relatives of the dying can demand health, hold out empty hope, say things like "you're looking so much better today," which I should think would burden the dying one with responses they might not want to make and responses that they feel are false. Both kinds of responses would isolate the dying, I should think.

But I don't know how Diane came to this judgment of a woman she observed who sat beside her husband on the bed and patted his hand. He took his hand away, and she still patted it. Maybe Diane heard or saw more, but I'm afraid she is reading into the act herself as the dying, one of the many people who love her as the hand patter, the person who won't let go. She suffers all the time from being held too tightly.

When we discussed my reactions to Ann's argumentative tones, angry outbursts, criticisms, I said that I can't allow this to happen. Diane tried to say, 'you mean you won't.'

I declared that I would hate to have the worst parts of my character, my arrogance, my anger, my refusal to listen to others all that was left of me at the end, and that I would hope someone would stop me from behaving that way. Diane responded that she thought I was condescending.

I didn't argue, but I should have. I can't allow Ann to mistreat me because that is wrong, against my principles, and against hers, too. I must tell her when she makes life miserable for me. Diane thinks that the relationship fades, that the person who takes care is only a servant of the dying.

Maybe, maybe at the end, I thought, but not now, not when the person wants to continue to be human as long as possible.

I should have told her that I have read a great deal

of the philosophy of caregiving and have formed principles – that the relationship is a mutual one, requiring mutual respect. I meant it when I said I can't just allow myself to be treated in angry demeaning ways and if I don't stick with what I believe, I don't live a human life.

We agreed that there is no literature of the healthy person's place in an old relationship when the other is dying, but I think I was wrong. There are the care giving books of ethics, and I've read many. Diane is going to try to shove me at a hospice therapist, but I don't think so. I'm put off by her judgments, and I also don't trust the intelligence of people I don't know.

I also want to point out, should have pointed out, that though Ann is losing life, I'm losing hope of what the end of life could be. It's hard to say this – you always sound so self-concerned – but Ann and I have both said this to each other – that she can pity me, who will have to face sickness and pain and loss of powers pretty much by myself. In the face of that future, "she won't let him go," is facile and cold.

December 10, 2002, Tuesday

Sunday evening the sky toward the southwest at 4:30 was swept by a flow of sharply delineated mare's tails. I called Ann out of the house to see, and we stood in the street for several minutes. You can't help thinking at such a time – the world is too much with us – but how to make a practice of ignoring the world and being with the beauty of the earth?

That same evening while I was writing in my journal,

Ann came in to tell me her checkbook wouldn't balance. She was almost in tears, possibly trying not to blame me for the problem – I'd used the computer program's balance, not the one from her book. I took the checkbook, opened up the program, looked over checks, saw that the ones since we reconciled had all been entered – except one, possibly written at Health Plus. I don't know why Ann cried. She felt frustrated, probably, or possibly she was concerned that I'd object defensively, as I had during the time she was becoming so terribly frustrated and angry. The prednisone days, I'll call them.

There was another time, perhaps Sunday evening, when she cried, saying she didn't know how she'd manage without me, that it would be impossible. I didn't have much to say to that – I don't know who would take care of her or how she'd manage if I were not here at all. I'd hope my children would, but that's asking more than is possible for them. If I were sick, I believe she would manage, would help me. These thoughts entered my head – I didn't think of reminding her that maybe the women who cared for her mother in her last days could help if I were to die suddenly, have a stroke or a heart attack.

The tears released tension in both of us, as I held her so that she wouldn't have to sob: the deep heaving breaths hurt badly.

December 13, 2002, Friday

After dinner Thursday Ann wrote letters, one to a friend and one to the editor of our local newspaper, then forwarded to several friends an *LA Times* article she approved of. Just before bed she said, "I don't want to see anyone. I don't want to see Dr. Borda tomorrow. I don't want to have to get up in the morning."

Then she told me about the terrible nightmare she'd had during the day, when I was gone out to lunch with Diane. The nightmare was terribly real – she didn't use the word hallucinatory, but I was reminded of dreams I've had when I've thought I was awake, only to discover I was really dreaming. She didn't give me the plot of the dream, but said she was angry, something had to be set right, but she couldn't do it, things seemed to disintegrate. Then she felt in her chest a warm flush; this seemed to bother her.

I listened, carefully. I said, "It's a lot like you, as I've always known you, angry at a group of people, struggling to set them right. From the beginning, I've always loved this part of you too."

She told me she was afraid she was getting too tense again and likely to become too emotional.

December 15, 2002, Sunday

Yesterday Addie, Ann's cousin, came, with her husband. I thought I heard voices while I worked, but Addie startled me when she stopped at my door on her way to the bathroom. I stood, because I have no extra chair in my office to offer. For several minutes I dealt with questions like, "Are you tired?"

I had no idea what she meant. "Do I look tired? "

"No, well, maybe a little." She then commented on my being addicted to the computer. This I understood to mean addicted to email or surfing so I explained what I was doing – typing my old, old novel into the computer so that I can rewrite it one of these days. She then asked questions about that.

She's short, maybe only five feet or so, grey haired, not thin, but not heavy, either. Trim, I guess. Stylish. A friendly businesswoman. In the end, I gave her copies of "Manzanita" and my own reading copy of *Staying Under* just to get her out of the room. Ann was grateful for my having been generous. She offered to pay for another printing of "Manzanita," but I declined.

December 17, 2002, Tuesday

In the morning, we'd sat down to read, Ann the paper and I a book, when the lights blinked twice, then stayed out. Without discussion, we got our flashlights and continued reading. Around eleven, I went upstairs to read where more natural light came in. When I returned downstairs, Ann was holding her hand over her face, the way she does when she's holding back tears. "I had another explosion," she told me.

I waited for her to explain. She had phoned the PG&E emergency number, where the woman who spoke to her went through a prepared list of explanatory items without addressing Ann's situation or giving any idea of when the electricity would be on again. As Ann told her about a ninety-two-year-old next door, who lived alone and was unable to walk without help, she began to cry. "It's not that I'm ashamed of crying," she explained to me, "but that I'm upset because I can't talk, can't explain myself, with tears in the way."

Late in the afternoon, the electricity still off, I drove with Harvey out to True Value to buy batteries for our electric lanterns. On my return, Ann was putting final touches to the clam chowder she'd prepared on Sunday, her work lit by flashlights. I performed chores like getting water, putting batteries in the lanterns, taking out garbage that couldn't go in the disposal, discovering a new way of moving, looking and seeing when you carry your light in your hand, or, as I was often doing, on my shoulder.

At one point Ann said, "If I knew what to say, exactly, I'd call police." I suggested she consider calling because they ought to be aware about this small isolated enclave of dark houses on San Jose Court and La Entrada. So she phoned, and the dispatcher called back to say PG&E would have the repairs done in two hours. We enjoyed a quiet, dimly lit supper – the lanterns giving a sense of candlelight – and afterwards we read with the lanterns perched on our shoulders. Before nine we heard the PG&E repair truck. Ann went outside and down the street to talk to them and I followed, as soon as I could get my shoes on. By the time I arrived, Ann was thanking the foreman, a round and short man, and pleasantly asking what was the trouble, commenting on how hard it must be to come out at night and do this work and generally thanking the men for doing a job that was hard and that the company they work for doesn't make easy. The lights came on again within an hour, and twenty minutes after that the pleasant foreman knocked at the door. Ann offered coffee, but he said no, they had to get on to Atascadero.

In our talk before bed, Ann worried again about her

self, the explosion to the PG&E. I reminded her that it was a response, a legitimate one, to her illness. She'd done the same last year, with the phone company. I opined, a little pompously, that the prednisone returns her to her basic self, the childhood self that was easily frustrated, that becomes angry and can only cry because childhood and illness are powerless states.

"What am I learning, then?" she challenged me. "What good does it do me to learn not to break down in frustration?"

I didn't have an answer, but did say I was proud of how she had dealt with our all-day crisis. I know she wants to be remembered for strength and courage and ability to fight good strong battles. I'll do my best to help

December 19, 2002, Thursday

Complying with her dentist's wishes, Ann had made an appointment with an endodentist. Tuesday, late afternoon, she was upset returning from the meeting. Although I'd offered to go with her, she'd known I wasn't enthusiastic, and turned me down. (I felt guilty again, something I have to live with, meaning, not get upset about it.) She had broken down and cried there – not that the crying bothered her so much as it was that she couldn't ask the questions she knew she should have asked. Dr. Karl was not the grim person Kathy, from Dr. Doyle's office, had made him out to be, Ann assured me. She told him she was concerned about pain and the drugs necessary to stop it. He told her the tooth was beginning an abscess, that it could get very painful, much more painful than the root canal would be. She would have to have either the root canal or have the tooth pulled. If she has it pulled, she has no more grinding teeth on that side of her mouth and the teeth on the other side are not well. She doesn't chew on them now in order to protect them. (She probably should have asked him how long she would be in the chair. I remembered a long complicated process, uncomfortable but not necessarily painful.) Dr. Karl said the tooth will surely die. She said to me, "But then so will I."

We decided she would have to speak to her regular dentist. And to Dr. Doyle.

December 21, 2002, Saturday

Ann worked at her computer, corresponding with essential friends, went to get her blood pulled in the afternoon, read the paper in the evening. Although she has several mysteries in a pile and the promise of a good western – one by the poet David Wagoner – she hasn't touched books this week. "I'm not interested in serious reading," she said. I'm not certain what she meant. At the time I took it to mean serious novels. She did, however, listen with pleasure to my description of scenes from *Within a Budding Grove* and Proust's analysis of Albertine's wish to please.

She also shared with me some letters she'd written. One of her letters was to a woman who wished to visit at Christmas. She'd been having a hard time writing the letter because she doesn't want to see this person, yet doesn't want to hurt her or let her down. Remembering the old friendship, she wanted to pretend the woman's recent desire to tell her "horrible things about her life, what she's doing to herself, what others do to her" didn't exist. Another letter concerned a war protest by women at the White House, and a third was an answer to the despair her email friend Susan feels because her urologist can't get around to removing and repairing a painful urethral stent until the end of next month.

That's my Ann!

As for me, I'm holding back emotion – but it comes flooding in every morning – anxiety with no habitation, exactly, or name. I don't know what I fear. I don't want anniversaries like Christmas – counting days, I guess. I want life to go on in bland accretions.

December 23, 2002, Monday

I ought to note here: getting out of the car at the doctor's office today, Ann said she was forgetting or sliding over essentials frequently these days. "I noticed," I said. "Stress," I said. "No more than I do when I'm stressed." Then I added: "That's the reason I keep saying not to let yourself get out of breath. Keep the oxygen coming."

This is, I think, the first time I've agreed with her about lapses or failures. She had forgotten to pick up her pocket calendar. This morning I thought she'd forgotten what I'd told her about Beth's carpet problem and she covered that up, after waiting for me to describe what had happened. I do think it's stress. But at the same time, her driving is a little worrisome – just a little. She drives too close to the right side, sometimes going over the white line, and this morning complained she's having trouble getting out of the garage.

But she does remember all the important things. She still writes well.

This afternoon I'm concerned that my agreeing with her may have distressed her more than she needs.

Yesterday she made a wonderful soup, which we ate with cheeses and good bread. She drank wine, and we were happy. Before bed Sunday night, we had a discussion about devils and evils, ranging from the gargoyles that my niece who believes in devils will be seeing in Paris this Christmas. We discussed the cruelties of tribesmen in the book *The Great Game*, which she's reading now. Torture is used as an example, to make sure rules are obeyed: Ann's suggestion. Competition blinds people to their own evil. The great weave of human society – original sin, Ann says – keeps us from perceiving the harm done to people.

December 26, 2002, Thursday

Our carefully planned Christmas pleased us. Tuesday afternoon we gathered the crab from Giovanni's (Ann worried about their size) and a few last minute things from Albertson's. We had a moment of distress there, when Ann, pulling into the handicapped parking place, pushed her bumper into that of another car. I could see no damage. Ann climbed out to make sure while I went into the store.

Outside, Ann had been concerned at the time I'd been taking, but we got to Giovanni's in plenty of time. A crowd was lined up inside the market. Eventually I had to shout for attention, but we were home in plenty of time to rest and get ready to go to dinner at Windows.

Sunset began on the way out, pale pinks and blues as we played Liebeslieder. No one on the streets except another older couple on their way to Windows also. We had to wait a few minutes because we arrived before the restaurant opened, but when we were seated, we were bathed in sunset – still water, silent masts, far off the sea a line of aquamarine above the dunes. Ann had oysters, a salad, duck, a cheesecake. I struggled with pheasant – about the same as spicy chicken – and enjoyed a bread pudding at the end. I told Ann I'd drive home, so was careful of wine consumption. Kept thinking last last last.

Went to bed early. Pleasantly. In the morning rose after waiting until 7:15. At the bottom of the stairs, Ann's door shut, a note outside. She hadn't slept most of the night and hoped to catch up this morning. I made my usual breakfast and read until I heard Ann getting up about nine. I came downstairs to find Ann upset because her insomnia had kept us from going out to breakfast, the first step for the day. Assuring her that all we'd missed was breakfast at Madonna Inn, I waited until she'd eaten. Then Ann made a call to her aunt Marge, I turned off my phone, and we opened the champagne, sipping it first in the kitchen before starting Bach's Christmas Oratorio. This was about 10:15. At first I was delighted with the sound of the big room speakers, then slipped into the music. As soon as the music began, Ann closed her eyes, apparently asleep, leaving most of the champagne we'd poured in her glass. Later, after the music was over, she explained she'd just been totally relaxed, soaring with the music. I wasn't, feeling more interested than sublimely impressed. I even made some lunch for myself, listening, drank Ann's champagne, left to slow-bubble in her glass. Together we decided to wait until after dinner for Messiah. Ann fussed about the size of the crabs again, so I went through the garbage hunting for the live weight on the receipt until I found it and she seemed to be satisfied. We enjoyed the crab, enjoyed the pie, enjoyed the Messiah, though I fell asleep here and there.

Before we started the Messiah, while we were doing the dishes, I spoke of Proust's having locked himself up for the last three years of his life in order to complete his work. Ann said, "I'm afraid you're going to do the same thing one of these days."

"I don't know what I want to do," I said.

After contemplation. What would I do?

I was awake until midnight. We'd congratulated ourselves on things going well. We talked about early remembered Christmases, and I amused Ann with the story of the cross for my mother. "Like something to decorate one of Anne C's rooms?" she asked.

"Yes, exactly." I remembered my older sister Bernadette laughing when my mother unwrapped it.

In the end, a day like others, that's the bitter part. Otherwise, sweet.

December 30, 2002, Monday

Yesterday morning before I left for Benton Way to be with the family, I tried planning with Ann. I don't remember now, but she may have asked me what I was going to do. If she didn't, then I spoke because it is a convention of our lives that she ask me on Sunday what my plans are. I said I was going to the grocery store to get supplies for Chris and Beth to have for dinner on New Year's Day, but that since it was hard to buy two orders at a time, I would come back home, hoping she could come with me to do the shopping we need here.

Ann became visibly upset because she wanted to say "no" to me, she couldn't go, because she felt fairly well and believed she must write some important letters. She said she felt "torn." I guess she felt guilty because she was putting a burden on me so she could write letters to others.

It's true, I've asked her to forward some of the letters to me, because we don't spend much time working through feelings, examining nuances, presenting ourselves and our feelings about life to each other, mostly because we are so much together we each must ask ourselves, "What is there to communicate?" And then I hold back much of what I think because I fear upsetting her, I fear her tears. The result is that I feel cut off.

"Be easy," I said. "It's okay to want to use your energy to do what you feel you have to do. It's just that I might not come back at two, as I said, because I'd planned to spend that time with you. But if you're writing letters, I'd stay with the family."

"I have so little time," she said, meaning, I think, so little time when she's feeling well.

"And that's when you need to get work done you want to finish," I said. I went on to praise the letters she's written to editors and the struggle she's made to keep people aware of the damage coming down on the United States. "I'm proud of you," I said. And, "You should be pleased with the life you've made. You need to feel strong and useful, and you have been." We stayed together for some time, until I was sure she felt calm. Or as calm as possible with prednisone.

Friday evening the family and I and Ann went out to dinner for my birthday, to the Galley, where we were placed at a long table extending inwards from the window. Ann sat next to the window and to me. She was uncomfortable most of the time, though she kept up a brave front talking to Claire and Noelle. At the end of the dinner she told me she'd run out of air in her Helios, so we left. I went back to Benton Way to be with the kids after I dropped her off.

January 3, 2003, Friday

Still balancing between the continuing day-after-day life (as if continuing is forever) and my fears, worries, tears. Last night I brought Ann a bowl of ice cream to her bed – she was hungry and I wanted to spare her the oxygen-depleting trip down the hall. As I handed it to her and she looked up to thank me, I saw the hollows under her eyes.

January 6, 2003, Monday

Yesterday Ann felt her shortness of breath to be severe. She seems to breathe heavily when walking around even when she has the portable oxygen receptacle on. I stopped to refresh my memory on how to fill it in the morning before I went to Harvey's, with the intention of filling it every morning for her before she gets up. But she said last night it wasn't necessary. In my head I said, not yet.

Possibly anxiety increases the problem – she's anxious about the root canal procedure she must undergo today, and I am too. More probably the non-threatening answer to her breathlessness is this: she's cut back on her prednisone, and the inflammation in her lungs is probably increasing. The threatening answer is that the cancer is destroying the remaining lung and she hasn't got much left to breathe with.

Dr. Doyle said she would, with the help of Ativan, sleep more and more without feeling the need to take great heaving breaths. I thought of that when she reported on how much she'd been sleeping recently, both in the morning and in the afternoon. She said she has been reading only a bit in the book *The Great Game*, which I renewed for her two weeks ago, some of the newspaper, and some of the *New York Review of Books*. Today I renewed more of the books – none of them read – she took from the library three weeks ago. I went to bed last night worried, woke worried.

January 7, 2003, Tuesday

Monday morning Ann learned that upping her prednisone intake from 16 to 20 mg in one day should be okay. As a result, her breathing has been easier, relieving my worries, especially those about the root canal procedure scheduled for that afternoon. She confessed at bedtime last night she was worried about the effects of prednisone on her temperament.

"I thought I'd managed to get it under control last week," she said.

I began to laugh, saying "Well, all except for the three cans."

On Saturday she'd pulled three cans from the can cabinet, two of diced tomatoes and one of plums, and wondered where they'd come from. I explained that the plums had been purchased in the first part of her illness when she was receiving major doses of chemotherapy, in the desperate attempt to get her to eat canned fruit, since few vegetables appealed to her. The diced tomatoes were a mistake: I mistakenly thought I'd bought stewed tomatoes. After my explanation, she'd still been unconvinced. She insisted someone outside our household must have put the cans on the shelf. Or possibly I'd just forgotten to take them to Harvey's house. Last night the memory of her protestations was funny, though I'd been more than a little irritated at the time, and Ann too recognized then that she was, as she termed it, "being bad." Strange – this way of behaving is so foreign to her basically generous and trusting character.

Before we left for the root canal appointment yesterday afternoon, Ann took 10 mg. of valium and felt fine throughout the root canal procedure, reporting to me afterward with some pleasure she'd been able to watch some of the microsurgery. Dr. Karl did discover a fracture in the tooth next to the one having the root canal, and while Ann was still in the chair, phoned her regular dentist about it. Because I could hear the call coming through about Ann, I was concerned something had gone amiss. But no, thank heaven.

January 9, 2003, Thursday

Yesterday (Wednesday) turned out to be difficult. Harvey had strained his left shoulder digging up the yard on Tuesday afternoon, so when I saw him in the morning he complained about stiffness. In the afternoon he said he was feeling much worse than he had in the morning. He hadn't got dressed, he couldn't lean down to pick up anything he dropped, and he was worried about pinched nerves and heart attacks. I offered to pick up food for him at the store when I shopped for Ann and me – then went to the bank to deposit funds and to the grocery store, back to Harvey, then to the drug store, and finally home.

This morning I'm still tense, although I'm telling myself I'm not in real, but imagined jeopardy. Harvey is about the same – complaining and still unable to bend down. I spent my time at Benton Way doing chores and making suggestions for comfort and assuring him the pain would go away. I also offered to help him get a shirt on. He thought he'd take a shower, but I discouraged him because it would only make his back hurt when he tried to get his clothes off.

Ann too is about the same. I bungled on filling her portable oxygen for her when I didn't lift it up fast enough and the two nipples stuck together, frozen. Then I bungled by pouring out too much milk for her breakfast shake. She came in while I was struggling and gave me a hug, and that warmed me as it always has.

January 11, 2003, Saturday

Yesterday was pleasant and easy – until bedtime. I took care of the Harvey problem, shopped for dinner, came home, did chores like folding Ann's laundry and filling water bottles, started dinner. Ann worked hard to fix a perfect salad, and we ate more or less on time. I began to get sleepy before nine o'clock. Ann urged me to go to bed. She worried about my becoming too tired, she said. I argued a bit, telling her that if I go to sleep too early I wake too early and then become sleepy again early the next night.

We were discussing my restlessness on Thursday night, my waking up every hour or so, and she began to fuss at me for not going to a doctor to get something to help me rest. I put her off, and she began to tear up. Unable to talk, she said she wanted me to leave – and I did, because I could see that my presence and the discussion we were having just made her less able to control her tears. After she'd gone to bed I came downstairs to say good night, to see if I could get her to rest easily. A mistake. My weariness, my headache at either Christmas or Thanksgiving – can't remember now – worried her and I was doing nothing to take care of the problem. I pointed out that my blood pressure and pulse were perfect and I don't really have a problem sleeping – just in staying asleep for long periods of time, and this happens just occasionally. So what would I say to a doctor? Besides, I don't believe in taking tranquilizers to deal with the kind of distress I'm having now – it's natural distress and I handle it with the kind of meditation I do when I write. I told her I remembered she'd said I might become a recluse, that she was afraid I'd shut myself up to write, and I said that I force myself to be with the people I love, even when it's hard on me, in order not to be a recluse. We spoke a bit about my work; I said this was the part of me I liked best, the writing part. She became tearful again, unable to speak, though I think she was trying to say she herself was losing her words and was becoming unable to speak. I think she meant this as a function of her mental acuity, and I would have reassured her, but she said – I see her lying with the head of her bed tilted upward, red plaid pajamas, red sheets, grey hair, eyes sunken, cannula in her nostrils, her face crumpling: "I'm scared."

I think now she meant about me, but at the time I considered that she was scared because she was losing the power of speech. Then she wanted me to leave, so I did.

This morning, back from Benton Way, where Harvey is somewhat better, but concerned because the pain is still there in his shoulder, I found her getting up. I offered to fill her portable oxygen and managed to do it without a problem. Then I mixed her milk.

"How are you this morning?"

"Droopy," she said.

"I wish I could help," said fatuous Carol.

Last night came up – I don't remember how – and I

said I blamed it on the prednisone. Then I left, turned on her computer so I could join the internet, and it came over me that she might think I was paying no attention to her concerns. I went back to the kitchen – she was about to cry again, head down, trying to control her mouth.

"I didn't mean to trivialize last night," I said. "I meant that the prednisone kept us from talking it through."

She tried to get out that she was glad, she was afraid I hadn't taken her seriously. She said, "I meant every word about you." But she couldn't stop crying. I put my arms around her, and she said that crying hurts. I tried to help her think of other things, but she really wanted me to go so she could remain in control of her thoughts.

And that's where I am, in my office, writing, while she reads the paper in the living room. I don't know that we're going to be able to talk about anything for a while, not until she's a bit more used to the higher dose of prednisone. I am tense and finding it difficult to concentrate on writing even this.

I remember a vow I took some time ago about finding moments of beauty in every day. I've been skipping that because with the federal administration imperialistic in the worst sense, repressive, aggressively avaricious and the state government forced by insufficient funds to compromise fire protection and help for the sick, the young, and the elderly, it's hard to feel good about anything. I'll have to remember to find those moments every night and share them with Ann.

January 13, 2003, Monday

Last night Ann prepared a rough draft of the notes she planned to give Dr. Doyle today while I did several chores, fixed dinner with a little occasional help from Ann, feeling active and confident. Even strong. I copied an article on Medicare fraud to Ann and another one on the nude women vigilists in the Bay Area to her. Talked about them briefly. Read and discussed Ann's letter to Ken Schwarz about San Luis Obispo's City Council vote against unilateral war. I also looked up aphasia for Ann in an online medical dictionary – printed out the description – and assured her she didn't have it. She has had trouble finding words when speaking from time to time, and I have no idea whether she really has trouble writing good copy, but I assured her what she does write is clear and pointed, as good as it's ever been, if not better.

After dinner Ann pulled turkey meat off our left over carcass and started to put a soup together while we discussed what she was going to say to Dr. Doyle about her difficulty with words. I insisted she make clear to him that she still writes well, if she is – subjectively – a little slow finding words. This she accepted. When it was time to go to bed, she had trouble going through the procedures, taking the pills, performing the last tasks. She'd put the turkey-soup in the oven at a low temperature. When I asked whether she meant to leave it there, she said she had to think. Which she did, silently, a spacey smile on her face. I saw something was wrong, she wasn't quite all there, so I asked to help her, but she wouldn't let me, exactly. So I just shut windows, doors, put the soup now out on the sink in the refrigerator, turned off her computer, and made my way to bed ahead of her. I heard her downstairs, getting ready, and came down to say good night. The lights were out and she was almost asleep.

January 14, 2003, Tuesday

At the doctor's Ann tried to explain her struggles with prednisone and her difficulties over the last four weeks. Hair still damp from her shower, pushed back awkwardly along the sides of her head, she was pale and breathless because she hadn't recovered from gathering herself together for the trip to the doctor's office – she tends to lose track of where she's put things these days. She was having a difficult time handing him the written explanations she'd brought along, so her hands were trembling. He sat to her left side, on a stool, his narrow head bobbing, his eyes moving swiftly from her face to mine. When we came to the part in her written descriptions about forgetting words, I interposed that she has no trouble writing. Nevertheless, he ordered an MRI. Or maybe I shouldn't say nevertheless, because if he finds a brain lesion, radiation might help. If he doesn't, then Ann will be relieved because the words will come and go with the oxygen. (I think.) He also ordered a blood test right then and there because he was afraid she might be anemic.

Then before we left the office, all my fears became real.

Dr. Doyle had heard more congestion or deadness or whatever – he didn't exactly say what, but I suppose it's that he heard no air as Ann breathed – in either lung. The carboplatin has not been working, he believed, and would think of some other medicine to try. He suggested thalidomide; someone with melanoma in her lung had some success with it. "It's expensive," he said.

Ann then explained that she doesn't have the money for expensive drugs. He chatted about ways of getting it from the company. Samples, maybe, to see if it does anything helpful. I was amazed and suggested to Ann that she did have the money through her insurance. But it was true – insurance may not pay for experimental drugs. She didn't think she'd try.

He made no more suggestions for stopping the cancer, and as he left the room he put his head down and looked grim. The news he was conveying came through clearly.

I had been expecting it, as had Ann. But in spite of its clarity, it had to overcome months of refusal to believe, so you might say it percolated through. Another way of understanding what happened: I've become so practiced in seizing the day that I immediately did and pushed away all tendency to cry. That is, I felt tears in my eyes, but blinked them back and refused to feel the emotion that went with them. I've taught myself that it's futile to think of a day without Ann, that I can and will take comfort in whatever a day with her now brings, even if it's the news that there will probably be very hard times coming.

But I guess I did this with great effort, because by the time I went down to visit Harvey, I was physically tired, aching, and when Ann – reacting to the news in a different way – was energetically putting a pot of food together for dinner, my stomach ached, my intestines cramped, and I thought I was ill. I wanted to run away from Ann's conversation and read, anything, a book, the paper, a magazine: my escapes. After several minutes I told Ann that – and we did, we sat down and read for twenty minutes before dinner.

Ann voiced what we'd been thinking at one point: "You weren't expecting this, were you?"

But I was – that's what was so strange. Late last night, alone in my room, I'd given myself ten minutes to feel a slight forecast of the pain.

In one way, I have been feeling pain, because I've noticed how circumscribed our lives have become.

Ann's response to the news was hard to determine. Although she said she'd been feeling that her lungs were filling up, she spoke of work needing to be done that she's been postponing for a year. A letter to her lawyer about the Bolsa. Organizing her checks. She wanted me to bring her accounting program up to date and spoke of calling her tax preparer to determine problems about income tax.

7
Consummation

January 15, 2003, Wednesday

Last night we started for bed without much conversation because it was late. I noticed as Ann was getting herself ready to go back to her room that she was inefficient, finding a difficult time getting all she needed – that is pills, her oxygen, etc. – together. At one point I asked if I should turn out the light in the living room, and her response was – "Didn't I turn it out?" I said no, then turned it out and checked the door. In the kitchen, I said, "Shall I close the window?" and she answered, "I was just going to turn it out." I puzzled over whether she was using the words for turning out lights for closing windows.

After I went upstairs, I could hear her turning water taps on downstairs. Then suddenly I heard "Damn," fairly loudly, and something else. Afraid she'd fallen, I raced downstairs to find her about to cry, on her knees on the floor. She'd dropped an Atavin pill and couldn't find it. I lay down on my stomach and found it under the bed for her.

"That's what I'm here for," I said while she arranged her pills, pulling herself together. When I was satisfied she was all right, I went upstairs reminding myself of how I'd tried to handle the first difficult days two years ago: Pema Chodron's meditation technique of pulling in all the sorrow and suffering that the incident or situation calls for, then breathing out peace and goodness to the world. I admit I've been absenting myself from feeling.

This morning I'm afraid that the MRI will show some brain lesions. If so, I don't want Ann to know. Doyle's office hasn't called, and the longer they don't, the more I fear the call.

It's 10 a.m. and Ann isn't awake yet.

Over the last three days Noelle, Beth and Claire have been worried about Ann or me or both. Beth called last night to find out what the doctor said, and so did Noelle. Each has a different approach: Beth encourages hopes and comforts; Noelle distracts me with information about an old friend's divorce, his having lost his wife to another man in their academic department. (I think I can follow the trail here. Ann reminds Noelle of the old days and thus her friend.) Claire tells me to find some time to let myself cry.

January 16, 2003, Thursday

This morning Ann had awakened at 8:30, she said, to answer the phone. A nurse from Dr. Doyle's office told her that her MRI showed that her brain showed no disease. "I expected that result," I told Ann.

"Well I didn't," she said.

But the nurse had been indefinite about when Ann should see the doctor again. I reminded Ann he had told her to see him after the MRI. Ann decided to wait for a while, since she expected the office to call her.

I didn't, so I'll have to remind her from time to time until something definite is settled. Much depends upon whether Dr. Doyle is going to follow through with more chemo or thalidomide or an old drug he mentioned whose name I didn't catch. Ann believed he needed time to decide. I wasn't confident he'd think about it until she made the appointment to see him. I would like to find out if there's anything more to be done about her difficulty breathing, whether a thoracentesis might help. At the same time, I'm worried about what he will say: time to go to Hospice? But now that I think about it, Hospice is no worse than where we are now. We know there isn't much time. What we want is for Ann to be comfortable and feel cared for.

I bought a few small birthday presents for her yesterday afternoon, the best I could think of, gadgets to help her keep her bed sheets smoother. Today I'll order, for both of us, the Beethoven sonatas. We're hoping to go out to dinner Monday evening, to Windows. If it seems possible, we may try for a movie that afternoon. Or if it's a nice day, a ride. I am amazed, now I think of it, that she's survived two years: the 19th marks the day two years ago when I insisted she go to the doctor because of her difficulty breathing.

I've been trying to follow Claire's advice, whether I'm feeling secure in the daily routine or, having noticed Ann's breathing distress, am fearful of what will happen in the next few weeks: I try to let the feelings expand, melt them, dissolve them, let them fill me, breath them in. I've enclosed them too tightly the last year. A hard spot within.

January 17, 2003, Friday

Ever since Ann heard from the nurse at Dr. Doyle's office about her MRI I've been urging her to call back to make the appointment the doctor suggested she make.

This morning she had an appointment with Dr. Borda at 10:45, then another with her urologist 11:15. She forgot the times, thinking that her first appointment was at 11:15, so that when I came downstairs at 10:15, she wasn't dressed. I reminded her – and she rushed off to get ready. The rush exhausted her oxygen supply, between dressing and collecting her papers, so that as she started down the hall toward the garage door she was breathing in great gasps. I turned back, thinking to tell her to slow down and found her leaning on the wall. I rushed for my office chair, telling her to sit down for a minute because we weren't late. But she thought I meant to push her in it as if it were a wheel chair, and refused. She was gasping as we got into the car, and although she seemed to be breathing normally – with her portable oxygen – she was gasping even as we went into Dr. Borda's office, enough to make the nurse pause, ask questions, say she'd wait to take blood pressure.

I stood by while Dr. Borda talked to Ann. She was able to give him an account of her prednisone and her diabetes checks without striving to breathe. She also told him about the non-call from Dr. Doyle's office and her puzzlement about what was going on there. He began to discuss Hospice as a possibility, describing its benefits and advantages. He listened to her chest for as long as thirty seconds. Before we left, he said he'd email Dr. Doyle suggesting Hospice.

Back home, she went to rest in her chair. Before I went upstairs I suggested she call Dr. Doyle's office to find out about making an appointment. Not long after three (I think) she phoned me upstairs, asked me to come down. She was sitting at the dining room table, still in the gray jacket she'd had on that morning. Her hair came down over the right side of her face, straight, stopping just short of her glasses. "I've talked with Dr. Doyle," she said.

What she told me about the conversation came in bits and pieces, as she got control of herself, then lost it, then got control. I'm not sure what the order was. At one point he was supposed to have asked whether I was there. She took this to mean, in the context, whether I lived there, because Medicare won't allow Hospice payment if she lived by herself, which sounds strange, because what happens to all those widows who watched their husbands go through Hospice when it's their turn? I still think he wanted to talk to me because he wanted to have my idea of how Ann was. She described this conversation this way: it sounded as if he had been taken by surprise or was offended. He repeated that she'd done very well to have lasted two years. He spoke of making her comfortable with morphine, which can be a two-edged sword because the more you're quiet with the morphine, the more your lungs fill up. What else she remembered, and what I remembered of what she told me is this: that they agreed there was no more treatment she would avail herself of, that the thalidomide option – the 1% chance he suggested –

didn't seem to be right. I simply sat there and listened, watching her cry. I questioned her, lightly. I probably raised my eyebrows at the refusal of the thalidomide.

She said, "What is it you want me to do?"

I had no answer. Did she want me to say let's try everything? I couldn't because that would be wrong. She has to determine what she can handle, not me. Finally she said, "We might as well both sit here and cry."

I stood up and pulled a chair up to sit next to her, and we both cried. Right then I believe I shed tears more for her anguish than for anything else. She began to talk about how she'd expected this and that's why she'd been trying to get things in order. She spoke of what she had accomplished in piling up checks. Then after a little while, she said, holding her hands up as if to ward off attackers, "I've always been someone who sets up the defenses. But not for this."

I'm not sure whether she meant there weren't any defenses for this or that she hadn't finished her defenses. Or rather, my defenses, for she went on to say "I don't want to leave you with any problems or difficulties."

Katy, a nurse from Hospice, phoned during this conversation. She said Dr. Doyle had phoned, that he would remain the primary care doctor, if Ann wanted him to. She then explained what Hospice could do, promised a brochure, and left her phone number.

At the end of the conversation, I suggested we see it as nothing different from what it has been. She won't suddenly get worse because of Hospice, but they will offer help. I hope.

January 18, 2003, Saturday

Conflicting peace marches today? One website, Supervisor Krejsa and company's "Passion for Peace," announced Mitchell Park as the gathering place. Yet the *Mustang Daily* said the government center downtown. Ann and I both searched on the web this morning and both of us found the Passion for Peace announcement. "Do you want me to drive you down there?" I asked Ann.

"I don't have enough air to go anywhere today," she said. "But I think you should go."

My sense of guilt about wanting to avoid the peace march rose to a crescendo. Then I went. Might as well have been the sixties or the nineties, but heads are now grey; there were not so many thirty-five to forty-five-year olds there as I remember from when I was thirty-five to forty-five. Same leaders, same songs, many of the same people. Three decades of protests, I thought, from Vietnam through Diablo, through Gulf war to this. I had to walk four blocks from where I parked and my feet and back ached in ways they didn't in 1991.

And I cried, for Ann, without Ann, for the solitudes of souls.

In the mail before I left, Ann had received copies of letters she wrote as an eighteen, nineteen, and twenty-year-old to her friend who lived in Denver. I asked whether I could read them. That evening, when I returned from Benton Way, she said I could. Mostly, they're about activities with and thoughts about friends and relatives – mostly friends – during the summer months, not an unusual set of thoughts for summer letters. But they were unmistakably Ann's, because of the joy she expressed about seeing her friends, the deep interest in their affairs, the sense of how she cared about every one of them. I said as much to her. She wanted to know if I saw what was missing. I didn't really.

Somewhere in this, perhaps in my comment on her closest friend – she wasn't showing as much feeling about her as about the others – Ann heard or thought she heard something, I don't know what, to bring her to say this: "I don't like your getting hold of the letters and making a novelist's interpretation."

"I thought I'd done too much biography not to know when I'm speculating."

We each said a few more things, none insensitive that I'm aware of, and she finally said, "I didn't want you to read these things. You see things that aren't there."

I fell silent immediately, and before going to bed, she said, "I've hurt you."

"It's just that I thought we were closer than that."

Later, upstairs, I thought, what did I mean by "closer than that?" If I'd been stomping around with any interpretation except the sense that she loved people and it was obvious then as it is now, then I could understand that I'd been intrusive. But I was, I thought, extremely careful. My conclusion was that she'd heard something I didn't intend, a symptom of not trusting my version of her – the way I sometimes don't trust the way my children see me. I wonder if I'm going to be able to tell her my feelings any more. I thought, before I went to sleep, whether she was deliberately pushing me away – and/or letting life go. I wondered whether I could let go. It's becoming hard to talk about things that are close to our cores, because we're both afraid of starting tears.

January 19, 2003, Sunday

This morning I told Ann I'd awakened crying. We then spoke of our not being able to communicate because of the tears. Ann was crying then, and so was I. In the midst of my tears I said that I wanted to keep every possible part of her. That I have a file into which I've put even the little notes she leaves me.

"I don't know what good you think that's going to do you," she said.

I considered the truth, whether I'll ever be able to look at them again, whether I'll ever be able to read this journal.

January 20, 2003, Monday
Ann's 73rd birthday

In the morning after I returned from walking with Jean and checking on Harvey, I took off my shoes and lay down on top of the quilt, next to Ann. We were quiet for several minutes. After a while, I tried to remember last year's birthday – thinking how thankful I am for the year we've had since then – and then told her I wasn't happy with my presents for her, and that I had no poems this year. They don't come easily, the way I feel. Ann began to be tearful then, so I stopped talking, called up calm and calming thoughts. I've been trying to project them into her mind, the images, not so much the recollections but the images

Later, I decided to try to find a poem in my files of half done or half-baked ideas that I could work with. Finally, I found something, worked out the lines, erasing most of what I'd written before, then turned to making a card to inscribe it on. After several trials and several errors, I managed a piece of paper on which I wrote in long hand. Not bad – the poem seemed more a poem in long hand. Then I wrapped packages. Just before noon it occurred to me that we could have champagne and a quiche for lunch, if I went off to capture them. Ann was pleased, and the birthday began to feel like a celebration. We exchanged presents. Ann became tearful over the poem – and I said, "I'm sorry."

She said: "This is what I would say, if I could find the words." She added that she was particularly touched by the last lines:

> Every morning for the past week I've been waking
> at five, and for a moment in the darkness I wonder
> if this will be the day when not even one thread
> of the mask that blinds me will loosen.
> But I have not been thinking of love.
> Only love releases the light
> of what we once wished for.

My girls had sent cards, all of them arriving by Saturday. Her Aunt Marge phoned to remind Ann what a "remarkable child" she'd called herself when still in a crib. A young neighbor came over with roses and stayed for half an hour in the morning. Ann's afternoon nap was interrupted by another friend, and Ann told her she didn't really want visitors just then, wasn't feeling well.

Late in the afternoon, the doorbell rasped as Ann was getting dressed for dinner. I ran down stairs to receive – a bouquet from her cousin Casey. Then Claire called so she and Annie could sing for Ann.

In the evening we drove out to Windows – Ann having said she wanted to avoid Anderson's – where, in a long, grey sunset, the boats and bay and dunes all various shades of grey blue – we ate oysters and cilantro-marinated shrimp, in a quiet atmosphere, pleasant music. Classical, but not insistent on our listening to it. Ann was feeling not bad, but still felt short of breath, toward the end of dinner placing the cannula from the helios in her nose. We decided to drink scotch, in my mind in honor of Fiona [the daughter of a woman whose suffragette writings we'd resurrected] and Ann, after tasting, chose 15-year-old Glenmorangie, and I McAllen. Our drinks lasted all through dinner. I drove home feeling just right, and as the evening went on, felt warm, pleased with our day.

January 21, 2003, Tuesday

The Hospice nurse called to make arrangements to drop by about 10 o'clock. I heard Ann talking with her, got up from my desk and joined her in the living room. She was smiling as she talked, and spoke her name – Janet – so I could share in her pleasure that the nurse was Janet, whom we knew from Dr. Doyle's office in Mission Medical.

She arrived promptly, a small woman in a skirt and a print jacket, like the ones women medics wear at work in the hospital, with a name tag dangling from her lapel. Her hair was greying, cut short, setting off a smooth oval face. She wore big horn-rimmed glasses. I've noticed before that her eyes, behind the glasses, express kindness and compassion. This morning, sure that Ann's memory of her weight the last time she was in the doctor's office was wrong, she said nothing, but pursed her mouth slightly and lifted her eyebrows. After she'd reviewed the rules of Hospice care for us and described the benefits, she commented that she wasn't used to all these papers because the social worker usually carries them. She'll be coming once a week, or two or three times, or even more, as necessary, and her visits will take the place of visits to the doctor. Ann can still go to the doctor, if she wants to, though. A home health aide will come too, and we agreed she was needed only once a week for an hour now. One rule that we had no problem with, but that others might: we are not to call 911, but Hospice instead, if Ann has a medical emergency. Stickers on this matter have to be placed on the phone and a "do not resuscitate order" pinned to the refrigerator.

January 22, 2003, Wednesday

We had a rather late dinner, because we were discussing the avalanche Hospice appears to be when you don't quite need it, when becoming bedridden seems several months away. We spoke of my feeling that Diane's promise that I won't be alone seemed not worth much. Ann had brought the topic up – I guess she's been worrying about becoming a total invalid. I said, that I might call Julie to come when I feel really alone. I meant right after Ann dies, but Ann didn't hear it that way. She thought I meant when she was bedridden and dying. "I wonder how the guest bed will be for her back," Ann said.

"I'll let her have the bed upstairs," I said, not realizing the misunderstanding.

"No," she said, "I don't want that."

When I'd finished the dishes, I asked Ann to whom she planned to give the wooden figure made by her grandfather, and we discussed then the several lists she's planning to make. All will be mine – with maybe a few exceptions – but she will make a few designations for whom to give things to whenever I break up the house. One cousin, for example, might want the furniture and carvings his grandfather made. Someone else might want the block prints on the living room wall. She began to describe how my girls should keep the silver and china sets together in order to maintain their value. Eventually, this became a grim exercise for us, and I tried to turn talk away to reminiscence. Ann did talk then about why she never went back to Cazadero for long summers after she started Stanford – quarrels with an uncle by marriage, her grandfather's wrath at the people who came deep into the mountains where there were no stores without bringing food with them.

We went to bed without reading at all. Before I went upstairs, Ann was becoming tearful at the thought of leaving me, and I tried to calm her with thoughts of the beauty of the north of Scotland.

January 23, 2003, Thursday

I'm afraid Ann's trying to do too much, since she's worried, now that she sees how sick she may become, that I may not be able to keep the world together for her. This last occurred to me when I arrived home and I discovered she'd been doing laundry, about which she told me not to bother.

In the early afternoon, Janet came with a nebulizer. Ann's oxygen level didn't improve with it, but we're figuring that was because when she was mouth breathing she wasn't using her extra oxygen while inhaling. Janet seemed almost concerned that oxygen blood level wasn't low enough to warrant the equipment, so had Ann go around the house without it. From 91 it dropped to 85. She also told us we only had to wash the equipment off once every two or three days, thank heavens. I was concerned that I was going to have to wash it out with vinegar three times a day.

January 24, 2003, Friday

At 10:30 Ann and I struggled to put the nebulizer parts back together, Ann finally figuring out the arrangement. I stumbled around, trying to race through the directions, trying to be helpful in making her comfortable, but in the end I was only able to fetch her a glass of water. She reported that when she got up this morning she felt wobbly, as if her limbs were not going to carry her. Shortly after the nebulizer treatment she reported feeling mildly dizzy. This afternoon after a long sleep, she said she felt quite weak. In addition, she was not thinking clearly, she felt. She'd gone looking for her glasses when she was wearing them.

January 25, 2003, Saturday

This morning as I left the house I picked up the paper, and glancing at the headline, read, "Bush Warns Nation to be Ready for War." The sun was turning the grass on the hill above me brilliant green, glistening with tones of pale yellow and white, and a meadowlark, the first this year, began to sing. I'd just filled the oxygen tank for Ann, who was still lying asleep in bed, the olive comforter across her chest, grey hair, plaid pajamas. She was breathing easily, and I hoped she'd feel well today.

What I learned yesterday: she still doesn't want me to rush forward to help her. I have to remind myself to sit back and wait for her to ask, or to help where it's unobtrusive. Last night I became anxious, the way you do when a child is crying and can't stop, as I heard Ann breath with great effort, taking big gasps, as she prepared for bed. She'd dropped pills, possibly had to return to the kitchen for something she'd forgotten, and had trouble fixing her bed. She was lying down, and I offered to fetch water for her, but she wouldn't have me do it, answering impatiently, because she is impatient with having to talk, that she had to stand anyway when taking pills. I offered other services, but she refused, always impatiently, as if she must explain – impatient, so that I couldn't say, you don't have to explain. Finally, I was allowed to go down the hall to get the cipro for her. When I got back, she was breathing more easily, but we were both upset, and I said I didn't want her to have to feel this way. After we were both easier, I said – and one of the irritating things about me, I'm sure, is my asking questions about whether she'd taken certain medications: "I ask too often because I want to know if you're having trouble because you haven't taken something or because you have."

I'm trying to warn Harvey these days that I may be in short supply soon. That I may not be able to leave Ann for long. I'm also going to ask Diane to help me with two things: I'd like her to help me with a big grocery shopping on the days we get together, and I'm going to give her the recipe and ingredients for the custard Ann likes so much. Then we'll see what works out.

January 27, 2003, Monday

I've just resolved to prepare a story for mailing today and post it tomorrow morning. I've been lazy about this.

And take books back to the library and check Ann's safety deposit box for her rings and get groceries.

Too much, I think, especially when I must also check with Ann what she wants to do about calling Janet about the drug used with albuterol in the inhaler, and the fact that it is contraindicated for patients with achalasia. Saturday evening I returned home from Benton Way shortly after eight. We'd had a strenuous afternoon, because Ann had begun to search the closet in her office for the rings she put away at the time of the remodel. She also did what she could to clean the closet out. She asked me to go through the clothes hanging in the plastic bag in her bedroom closet, a painstaking task, and a somewhat painful one as I ran my hand into the sleeves of jackets she's worn on celebratory occasions with me or felt the soft cloth of a blouse or scarf I remember she had in England. It was also painful to hear her gasping as she walked from the closet to the dining room table, where we pulled things from boots and smoothed out pieces of padding. When I arrived, Ann had already eaten her dinner, but was mildly upset because she had burned some food she was preparing, having caught the cannula to her portable oxygen in the telephone cord near her computer. I chatted with her about the need to complete the washing of the humidifier bottle attached to her concentrator – we had removed the bottle, then washed it with soap, and Ann had later filled it with vinegar. I wanted to complete the task and was willing to do it on my own, following instructions in the book, but Ann, impatiently, insisted on coming too so she could give instructions for every move.

I've become more patient with her need to instruct, though I do try to move faster than her instructions will allow me. I rinsed, waited to air dry, as required, but she said it wasn't necessary. We pulled out a new cannula to attach to the plastic tubing, Ann demonstrating how to attach it – twist and pull, but more twist than pull – and then I filled the bottle with air, put the top back on, and sat down on the floor to try to replace the bottle on the machine. I guess I'd made a mistake about the direction it screws, thinking clockwise since it seemed to have come off counterclockwise, so I struggled to no avail. My arms aren't strong enough to hold out for the length of time it would have taken me to figure out how to screw the bottle on – I was lying flat on the floor trying to do it, golden light on golden floor, the machine, the tubing, catching the light, glowing. Ann had been breathing heavily the entire time, so I was troubled but finally she sat on the floor and got the bottle back on the machine. We turned the concentrator on, and it shrieked at us, the bubbles bubbled properly and the indicator showing a level of "2" popped up into place. "I never have been good at listening to instructions and following them," I told Ann. "I always have to read them."

We were right next to the nebulizer and the medications you're supposed to put in it, and I decided to follow my inclination and discover what the second medication was and look it up on the internet. The name was ipratrobium bromide. I was about to look it up, when I remembered that I couldn't because my computer was in the midst of a "total" backup. Ann suggested I use hers. I did, and reached a page with a discussion of precautions. Among the warnings were these: tachycardia, autonomic neuropathy, and achalasia. Triumphant that I'd solved the mystery of why Ann had felt so awful Friday, I read out to her the warnings, thus stirring her into anger, and tears. She cried for an hour, sitting on the couch in the living room, her head in her hands, trying to stop the sobbing, shoulders humped. I sat with her. She was angry first with Doyle, calling him and the medical profession "Murderers" because he'd made this mistake. Later she cried for her two years, for the effect it's had on me, for loss, always coming back to her anger. She wanted me to phone Dr. Doyle and tell him what I thought of his having prescribed it; she couldn't speak, she'd start to cry, she said. I did what I could to mitigate; I said her tachycardia was controlled, we didn't know whether she'd had autonomous neuropathy, that Janet had been careful not to give her a full dose. By this time the exertions connected with the concentrator, were having their effect, I thought, and all I wanted to do was to calm her. One worry that came forward – that I wouldn't be able to handle the extra work and would leave her – a deep worry, one she's never expressed before. So I have to be more patient and reassuring. I talked about our being together in this, each suffering in a different way. I talked about the community of all human souls, trying to use, for myself, the sense that I wasn't alone, we weren't alone, there are millions of us suffering in this way. At last, she became calm. When I went upstairs, I calmed myself with the poetry of Jorie Graham.

In the morning, all was well. We talked before I left for Benton Way, discussing the list I was going to ask Diane to help me with, Ann adding one new item to it, the making of a sign that says "Do Not Disturb" which could be hung on the outside door when she wants to sleep and would not like to have anyone wake her up. At Sandy's I bought sandwiches for Diane, who arrived about 12:20. We took the sandwiches back to my computer room, chatted about her trip to Pasadena, and I told her, without whining, about how difficult January has been and that Ann has signed up with Hospice Partners. I described the services provided. Diane asked for a list, and I asked her to help me with shopping on Thursdays, when we eat lunch together, and to make the sign and to make the custards from time to time. Diane drove me over to the Cal Poly library, so I could get a book for Ann, *The Stripping of the Altars*, by Eamon Duffy, a history she may want to read now that she's finished *The Great Game*. All day yesterday Ann stayed in her pajamas, tried to rest. After dinner we listened to the Beethoven sonatas I'd ordered for her birthday, and she closed her eyes, leaned back in her chair, and appeared to be breathing easily: bright blue robe, red pajamas, soft light.

At one point, in the Sonata 28 (I think) the second (and last) movement sounded so like some Schubert we knew that Ann, eyes closed and all, and I were both smiling with the delight of it. Harmonies, melody and all.

January 28, 2003, Thursday

Around noon yesterday Ann and I set off to the Four Seasons Outfitters with Ann's revolver. With some directions from Ann, I found the Outfitters: SUVs and pickups in the parking places, bars on the windows, battered ads for Winchester behind them, and dust all over everything, including what I could see through the door. Ann went in by herself, portable oxygen and purse over her left shoulder, revolver and ammunition in boxes in her right hand. When she came out, she was laughing: she'd left the gun on consignment, but had to be warned by the clerk who wanted to tell her a story about what she'd have to do to get the gun back.

"If you'll excuse me, a little old lady . . ." he began.

"That's all right," she said, "I think I qualify as a little old lady."

"This little old lady left her gun here, and then she wanted to get it back. But she had to go through a complete background check in order to take it out, I mean a complete one . . ."

"Look, I have lung cancer, I don't need this gun any more. So it's okay, I won't want it back." Before she left they agreed that it might take a long time to sell, that it probably won't bring more than one hundred dollars, and that after she'd gone (there was some joking about change of address) her heirs were to check in every once in a while to see if it had sold.

February 1, 2003, Saturday

Maybe speaking of the past doesn't provide Ann with a sense of calm, the kind of serenity I derive from it. Last night I tried to recall the time when we were working on the index to *Feminist Quotations* in the house on Lawrence Drive. I couldn't quite remember the panel we'd used to put the index topics up on. I saw the plastic imitation glass, either amber or green, but I didn't know how we stuck the topics on (now I believe we probably used gummed labels, like name tags, easily moved). Ann and I tossed the recollection around, bringing up paintings – the kitty over the dining room table, the ocean above the couch – where they were then and where they are now. Then Ann told me about the strange dreams she was having about the house where she'd lived in Morro Bay. It had become a ruin and she was feeling anxious or troubled, though not necessarily about the deterioration. I switched to a discussion of the Baumans, and where they'd been at her mother's house in Pasadena – on the north wall behind the piano – and where the trays had been. Then Ann asked me to stop talking on these topics, because they weren't bringing comfort.

February 3, 2003, Monday

This morning I woke early and tense, rehearsing the difficulties of the day and troubled about the difficulties to come – increasing housework schedule, decreasing times to escape in my habitual way, through words and stories, and no pleasureful rewards in sight. I don't even know what would give me pleasure any more, except maybe having another story published.

Here's something I think of frequently and wish for – the fun established couples have in retirement, attending concerts, socializing, traveling.

This morning these thoughts piled onto my emotions – I'm trying to find a word for the boredom and slight restlessness I felt with both Harvey and Jean. No lift, just sag.

February 5, 2003, Wednesday

Ann's pain wasn't under control yesterday (Tuesday) until late afternoon, early evening. That is, it went from the early morning mid-chest pain at about the level 6, she said, to about 3 by noontime, and then late in the afternoon was down farther and diminished to about a 2. On coming downstairs after a nap, I found her working on a list of medications for me, noting what she takes and where it is, and when she takes it. She was sitting at the dining room table, leaning forward and I had a sense that she was struggling. I've put the yellow sheets on which she made the notes in the cupboard with the medications.

My reaction to her pain was fear for her, fear that I wouldn't be able to manage appropriately, fear we wouldn't be able to get the pain under control, fear that the pain and the consequent debility was going to continue day after day. I feel it most in my gut, which cramps. I also feel it in my head, because I have a hard time working on writing anything but this journal. In a way, too, I feel cut off from her – isolated – because there's nothing I can do to alleviate the suffering. I keep trying in my mind to go back in time, too, just to a few days ago: if only she were as well as she was last week, I tell myself, and recall what it was like. What it was like when she made the salads every night – just three weeks ago.

Today (Wednesday) was quieter than yesterday, but more troubling. Ann woke at the usual time (nine or so) and would have gone back to sleep, having taken her pain killers and relaxants, but I started talking about bank problems, and that woke her up. I fixed her breakfast, and after drinking it and taking her morning medications, she sat in her chair, reading. Near 10:30 she fell asleep. Lunch over, Ann took her after lunch meds, sat down in her chair and went to sleep again – black jacket, black sweats, black shoes – white hair, waving a little now. I thought of the hair waving, her not having chemo, and my puzzle – why did we stop. She's gone down hill much faster now, and I want to know, why was the carboplatin stopped, how did the doctor determine it wasn't doing any good?

When I came out at seven to finish fixing dinner, Ann said she was having serious troubles at her computer. She gave up, sat in her chair with the paper while I fixed the dinner – mushroom risotto with shrimp and red bell peppers, cooked, and Italian herbs; peas; bread. Her talk was slow, and she was having trouble finding words. She did advise me about dinner, but slowly, missing a few essential words. At some point – while I was waiting for everything to heat up, with her permission, I went in to see what was happening to the computer. Nothing, really. Ann was having trouble typing. Or spelling. Or expressing herself. She'd sent off two garbled messages. While I was doing the dishes, I told her that nothing was the matter with the computer. Earlier in the afternoon she'd said she wished they would tell her if she should expect this – meaning losing her powers.

After dinner she requested hearing the new "Bagatelles" recording we bought. I put it on, and she was asleep almost immediately.

February 7, 2003, Friday

Yesterday, Thursday, began well enough. Ann was much more alert and close to her old self. I spoke briefly with a neighbor as I left to visit Harvey. She offered baked goods, apologized for not coming by. I told her Ann was sleeping a great deal. She wanted to know about the x-rays, and I noticed how I flubbed the answer: as far as

I'm concerned the last x-rays were taken last October. At the last she said, "It's hard, I know."

I looked at her, and said, "Yes, it's hard," meaning what she was meaning, watching someone you care for disintegrate before your eyes. No matter how slowly it takes place, it's hard.

When Diane arrived to help with grocery shopping, we went off, leaving the "Do Not Disturb" sign on the door so that Ann could sleep. The shopping trip went well. We had time to talk over a few poems. I also discussed with Diane my sense of having been pushed into Hospice without a final word; I wasn't clear about what had happened to plans for Ann's treatment. I wasn't satisfied with the reason the doctor had dropped plans to continue with the carboplatin treatment after New Year's. Yes there was the MRI, but it was supposed to have shown nothing. Then the next thing we know, she's enlisting with Hospice. Wouldn't more carboplatin have held the cancer back another little while? Diane suggested I talk with the doctor.

When I returned, Ann was at her computer, having no problems at all, and this made me happy. She came out early, and we sat for a while reading the papers. Then it was time for dinner – and Ann saw that I had made a mistake in the kind of rye bread I bought for her sandwiches, and pointed it out to me. I suppose if she had just pointed it out to me, I could have handled my sense of failure. But she began to explain why it was wrong, and I tried to explain that I knew it wasn't exactly what she ordered, but had hoped I'd made a sensible decision. She wanted to know why I bought it at all; I tried to explain that she would run out of bread in the next week and I didn't want to have to go to the store again. She said she would have to go then.

Then my tears started up, for I believed she was trying to make me feel bad for not taking perfect care of her. "I'm doing the best I can," I kept repeating.

And then Ann started to cry. The two of us cried for a couple of hours, at first Ann because she was upset with me, and me, because Ann wouldn't listen to what I was trying to do, how I was trying to make more time to be with her by consolidating and organizing the errands and the shopping and getting it done all in one day. Over the two hours we exchanged some words hard for each of us to take – she said I may be tired, but she's the one who's sick. I said, I feel all by myself right now. She said at another time, how she was upset about having lost some money because not having enough put too big a burden on me, and I said, in reply, what can money do, at this point?.

Finally Ann asked me to stop talking, and I did for a long time. Then, sitting on the couch while Ann leaned forward in her chair, trying to control her sobbing and the pain of it, trying to keep her nose clear so she could breath, I described exactly what I had thought, how I had balanced the fact that Ann would need bread before the week was out, that what I bought was not exactly what we'd bought before, that I didn't want to go into another store looking for the special rye bread she likes nor did I want to have to go back; how I'm trying to save my energy for other efforts to help her; that I'd made a choice, and then, when she objected, realized I'd made the wrong choice and felt – because of her lecture – that I'd failed. Within a few minutes, her crying contained, Ann told me she'd experienced a failure to understand what I'd been going through, that she'd spoken thoughtlessly.

We got up after a while, both of us still tearful, I more because I'd exploded and caused Ann to cry hard and thus put her in pain, and because the dinner I'd fixed we couldn't eat, because the calming routine and ritual of our life couldn't continue just then. We put away the food and washed what dishes it was necessary to wash. Ann then went to bed and I remained, took a drink of vodka, and ate some bread and cheese. I wished Ann good night and told her to keep my love with her overnight, and went up to bed.

This morning, Friday, I woke with tears still in my eyes and rolling down my cheeks. When I had prepared her breakfast protein drink, she got up, tearful, rebellious about her illness, hating herself and the way she felt. In her blue robe, green pajamas, she walked the hall kicking at the tubing, crying, and when she arrived in the living room, she pulled it out of her nose. After ten o'clock and a cup of tea, I offered to call – or did she ask me? I can't remember – the pharmacy to find out if Hospice had sent in an expected order. The report was that it should arrive at the house before one. I spoke to Ann then about going for a ride after it arrived. She said maybe. Then, in a burst of distress – I'm sure it was that, though now I can't remember exactly what we were speaking about when she said, "I thought you were going to call and talk with Dr. Doyle."

"I am, I just needed to know if you thought it was a good idea."

So then I phoned the office, and avoiding an immediate conversation with him, I made an appointment for Monday, February 17, after promising his office staff to pay in cash – a promise made to an implied demand for an answer to the question: how was this going to be paid for, since no insurance will pay. I'm hoping Ann is well enough to come with me, but she seems to be failing fast, and I'm wondering where she will be in a week. Yet the Hospice nurses aren't hearing a lot of change when they listen to her chest with the stethoscope – top of left lung, some air; some air throughout right lung: is the failure rate because of pain and the consequent narcotics?

February 8, 2003, Saturday

Last evening I found Ann sitting on her bed disconsolate because unable to determine which pills she should take. I couldn't be sure just what the problem was; it looked as if she had the right set in front of her. She asked me what was the matter, she felt so sad, she was such a baby, a spoiled baby, and she wanted to give it all up and she was ashamed of herself for not being strong, for crying, for not being able to cry. My tears began to fall, and we cried together, holding on to each other as if we were in cold water, drowning. She kept saying she didn't know how she deserved to be so lucky as to have me. I assured her I was going to be okay. I also told her she didn't seem to be slipping so much – if you took into account the way alcohol used to affect her in just this way when she'd had too much. Eventually, we calmed down and I reminded her we were like soldiers, together. "Yes, but what am I able to do for you?"

My answer: "It's like this, we've started up a high mountain together, and you've broken your leg, and right now you're leaning on me so you can go forward. You've got to accept the fact that eventually I'll have to carry you."

She thought about that, then said, "I used to read books about things like that."

I went to bed feeling peaceful, meditative, acceptant. I hope she did.

February 10, 2003, Monday

Sunday morning I waited until she was up and dressed before I left for Benton Way, much concerned about leaving her. We chatted a bit before I left about what we could do to ease both of our concerns. I feel I have to keep Harvey in a routine in order to stall any emotional, and therefore possibly physical, effects on him that may create a difficult problem. Ann spoke of having someone come in to get her meal on Saturday, and I said that was possible, but I could also fix it before I left or come back early to fix it. We'll deal with that the first of March. This week, Claire is coming, and the week after that, I have a family wedding which I will plan to leave early and be home in time to fix her meal. Sundays – and we didn't talk about this, but I thought about it – we can get small helps from the neighbors until she needs people to be with her to help her up.

She emailed me a meditation website, which I read, and thought again about vipassana meditation, the kind in which you watch the flow of thoughts and notice what they are. I wasn't meditating yesterday, but I thought several times of the page, and watched my thoughts. They are in a narrow compass now: Ann, how to deal with Ann's problems, how am I going to manage the physical difficulties that may come, how am I going to manage the emotional difficulties, how have I been managing, and so on.

February 11, 2003, Tuesday

I got my hair cut at noon – no more flip, no more long hair to push behind my ears. Susan the social worker arrived shortly after I reached home. We chatted about Ann's stress about my back – and I assured everyone again it was getting better. She's good at her work, Susan is: she asks open-ended questions – some of the ones I've become familiar with through Diane – like, what would you like to do in the time you have left. "Find my lost rings," Ann said. She didn't elaborate, and Susan didn't press, and I was glad, since Ann was about to shed tears after that question. Ann also discussed her struggle with seeing people – the crying, the irritability. I told Susan I dealt with the irritability by dodging, if I noticed it. Later in the interview she asked Ann what she felt she hadn't accomplished that she'd like to have accomplished. Ann had already spoken of her review of her life for the book on girls' schools, so in answer to this question she spoke of the way she felt she'd been deserted by her family when her mother was ill and she wanted to move her to San Luis; how difficult it had been; how she and I might have succeeded as feminist writers then – we were on a roll, but couldn't recoup. She also spoke of the smoking she did – and I added that she'd just taken a course on stopping smoking at the time – and the stress that may have brought on Sjogren's. I described for Susan at one point Ann's natural leadership ability – I think before that Ann had spoken of how she felt the local Commission on the Status of Women a great accomplishment. Susan asked me also how I dealt with tension and grief: I said – I talked to my children; then I added something about how, when we first learned of the lung cancer and its prognosis – two years ago – I'd listened to meditation tapes. I also mentioned the spa. "Is it outside?" asked Susan.

"No" I suppose she was going to talk about the sky. As she left, she told me to call her any time I needed to talk and the kids weren't enough.

That afternoon I lay on the couch to nap, and put out my hand to hold Ann's from time to time.

February 13, 2003, Thursday

Harvey phoned midmorning: he'd blacked out and fallen and just managed to get to the phone. I found him sitting on a chair in the dining room, no glasses, a t-shirt and pajama pants on. He was fine, no lumps, no serious strains, just the fear of falling again. He'd been feeling light-headed that morning and had bent over to look for his suspenders, when coming back up he blacked out. He'd had a container of urine in his hands that spilled all over his bedroom and he'd already tried to mop it up. He cried a little, just as I would have done. I mopped up the urine, put what was wet in the washing machine, and reassured him. We theorized that what he probably had was the hypotension of the elderly, so I advised him to exercise a bit to get his blood pressure up.

February 14, 2003, Friday

Today we visited Dr. Borda's office. After a brief discussion of managing her blood sugar, Ann asked him directly how long she had to live.

"One month to two," he answered, his head turned down compassionately, looking into her eyes. He had a smile that wasn't a smile, but a recognition, a saying, I love you.

She looked straight ahead at him without flinching, asked another question, about pain and shortness of breath. He answered that patients in her situation judge for themselves how much discomfort they can cope with, how much mental failure they can cope with, and balance the amount of medication they take.

After we left the office I said nothing, waiting for her.

"Let's go to lunch," she said.

We went to 1865. It was early yet, the room almost empty. Ann had two gin and tonics. I said nothing; Ann said nothing about the time she has left. What is there to say? I was thinking. We were both feeling the heavy weight of sorrow. Life was narrowing to a tunnel, life as we knew it. Should I call in people, have them around?

February 16, 2003, Sunday

Keeping this journal is getting difficult, partly because I have been busy in the mornings and partly because my back hurts when I sit in the computer chair too long. The last time I wrote in it was Friday, trying to catch up with the week that had just passed. Notes I made but didn't have time to fill out say that on Tuesday either we felt or I felt that there was a sense of things getting beyond us. After Susan left, we both felt a desire to have an early drink. We talked then about religious concepts – at least I think it was Tuesday, because I remember it was still light out and we sat facing each other across the living room. I now suppose it could have been Thursday, after the lunch and grocery shopping expedition with Diane.

I say this because Diane wanted to know whether Ann and I ever spoke of spiritual matters, mentioning her knowledge that Catholics often return to the fold at the last. I told Diane about Ann's concern at one time about how her family and the nuns who taught her might all have been right, and how we had discussed that possibility and set it aside for the concept of a loving God, if indeed there is a personal one.

On the Tuesday – or Thursday – I mentioned to Ann my feeling we are all moving toward becoming one with the universe. Ann snorted – but just a little – and I went on to consider a) human consciousness and its awareness of the universe, how this in itself is an end – or a beginning; b) that we have to consider a first cause, for how come there's something, or we're aware of something, rather than nothing. I said I sometimes wish we had the sacraments to share with people we could admire and respect and love. Ann agreed that we'd have a hard time finding people who accepted our concept of the sacraments as reminders, and I added "Of the community of saints, the community of humans."

At some point I wished Ginny and Elizabeth here, and Ann expressed her opinion that Ginny wouldn't quite fulfill the idea of someone who agreed with us about the sacraments, but that maybe Elizabeth would.

We went on to discuss Ann's leadership qualities (which makes me think this took place on Tuesday, not Thursday, because we'd been talking about those qualities with Susan), Ann beginning with, "I would have made a good abbess." She went on to play with the idea of the convent she would found, how difficult it would be to find the right people.

February 17, 2003, Monday

Before I left for my visit to Dr. Doyle, I asked Ann to read over the questions I planned to ask him. They must have been the right ones, because he'd foreseen all of them. He admitted that he'd been unable to decide January 13 whether more chemotherapy would help. Perhaps it might slow the cancer down, but it wouldn't stop it. Between the low platelets and the lack of immunity caused by chemotherapy, he was concerned about pneumonia if she continued. He'd been upset when he left the office, as I'd thought. Basically, we parted friends, and I felt relief that everything had been done that it was reasonable and compassionate to do.

In the evening, I became more than usually tired around 9:30 p.m., and asked Ann to get ready for bed. We had another minor struggle about pills. Had she taken the cipro? We straightened this out, and each of us went to our rooms, I having checked that windows and doors were closed and turned off Ann's computer. She reminded me to turn off the heater.

Upstairs I found myself frustrated and frightened. Ann's mind often wasn't completely with us today, and her tendency to obsess about things she needed to have control of was making it difficult for me to substitute my mind for hers. For example, this evening, she'd said she had taken control of pills, like the cipro, but then hadn't and asked me what happened to it. I began to cry, lying on my bed and sobbing for about ten minutes, tired and scared and not knowing how to relieve the workload that Ann creates by insisting on doing certain things herself. Then I came downstairs to say good night. After her shower this afternoon, she had left water running over a shirt in the bathroom sink, and it spilled over the floor. I'd found her mopping up water on floor, wheezing with the effort. When I got downstairs this evening, instead of finding her lying peacefully in bed, I discovered that she had emptied all the drawers and shelves from the right side of her bathroom sink. I didn't understand what was going on. My first thought was that she'd decided to rearrange the shelves. I burst out, without thinking: "This is worse than taking care of a two year old" then regretted what I said immediately, especially after Ann explained, gasping for air: "Neither of us had the wit this afternoon to look into the drawers to see if the water had got into them."

The drawers and shelves had become soaked, their contents, too, and Ann had tried to do the work to spare me. I helped with the shelf right under the sink, lifting out the spare tile and drying the surface with paper towels. Then I got out of the way while Ann got ready for bed. I did apologize for my outburst, but at Ann's request I said nothing until she was under the covers. Then I told her that she kept forgetting there were two of us in this, that this uphill trek requires me to help her more and more, and that she should have called me on the phone and asked me to come down to help her because she was harming herself by pushing until she ran out of oxygen.

I think she listened to me, because she seemed quite content the next morning when I left to visit Harvey and she took her morning pills with good grace, without questioning me.

February 19, 2003, Wednesday

Yesterday became difficult rapidly. Ann got up to meet Janet in the living room. I'd just managed to finish the journal entry above and make out the rest of the month's bills, a fairly easy start to the day. We had some discussion about whether Kathy, an aide, who had phoned to say she was coming, should come. What could she do? I suggested we keep to the schedule Ann wrote out at the beginning of our Hospice experience: the aide was to change Ann's bed and clean up the room on the weeks the Webers weren't coming; on weeks like this one, when the Webers were coming, she could help Ann with personal care – foot bath, shower, oil rub, massage. The issue was undecided when Janet arrived, for Ann had just begun to tidy up the bathroom herself. I'd stopped her, for her face was pale and she was gasping for air. Janet persuaded her to use the nebulizer immediately, measuring the oxygen concentration in her blood both before and after. (86 before; 91-92 after.) Apparently I embarrassed Ann by talking about the bathroom spill, because at one time when Janet was not in the room – she was attending to the arrival of the oxygen tanks, which are to supplant the portable oxygen carrier – Ann told me how angry she was with me.

Later, after we'd fussed about the oxygen tank's place – in the back seat of the car – and got ourselves an extra tank to keep in the house, Janet and I placed the spare tank on the guest room bed. It has to lie on its side, Janet said. So since that seemed an easier place to lift it from, we decided on the bed. As soon as Janet left, Ann asked where the tank was, why she hadn't been consulted about where it should go, why I'd put it on the bed where it might ruin the new spread. I answered as best I could, but Ann's mind was slow. She had expended much energy for the oxygen deliverery and for Janet, and maybe the extra morphine also overcame her.

Let me explain the extra morphine. Ann's directions for taking pills were what I followed in setting up the directions for them, the ones we were trying to work through so the process of making notes about every single thing wouldn't keep Ann laboring over her notebooks for hours, becoming frustrated and a little scared because she was confusing things. Ann's original prescription for oxycontin was for 10 mg doubled, or 20 mg. At some point, possibly when Hospice took over, the size of the pills was increased to 20 mg., so

Ann for a few days had been taking 40 mg. of oxycontin three times a day. It was my fault because I had simply repeated the instructions from her original list and hadn't checked the content of the pills in the new bottle. I'm hoping now the extra morphine explains her slowness. So far, I've confessed my mistake to Ann. I'll have to let Janet know, too, I suppose.

I offered to fix Ann lunch after Janet left, but she didn't want me to help her. I guess she was feeling a need to be independent; this has been a struggle all week.

I think it was at this point I went upstairs and cried hard again, sobbing. Ann phoned to ask where certain pills were, as if I'd taken them from her. But then she found she had them. I went downstairs to make sure. What was I feeling as I cried? The grief of not being with Ann in spirit, not having her trust me to take care of things in a reasonable fashion and for her benefit, the frustration of having to explain the simplest things as if to a four year old to someone whose mind had always been as quick as mine, the horror of knowing that time was slipping away in frustration and irritation.

That evening just as she was getting into her bed, Ann became irritated again at some simple thing – some very irrelevant thing, because I can't even remember it now – and I objected. She wanted to rehearse her problems of the day with me then, and I became upset again. This quieted her, and finally I said what I'd been feeling: I hated to use up our time with irritability; I know that she feels desperate, but her irritability makes me feel desperate too. I said we're like people on a life raft, fighting over nothing instead of making use of the calm time we might have. I said I didn't want to spend time discussing the day; I wanted our time to be quiet and peaceful. She agreed – with a few tears herself. I told her about the latest Proust, and we then said goodnight.

Noelle called this day, telling me that Ellen has been notified Ann has less than a few months to live. Ellen wants to see Ann, partly because, and I love Ellen for this: it is so typical of her age, that is, it's because she didn't get to sit next to Ann at my birthday party.

February 20, 2003, Thursday

Except for my back getting worse, probably because of the work at the computer all morning, we had a decent evening. We enjoyed a stew, read and commented on the papers, and at bedtime we were laughing as we imagined Lyndon Johnson's take on people like Bill Clinton. I went upstairs amused by what we'd imagined Eleanor Roosevelt might have thought about Hillary.

This morning Ann told me she had a very difficult time in the night, wheezing and unable to stop. She took her medications shortly after midnight and again at six. I suggested we might consider whether I should come downstairs to sleep in the guest room across the hall from her. She seemed amenable. We'll think about it.

February 21, 2003, Friday

Last night I dreamt we were sliding down a mountain;

the vision came with nightmare emotions. I felt at first waking it was a reversal of the imagery I've been using to keep Ann aware that I'm helping her and she's got to let me help – the climb up a long, long hill, she with her leg broken and becoming more and more helpless.

In a way, though, yesterday was better than the preceding days. After using the nebulizer late in the morning, she made herself a big lunch of olive bread and melted cheese, then, when I returned with Diane from buying groceries for the week, she offered her a glass of wine.

The conversation with Diane was good: imaginative, funny, interesting and responsive. Ann searched for few words, made comments about "metaphorically speaking," and described, in answer to Diane's question about Catholicism and the sacraments, not only a book comparing sacraments to chakras (I think) but also a form of retreat used by the Jesuits and those following the rule of St. Ignatius. We talked of Annie and Ian, of Rigoletto, and music teaching. Afterwards, though, she began to feel queasy, and about 6:30 took herself to bed. As I tried to be helpful, she was troubled when I made mistakes bringing her what she needed or wanted/ didn't need or didn't want. I asked, did you want a professional nurse? I meant this sincerely, asking if my mistakes were so upsetting that she couldn't bear it. But, once settled down, she read to me from the book by Eamon Duffy about the ancient village of Morebath and made ironic comments about archivists.

This morning she woke up a second time around 10:30, called me for breakfast and her breakfast pills; she hadn't remembered she'd already awakened and taken oxycontin and Atavin. After I took care of her needs, we discussed the methods of keeping track of pills. She believes her written method to be the best. It went to pieces only when she began having too much oxycontin, she believes. We agreed to go back to the written method. We agreed she was to tell Janet she wants to control her doses with mental acuity in mind.

Everything improved as the day continued. Janet arrived at 1 o'clock. We talked over the drug problem, worked it out with her. Janet noticed the difference in Ann, and commented to me on her way out the door, "I'm sure glad we found out about the drugs."

Ann was able to express herself about preferring mental sharpness to comfort. "What I want is to find a balance between the comfort of mind and the comfort of body," she said. She made a couple of slips – thought her jacket was Janet's and confused people when talking about a friendship, but otherwise was all right. In the afternoon, she spent almost an hour talking with a neighbor, who'd brought custards over, and after that she sent several emails out. She wasn't satisfied with that effort, and she was quite tired by the time dinner was over. But she knew who she was and wasn't frustrated by being unable to think through her needs.

I would love feeling confident about using the old method of recording every pill taken. There's too much strife around these pills . . . or am I trying to go back to an earlier time. I notice how the times I want to go back to are just a week ago, just two weeks ago – I think of people on difficult journeys, who having met another obstacle, the one they're struggling with, think of a preceding obstacle, maybe even one more difficult, as the one they'd really like to be encountering.

I went to bed comfortable and pleased, almost believing we'd been able to step back a few weeks, back to sensibility and sense.

February 22, 2003, Saturday

I've been trying to record what's going on around us, but Bush and Cheney's march to war adds to the darkness of Ann's approaching death, and it's hard to find any light at all. Narrow is the word I think of. I can see the outer world only through a narrow slit, and what's there is grey. The world here, inside, if it goes as well as it did a month ago, is bright. Focused light? Focused attention?

I still haven't had the courage to ask Ann to work out an obituary for Stanford and for Los Angeles. I still haven't found the time to work through the way the extra oxygen tank works.

But we're just starting a new day peacefully. This morning, Ann was awake and sensible at seven when I came downstairs to be with her. Her eyes were clear and alert as she checked with me what pills she was supposed to take. I told her, provided water, and she took them, sitting on the edge of her bed in her green pajamas, hair just right at the sides of her face. Then she wrote down what she'd taken and the time she took them. I stayed with her a while, until she was breathing easily, then I went upstairs to breakfast, checked Harvey, returned, talked to Noelle (who is in town with Ellen) about the plans for the day. Shortly after nine, Ann got up. I fixed her breakfast, she walked out to the living room – was quite winded, wheezing – she took more pills, an extra Atavin I think, and I helped her take the nebulizer after she'd eaten.

February 24, 2003, Monday

I try not to think of days as last days, for that emphasizes the weight of their never-ending-ness. Yet I must, because otherwise I might not let myself flow with love as I try to bring peace to Ann. Last night Ann lying in bed couldn't seem to catch her breath for several minutes. She tried Combivent, then lay down, and as her evening medications took effect, the breathing slowed. All the time she lay, panting, I worried, unable to do more than attempt to send calming telepathic messages. What I hope are telepathic messages. (Right now I'm wondering if those messages, if established could communicate with Ann after her body loses life . . .) Then as she was more able to breathe, I told her how proud she should be at having brought light into so many people's lives. Copper, I said, once in a poem. A copper light . . . she smiled, and that made me feel comfortable enough to go to bed.

Saturday had been pleasant. Ann wore herself out, though, first, finding a small book of songs composed by a Californio, songs her mother once played, to present to Ellen. She'd hoped to find another set of sheet music, one published by Lummis, but couldn't. This little booklet she put in an envelope, decorated it with a picture from her collection of California impressionist prints, and wrote a note, explaining the booklet. Ellen played both her oboe and her piano when she came

– the oboe gave her trouble because the reed was new and not broken in – she couldn't hit the high notes. But she carried it off with some aplomb. Conversation was pleasant and general, and Ann enjoyed her old self.

February 26, 2003, Wednesday

Keeping this journal is a joyless act, I'm thinking. Also, I'm not attending to the details of the historical period. Its effects upon me now are so remote – though remote like the distant sound of thunder rather than remote like the flight of a hawk over Bishop's peak – that they provide a general background of mild foreboding and helplessness, nothing that can be noticed sensibly day to day except to note the march to war and that Congress is doing nothing about the plight of the community of US citizens.

February 27, 2003, Thursday

Ann rose late again, and this time dressed: to be civilized, she says. It occurred to me she might be expecting visitors, especially when, out in the living room, she noticed that she had a black jacket and blue sweats on and would have gone back to her room to change if I hadn't gone for the blue sweat jacket. The day brought no visitors, though, and I began to wonder about the failure of her closest cousins, both of whom have tried, but who haven't been successful in finding the right day, to make plans to come see her. I think she expects them. A week ago, when I said something about a neighbor tiring her out, she complained that no one was coming to see her, that she was alone. I myself have been proud of my old-fashioned daughters, who make efforts to come great distances with their children to visit. They obviously feel it's the thing to do. But why? Do you inherit it by growing up in small town San Luis?

The move from bedroom to living room had cost her oxygen; she reached for air several minutes. "I don't feel well," she said. Her abdomen and the muscles in its lower part bothered her, I'm not sure how, but I didn't want to force her to answer. After lunch I lay down on the sofa next to her, just to be spending time with her. Sometimes her long morning naps and my time at the computer keep us from seeing each other, and I fear I'll regret not being with her in days when I don't have to be isolated.

We'd decided earlier to postpone seeing the Hospice social worker because Ann's energy didn't need any more demands made upon it. So I called Susan and expressed that sentiment on her voice mail. Around four-thirty, Ann wanted to take a shower and wash her hair. I'll help, I insisted.

So we went back to the bedroom, a big undertaking these days. When was it that it was an easy walk for Ann? I can't remember? Not a month ago, I guess. She's out of breath taking her robe and slippers and pajamas off. Her body is small and white and thin. It looks to me as if she's losing weight. Her back, no longer squared, has a hump. She bends over as if carrying the cancer. She kept the oxygen going in the shower, even while she sprayed herself over the top. I scrubbed her back at the last, trying to get the itchy skin off. I asked if she wanted oil rubbed on her, but she said no. She was so breathless I worried about her falling. I offered to bring a chair into the bathroom, but she shook her head no. Then, while she dried herself, she described what kind of rub down the tiles and the chrome in the shower and the glass door needed so I could do it properly. It's a big job, and I'm afraid the last time she took a shower she exhausted herself.

At bedtime she fussed because I've spent so much time, all day, doing things for her.

"No," I said, "I'm doing them for us. We're in this together."

February 28, 2003, Friday

This morning as I took my vitamins and pills I noticed how comfortable – that is, unworried, calm, reflective – I was. Any small act that is part of a composed routine becomes these days a refuge. I remembered the "awareness" meditations, where you simply think about your thoughts, noticing and possibly classifying them, and considered whether the routine of it, the constancy of it, achieves for us presence and the quiet of presence.

March 1, 2003, Saturday

Yesterday's difficulties begin when Dr. Doyle phoned just when I was having a technician replace my monitor. I told him Ann is gasping and wheezing a lot; but she's better than she'd been when taking too much oxycontin a couple of weeks ago. "Would you like to talk to Ann, if she's awake?" I moved into her room with the phone.

She took the phone with alacrity, her eyes sparkling. I listened to the sound of her voice rather than to what she was saying, which wasn't much: phrases like "not bad" and "all right" and "Oxycontin? Increase it?"

They said goodbye, and Ann, who had, I thought, laughed her social chuckle, began to cry immediately. She cried off and on for several minutes, I holding her hand, then, when she was sitting up, putting her head on my chest and patting her back. She wished he hadn't called, believing it was a goodbye call. Why did he ask her if she was reading and advise her to take more oxycontin. I told her he's fond of her. "You'll probably hear from him again and you can go see him any time you want."

That evening bedtime was near eleven, and Ann was unhappy. She doesn't want me to have to do everything. "You wear yourself out," she said.

"I'm happy doing it," I responded. "Let's just be calm, let's be at peace."

"How can I be at peace when I gasp for breath just brushing my teeth?"

Earlier in the day she'd expressed the thought she couldn't bear to be the way she was for another three months. I tried to tell her to focus on important things, not on having to get up to brush her teeth. I could bring her the stuff so she wouldn't have to get up.

"That would make a big mess."

I then began to talk about how I've been feeling Claire Sullivan, [a dear friend, a nun who had died two or three years before] with us, and maybe, just maybe that calmed her down. She did mention, though, before I left, that she'd told her Aunt Marge, who'd called last evening, that no, it wasn't laryngitis Marge was hearing, but the cancer. Marge immediately shifted the topic to her daughter-in-law. Ann was worried about her.

March 2, 2003, Sunday

At bed time Ann felt awful. I plied her with Atavin, oxycodone. She calmed down, and I climbed the stairs to bed. By this time it was almost eleven. Then, at one o'clock or more, I heard the phone. I picked it up. No sound. Heart pounding I raced downstairs, and Ann said, "Be careful now. The light went on outside about twenty minutes ago, and since then I've heard this pounding as if someone was banging a rock against a rock." I turned the lights on beside her porch, I turned lights on all down the halls, in the living room, looked outside into the yard. "No one," I said.

"But I still hear the sound. There, hear it?"

It turned out to be the oxygen compressor which gives a little throb every once in a while. We'd identified that sound earlier in the day.

March 4, 2003, Tuesday

Every morning I wake with fear of the day. Questions: will I be up to it? Will I be able to manage the detailed work that makes the work seem endless – though it's not – it's really quite easy and usually takes up no more than two hours, if they were all jammed together. It's the thought of having to keep the details in mind that make it seem endless, because they take up most of my consciousness, leaving only a few calm moments for reflection. I do have a sense of comfort here and there in the day, connected with my computer, with my bed, with the drink in the evening: these are times of routine, of pretending to myself all is well and all shall be well. But I don't meditate myself out of anxiety; I distract myself with reading or games or composition.

Monday morning, Monday afternoon, Monday evening were all three totally distracting, but not comfortable, because the distractions have to do with the detail. The routine for Ann is the same. She took early morning pills before I went for my visit to Harvey and my walk with Jean. Then around nine I brought her breakfast. I also promised to write those of her bills that require attention as I write mine. At three I set out for her tax accountant's with papers. I arrived back at Harvey's around 3:30. He was washing dishes and turned to tell me Ann had called. I ran back to the car, terrified that Ann had fallen – and worried that she simply wanted to know what pill to take or what to do about a symptom. In a way, this worry was more troublesome than fear that she'd hurt herself, for it would mark the loss of the Ann I knew, her disappearance into the illness. I was going to say passivity, but it's not really that nor is it dependence. Anyway, the fear took over as I drove up the hill. When I arrived, though, Ann was in good shape, having just received a call from her cousin Carmelita to announce that she's coming. Small, bent over, as she sat on the couch, Carmelita appeared agile and competent. Ann was her strong, outgoing self, and remained so, since Carmelita left within a reasonable time and had brought conversation to Ann.

During the evening Ann listened to music, and though I settled myself to listen, I fell asleep.

This morning she seemed dopey, still lost in a hard night. She took her pills, but didn't want to be conscious. She refused the Hospice health aide, who was to have bathed her this afternoon. She wanted to refuse Janet too, but I couldn't let that happen. Tomorrow won't do, and neither will Thursday.

This afternoon when Ann asked me to turn the heater on, because she intended to take a shower, I did so mentioning that she could have had the Hospice aide come, that it would have been easier on me. At her request I did nothing but wait and watch while she showered, acting only to dry off the stall, to empty the bowl in which she soaked her feet, to dry her off. While she got dressed, I moved back and forth, putting things out in the living room, in the laundry room, filling bottles of water. I came back after my last foray to find her lying on her bed, one shoe on, one off, in distress. I wish she hadn't insisted on doing all this showering by herself, but I believe she did because I made the remark I made about the Hospice aide. (I feel guilty) She wanted to show me as well as herself that she's capable.

I can't help but admire the fortitude that goes on with soaking feet that may not need soaking in a month or two. This makes me weep internally to write it.

March 5, 2003, Wednesday

When I woke this morning, I felt tense – as usual. This time I grabbed Beth's predicament to worry about: Chris is being transferred to Washington D.C. and that means she will be leaving California. I fretted until I realize I'm displacing my worry: Ann is weakening obviously and quickly. She needs my help, either brain or legs and hands, almost continuously. I don't know how much longer I'm going to have her. As soon as I feel the familiar falling sensation, the knowledge of irretrievable loss, I turn to thinking how to set up the days and nights for our comfort. For new routines to hold back the days, to find peace in them.

I have given up hoping she's going to be able to write her own obituary. I've started one and hope to talk over the empty spaces of it with her.

March 6, 2003, Thursday

The morning began tearfully. Ann woke, desperately uncomfortable, breathing heavily, wheezing, when I tiptoed into her room to see how the night went. I gave her oxycontin and Atavin, noticing she hasn't taken more than one of the medications I'd laid out for her last night. I took her hand; it was warm, and I wondered about fever.

I'm deeply worried that she's so uncomfortable now; how uncomfortable will she be when she dies?

Is she already starting to leave me – in the worst way – like last night at bed time, when she began to get her shoes polished and ready for the next day? I thought, but why shoes, she doesn't have to wear shoes, she's not going anywhere tomorrow. Is it a matter of pride? I had to tell her that I was tired, achingly so, that I'm not tired in the morning, when we can deal with the shoes. She agreed, then moved on to get herself ready for bed. After she brushed her teeth and put her eye medicine in – on my reminder – she sat on the side of her bed to use the nebulizer and the inhaler. Then I directed her attention to the bottle caps where I'd put pills she might need to take during the night and the notes I'd written for her. She couldn't read what I'd written nor understand the instructions. I had to go over them several times. Finally I went out to the kitchen, found masking tape, and brought it back to her room. I put a piece of tape reading oxycodone and one saying Ativan on the table and put the bottle caps holding the pills on it. Hoping she'd remember this in the night, I lay down beside her on top of the covers and talked about peace and love and harmony.

Frankly, I'd been startled at the change in mental acuity from earlier in the day. Just before bed we'd been listening to a Ferrier recording, and she had been keenly checking the production dates and discussing the singers. How could her mind have slipped away in the period between the living room and the bedroom? This morning, remembering that last night she'd taken pain medication before we left the living room, I compared it with the effect of oxycodone on her when Janet came last Tuesday: it had combined with lack of oxygen to bring her down. So after she was up and breathing well, reading the paper, remembering recipes for me, I described, perhaps more for myself than for her, what I'd noticed. "Let's both keep in mind you have about forty minutes of blurriness after taking oxycodone, but after that it usually passes."

Afterwards we spoke about our wishes the national and state news were more encouraging. What is encouraging is the number of people worldwide protesting the American war. What is awful is the number of people in the US who thrill at the thought of it. Including our president and probably the Supreme Court who handed him the election.

March 7, 2003, Friday

Yesterday Janet urged more help from Hospice. We should have someone in to bathe Ann three times a week. She herself will come twice a week. We should have a wheelchair and a walker, options Ann can use, if she needs them. I seconded the idea of options. Ann agreed, if only to help her get out of her bedroom in the morning. Then Janet went down the hall to the bedroom to look at the place where the equipment could be placed, and I followed her. Privately, she expressed concern that Ann may do something rash in a confused state. She was also worried about her falling out of bed. Perhaps I might want to be closer at night – come downstairs to the guest room, for example. She promised to have the social worker call me and perhaps come see me next week.

Diane arrived to help with the grocery shopping and we left the house immediately after Janet left, in spite of my feeling intensely that I shouldn't leave Ann alone. I couldn't help rushing about the store holding tears back, biting my lips. I'm not sure what upsets me more, the realization that Janet believes Ann's mind is not going to get better, or my sense that it's going to continue to move back and forth from clarity to blurriness. She's even been blurring what she hears; I noticed that today (Friday)when I named the people coming, Wendy and Kathy, and she heard Dave and Joan.

Back at home, the groceries unloaded, tears in the kitchen for a minute with Diane giving me a hug, I felt terribly sad and terribly inadequate. Ann was trying to get me to clear up every evidence of medical supplies in the living room; it offended her, and I suppose it should, but I wanted to postpone the task. It frustrated me that I couldn't postpone without upsetting her, and I was frightened too that as time goes on I'm going to have to keep upsetting her.

When they heard how troubled I was, my daughters wanted to help. Beth and Claire were each ready to come down this weekend. Noelle wondered when Harvey would come to visit. To Susan, the Hospice social worker, who called, I said, "I need to know what to expect as Ann's health declines so that I can plan, especially to see if I can get some help from my daughters."

"Oh," she answered, "It's nice to know your daughters will help out."

"Not with Ann," I explained, "but with their father." And I tried to outline the situation for her.

All evening I was troubled about having tried to explain to Susan. I understand that I want the community to understand what my situation is, yet object to having to explain it, or worse, don't believe they can understand, because it's not usual. They'll interpret according to what is usual, not what is factual and unusual.

Another part of the trouble I experience is feeling the community pressure coming down from Janet. I have to see her as someone who worries too much, who has experienced horror and harshness from circumstances and from people; I must not let that kind of worrier determine all my actions. I will leave Ann in the morning, I determined, for the 45 minutes it takes to see Harvey and check on Jean. Ann is asleep then. She won't fall out of bed.

(So much is happening I'm unhappy with this journal: no time to reflect, and maybe long ago I should have made it a reflective journal. I don't know whether it's going to help me understand this experience later.)

March 8, 2003, Saturday

Just now – at 9:40 a.m. – my eyes filled, and as usual, I pushed the grief away. This time, thinking of what Jean said this morning when I spoke of Ann's confusion: heartbreaking. I remembered Ann crying when she wouldn't work easily at her computer anymore – "They didn't prepare me for this." My heart broke then and broke again and again. How many times can the center of yourself fill with anguish? Then I open up this journal and see – moments of grace.

Yesterday afternoon went much better than the morning. By the time Kathy, the bath aid arrived, Ann was all right, knew I was going to the bank and why. She had even corrected the way I filled out the duplicate deposit slip, and when I returned, she was feeling good after the bath and massage, and tired but clear. The rest of the evening passed easily, for she was able to read and to enjoy what she was reading.

In the long run, I think having an aide come in Thursdays for four hours in the middle of the day would help. But I need to find out from the volunteer if she is willing to come – and from Ann if she's willing to be with the volunteer.

That's what I'll work on for a beginning. Then, after I find out from Susan what to expect, maybe I can plan more carefully.

If the volunteer calls today, I'll have to think through with Ann what she's willing to have happen. This Thursday? Or help in getting to the doctor's office on Friday?

Meanwhile, I think I need to compose a letter to Clare and Addie.

Definitely – I also have to ask Ann if she's willing to see if we can hire someone in here on Thursday, for starters.

March 9, 2003, Sunday

Here's the letter I sent out to her cousins and to members of the small group of Sjogren's syndrome friends:

I thought I'd better write to tell you all how Ann is getting along, since she's been having trouble using her computer and therefore hasn't sent any of the reports she was so good at writing last year. I don't believe she's sent email for over two weeks, and I don't think she's read any of her email in the last few days, not since her breathing difficulties increased last Monday.

I'm not sure whether she told you that she started with Hospice in late January, having decided with her doctor that nothing else could be done to stop the cancer. At first a nurse/case manager (Janet, an oncology nurse specialist who was formerly with Ann's doctor) was coming in once a week to check on her. These house calls take about an hour and are as comprehensive as a doctor's visit, for the nurse probes for and considers symptoms and then tinkers with the varieties and the amounts of medication that will help Ann remain comfortable.

This last week Hospice began to increase the number of visits Ann has from Janet. We had three visits last week and a call this morning (Saturday) to see how things are going. But since Ann's breathing has improved slightly with a new medication for the nebulizer she uses and because of an increase in the prednisone she takes, maybe the visits will drop back to two per week. The new medication for the nebulizer is lasix, used twice a day, and it has loosened up some stuff that Ann has been able to cough up.

I'm not sure whether you all know this, but since last fall Ann has been using an oxygen compressor, which delivers extra oxygen through tubing long enough to let her get around the house. At first she used it only at night and at a delivery rate of "2." Now she must use it all day and all night and the delivery rate is between "3" and "4." Although she could take a portable delivery system with her, she hasn't wanted to leave the house for almost a month. Next week we expect a visit from

Hospice's respiratory therapist, who will see whether Ann might do better on liquid oxygen. I hope this therapist comes. She's a very busy person, apparently. She's been requested by our Janet, but has sent her instructions rather than herself for at least three weeks.

Meanwhile, Janet has decided that since Ann's increasing weakness may cause her to fall in the shower, she is sending in a "bath aide" three times a week. Yesterday the bath aide also provided a much-appreciated massage and shampoo.

We are getting along quite well on a day to day basis, though changes are coming upon us more quickly than we've been ready for them. Ann rouses at seven or eight just enough to take her very early morning meds. Then she sleeps until nine or ten, when I bring her breakfast and the next round of pills. At this time she regularly chooses to go out to the living room because she's due for a nebulizer treatment, which she prefers to take sitting in her chair. Then she reads the paper and dozes until about two – time for lunch and more pills – and reads and dozes until four or so, when she is usually more alert. All this happens on the days when we have neither a nurse nor a bath aide functioning. When they come, she exerts herself – or, in the case of the bath and massage is exerted – and becomes exhausted.

Hospice does help with the changes in Ann's condition, coming to the rescue quite readily, as a matter of fact. We feel sometimes as if we were a platoon on the front lines, needing a bit of help to carry on, and when we call for the help, a whole army (Hospice) descends upon us, with volunteers and substitute caregivers and equipment that threatens an ominous future (a wheelchair, e.g.) Next week the Hospice social worker is going to discuss with me what kinds of changes to expect.

When I know more, if I know more, I'll write again. In the meantime, Ann is peaceful, but in her own special way, of course, and as usual full of love. She's not in much pain, but the difficulty breathing does make her uncomfortable, and she's not particularly happy about her loss of motor skills and some language skills when she has to take extra morphine to make the breathing go more smoothly. Her reduced oxygen and the consequent lack of energy make it difficult for her to chat on the phone or to have an easy visit with people she loves, and sometimes she begins to cry – not for herself, she says, but for the feelings of the people she's talking with. All this last week we've been listening to music after dinner – a little Bach, a little Handel, and last night Lucia Popp singing Dvorak, Brahms, Mahler. We keep assuring each other that we're managing this very difficult journey together, and I think that so far, we have managed quite well.

I know that when she sent out word about giving up on finding any more effective treatments of the cancer that she asked you to use discretion about whom you told. She tells me this request still stands. I think she feels especially protective of your mother, Clare.

And – I've shared this letter with Ann before sending it, so you'll know this is what she wants me to say. As a matter of fact, as usual, she edited it!

One of the suggestions she made that I haven't incorporated yet is this: that if you call, using either my number in Ann's house or Ann's number, that you understand that sometimes we have to let the message be recorded and that sometimes it's hard to find the time to call right back.

Another suggestion: Ann doesn't check her email very often these days, but I check mine. If you want to write Ann an email and be sure she gets it, send it to me. I can print it and give it to her. I don't belong to any lists and get very few messages a day, so it would be no problem for me.

March 10, 2003, Monday

A resolution, if temporary today, of many of my questions. I'm still busy, but more at peace, partly because Ann is more herself than she's been for several days. On Sunday, almost at the same time I began to receive answers to my email, she went into her office and began to work at her computer. At first I thought she was just reading or editing and getting rid of old mail, but when I checked my computer before dinner I found copies of notes from Susan C and others in her small email group. She'd been writing to at least one of them. It pleased me and helped me relax last night, convinced that for the time being Ann will be all right.

What is all right? Able to understand what she's saying and what I'm saying, able to understand – what? I'm thinking here of the occasional desperate struggles last week when she asked me, "What can I take to make it easier to breathe?" She was checking to see if she'd already taken all that was possible. So I guess it's not whether she understands, it's whether she's struggling for remembering what she believed she should know.

Janet was pleased that Ann seemed to be doing well. I too am pleased Ann seemed so well, but I wish she weren't so weak. As Janet filled the tubes for me for the lasix nebulizer medicine, she looked up. "You're doing very well, too." We went over the week's schedule – the volunteer, the call from the social worker, the bath aides.

The volunteer turned out to be a pleasant woman, about our age, easy conversationalist, easy with people. She made herself known to me subtly, and I, not so subtle, told her all I could about Ann's and my co-authorship, Ann's developing Sjogren's Syndrome, my writing, my journaling – though not what's in it. She'll come on Thursday, so Diane and I can grab lunch and shop for groceries. She introduced herself to Ann by commenting on her works of art and her antiques. They compared hometowns: Glendale, Pasadena.

Meanwhile, the federal administration marches us to war.

Ellen and Noelle have been subjected to a first class nasty demonstration by Operation Rescue at the Unitarian Services on Sunday, frightening Ellen.

I phoned Ellen this evening to suggest she ask her mother about her experience with the "Abalone Alliance" and non-violent protests in order to help her through the Operation Rescue memories. Noelle said Ellen came away from hearing the shouting and screaming fearful of protests in general. "Our teachers,"

Ellen told me, "said they would protect us and they showed us how to get out if the people tried to blockade us."

I hope Ellen writes this down, now, so she can remember exactly what happened. I hope this isn't her last experience with protest.

Then Noelle told me on the phone Monday noon, Ellen also learned on Operation Rescue day that she hadn't made the basketball team at school. She took it easily at first, then began to cry. Noelle found her in her room crying and taking down all her sports trophies, replacing them with pictures of horses. She wants a horse. She and the horse will be a team. When I described this day to Ann, she burst into tears for Ellen: "Poor, poor baby," she said. I thought of Ann's childhood and her inability to succeed as an athlete. But maybe I'm wrong. Maybe it's because she did succeed in getting on teams at the small school she attended that she knows what a loss this has been for Ellen.

March 11, 2003, Tuesday

I worked hard all morning, part of it counting pills out, part paying bills, part running back and forth with nebulizer and breakfast and arranging to cancel Ann's appointment with Dr. Borda. I was just about to open the door to a kindly, quiet and efficient neighbor, who was going to stay with Ann for two hours, when the phone rang. It was the respiratory nurse informing me she was coming right then. "I'm not going to be here," I said.

"Well, this is the only time I can come."
"I'll be back at two. "
"I can see Ann without your being there. "

I explained that I have to take notes. Then she wanted to know if I was family. I said no, I had power of attorney for health care and have had it for many years.

"Well, like family I guess," she says.

This introduction stiffened me. And Ann said she treated our neighbor like a servant. She came and left while I was gone, leaving a new set of instructions, which she had promised to call and explain to me this afternoon. Or tomorrow. All right, I thought – except Ann was a bit upset about it. Especially when I talked over the directions our neighbor had written down. Because she didn't know the treatments Ann was getting, her notes were hard to figure out. Except – nebulizer 6 times a day. Before breakfast, lunch, dinner, and bed. And lasix in the morning and at five o'clock.

March 12, 2003, Wednesday

Peace at last, Tuesday evening. For me, not Ann, who felt short of breath, generally weak and not well and this morning woke up at 6 wheezing. We were able to listen to music after dinner last night, Dowland's lute music. Both of us were tired and we went to bed early, Ann allowing me to push her down to the bedroom in the Hospice wheelchair. I persuaded her by suggesting she might be less air hungry. At first we tried it with the tube, but then we decided it would be faster and more effective if I take the tube down first, then Ann. Ann took oxycodone as well as Ativan and oxycontin before she slept. We smiled about Tennyson's "Lotus Eaters," and I promised to read it to her one of these days.

I slept through Ann's risings from bed, until around 2:30, and, anticipating her turning the light on, I dozed, tense, in and out, until five, when I decided I'd be able to sleep until 7 – and then Ann needed me at 6. The nebulizer and meds appeared to help.

March 15, 2003, Saturday

Yesterday I saw the volunteer outside in her car, and I waited in the chair for her to decide it's time to come in. She wore a green sweater about the same color as Ann's duvet cover, an orange and black knit scarf tied around her neck. Smiles. I showed her the list, the phone, our signal system. Ann was awake when I brought her back. I left, knowing I had just enough time to get the errands done. First the banks. Then mail the letter, then the drug store and the grocery store. It was after two when I was standing in line at the grocery store and I felt frightened and tired and frightened of being tired. Thirsty, I'm terribly thirsty. I worry about fainting. I worry about how tired I am. I tried to slow down, but slowing down isn't the answer – except for my arthritis. In the car I took meditative breaths. Finished my errands, home by three. The volunteer had been happily reading in the living room. Ann hadn't stirred. I chatted with the volunteer – discovered she went to Immaculate Heart in LA and that her sister had been in the order, left, left Catholicism, and became head of a famous international language school in downtown LA – on Sunset. Finally, she departed. I spent a few minutes with Ann, then the social worker arrived.

Her face reminds me of those in Italian Renaissance paintings. She's about 50, I'd say. Quiet, but not calm. A sense of restraint. She didn't begin the conversation, waiting for me instead. I need to know what to expect, I said, and later I confessed to being tired. To making blunders. What kind of blunders? I remembered one, easily corrected, mixing up the distilled and drinking water. We talked about my seeking paid help. She believed I'd need it at some time. I told her I want to do things right for Ann, find moments of peace with her, giving as an example my reading of "The Lotus Eaters" with its murmurous, soothing sounds last night. Eventually, after half an hour, she began to describe what is likely to happen, and fairly soon. Growing weakness, inability to leave the bed, gradual withdrawal of interest in everyone, incontinence, and at the end, great agitation before a final quiescent state, whether coma or not. The drugs Hospice provides don't necessarily work right away on the agitation, she said, sometimes it lasted twenty four hours or more. When it's over, the coma begins, as parts of the body go. She thought the coma gave the brain time to work through unresolved problems from the person's life. I didn't quite know what she meant by that, and asked "How does anyone know that?"

Her answer: "This is a surmise. There's no factual evidence, meaning I guess no brain scan that can tell us."

I said: "This is hard to absorb. I'll probably forget some of it," thinking she might have a book to give me. No book.

The possibility of agitation scared me. The next morning I mentioned it to Jean who told me that when her son died, he was so agitated it took three people to hold him down. Then he became quiet.

I'm frightened. I've never thought of anything like this happening to my Ann. I'm not just frightened of the event, that I won't be able to handle it, that it will happen when I'm by myself with Ann, that I won't be able to get help, that she will suffer horribly: I'm frightened of the future images of Ann in pain, screaming, angry. Thoughts of peace – projecting them – be damned.

March 16, 2003, Sunday

Back to Thursday. Too much is happening too fast.

The social worker stayed too long and I wanted her to go. When I finally got back to Ann in her bedroom, she was upset, staring at me with her eyes wide, wild-eyed. I'm beginning to think these are the times she's not quite herself. I told her I was talking to the social worker about what to expect.

"Well," Ann demanded, "what did she say?"

I described how she would become weaker, eventually not wanting to leave her bed. I noticed Ann's eyes opened wide, seeming more hazel than ever, presumably because of the narcotics she's taking. She knew I wasn't telling her everything because she kept asking me over and over again: "What else did she say?"

My answer: "She thought it would be a good idea for

me to have someone to help take care of you when it's hard to get out of bed."

Later, when Ann was up, I discussed hiring care. She appeared reluctant at first. The money. I argued that two months of it won't be as costly as our trip to Oregon was, and for which we still owe her account the money.

"But what about after the two months?" she asked. I looked at her, wondering what she's thinking. Does she imagine her condition will continue for longer than two months? It might, yes, but is she aware? For two or three weeks, I've tried to remember to pull back when I'm not sure about whether she's really with me. I assured her that we could go on for more time, especially if this will help me keep going. She remained reluctant.

"I'm letting you down," I said. I'm wondering if she wants it to be possible for me to do everything for her. Perhaps she imagined it so, as I have. Perhaps she sees herself as a burden, and that's hard as hell. I know the tightening in my stomach when I feel I'm burdening my children.

I couldn't bear the way she was staring off toward the kitchen, fearful I was going to see tears trickling down her face. We both had hoped I could be with her quietly to the end, and it doesn't seem as if that's at all possible any more unless I have help to take care of the details. I've been trying to imagine us on a trip, spending whole days together, just living. I've tried to share that concept with Ann, but she doesn't understand what I mean, probably because I've brought it up only when she's not quite all there. Or maybe not. Often in the evening and in the morning these days, she's been excruciatingly aware not only of what we're going through but of our being together in the most difficult experience of our lives. As for the trip, I should stow that.

I'm skipping all the difficulties of Friday here – Ann wasn't feeling well – but Saturday, with no Hospice calls, passed reasonably well. I even had some quiet time with Ann in her room, sitting on the green chair I'd brought up from my old home.

On the way to bed, after helping Ann through the bedtime rituals, we were able to give each other fifteen minutes of peaceful meditation. Still, I went upstairs troubled about the warning that Ann would become extremely agitated before dying, enough to try to read about it in one or another of the books we have. I finally turned off the light after twelve, then woke up, restless, half an hour later, then two hours later, and then at five for good.

Luckily, Harvey has gone north to be with Beth. He arranged his own transportation to the bus station, and I've asked him to arrange it back again to the house. He arranged the care of the canary–John, his neighbor.

And I have arranged to have help come in next week.

Today, Sunday:

Because Ann worried about theft when helpers from an agency come in, I asked Diane to stop off on her way back from church this morning to help me put Ann's jewelry – kept in her bedroom – away upstairs.

"If you'll give me lunch," answered Diane, and I promised to get her some lunch.

She arrived in her lavender suit. I'd already taken the jewelry out of the drawers and put it on the stairs.

"Is that all?" Diane asked, seeming a bit reluctant to go upstairs (Ann, by the way, was sleeping), but she went.

I'd chosen overhead cupboards to place it in. "I'll hand it to you, if you shove it way back," I told Diane. Again she seemed hesitant. I know now I'd forgotten her fear of heights, or, even if I had remembered it, I'm not sure I would have seen fear of climbing a step stool as fear of heights. But she climbed up and shoved the jewelry boxes way back into the cupboard.

"Now I'll get you lunch," I said.

She was going to go: "Honey, you don't have to do that for me. I should never have said what I said."

"No, it's all ready. Or almost ready." And then I began to cry, because I didn't want her to go off and leave me like that. She reached out and put her arms around me and I kept on crying.

March 17, 2003, Monday

Diane was supposed to be coming in to be with me when I asked Janet about the final processes, the ones the social worker had scared me about. But she hadn't arrived before I began asking Janet. Broaching the subject wasn't hard at all I found, with Janet replying sincerely and honestly, even gently, that what may happen is disorientation, hallucinations, falling when getting out of bed because not realizing where she is. "It might not happen. That's why I'm coming more often," she told me. She couldn't guarantee that anyone from Hospice will come to my aid, but she said I will get help over the phone.

March 18, 2003, Tuesday

Alone again, but so far it's a calm day. Ann has been tired, but clear-headed. Last night I kissed her hand goodnight, and she seemed troubled, saying, "You seem to be asking for a response from me."

"No, just want you to know I love you." I went upstairs then, considering how all day she'd been responding, to the agency help, to Janet, to me, and understanding how this had tired her, so that she asked to go to bed early, before 9 o'clock, though she hadn't been up long. I wondered whether she was entering the stage the social worker discussed with me, withdrawing from life.

But earlier she'd read the paper, commenting on it. Listened to my comments. She wanted to talk about the war and Bush's aggression, about Spain as an ally. Britain's foolishness in following us. The end of the Labour Party.

At this moment of writing I think how I've been putting off getting information for her obit, having her tell me how it should be phrased for the *Los Angeles Times*, for the Stanford magazine and Cap and Gown. Maybe today, I tell myself every day, and will maybe tell myself every day, until there are no more days. I know the day will come when all of this will be over, but I can't imagine it.

Each month of this ordeal was at first a separate country; now it's every week; soon it might be every day.

This morning I took her hand, said "I love you and you don't have to respond." Her eyes turned green with tears. Her hand was warm as it grasped mine. "Just let me love you," I said.

"And I love you."

"But you don't have to say it," I reminded her.

Then on to the practical matter of the nebulizer and pills and capsules and inhalers. I sat in the green chair for a time, watching her with the long pipe nebulizer, breathing in, out, listening to the steady hum of two machines – the compressor and the nebulizer drowning out everything. I thought of the green in the duvet cover, how the shade is just like the shade our eyes get when we cry.

This morning I arranged for an agency woman to come in Thursdays, Friday afternoons, Saturdays and Mondays until the end of March.

March 19, 2003, Wednesday

Late this afternoon, before I wheeled Ann out to the living room for the evening, she wanted to review the day when she called in Hospice at Dr. Borda's suggestion. Since then she's felt as if she's no longer at home, perhaps in a hotel. We talked about her bedroom at night, and during the afternoon. "Is it all the people coming in," I asked. "Like hotel cleaning women?"

Then last night we returned to the old days, talking before dinner over drinks, then not so much during dinner, for I would rather we listen to music and Ann focus on eating, not trying to absorb what I say and feeling or thinking about a response. Then we read after dinner, Ann sipping the last of her whiskey, I sipping wine, until it was time to go to bed. In between dinner and dishes, I set the snake-coil flashlight in the upstairs window, part of a vigil for the peace we're not going to have. We spoke of the vigil, of how Bush, Cheney and Rumsfeld are not only destroying the present peace, but all the work of the idealists of the twentieth century who wanted to substitute negotiation for conflict. Ann lectured me about my aching neck. I brought up my difficulty in finding the information for her obituary. I recited some of my favorite tags from my draft.

Once she was in bed, I read to her Spenser's "Prothalamion," each of us enjoying the rich melange of sound, the occasional glimpses of an earlier Thames, while ignoring the hints of corruption and favoritism in the Elizabethan court.

March 21, 2003, Friday

In the morning, yesterday, Thursday, Ann was awake when I came downstairs at about 7:30. She used the nebulizer, the Advair, took Prevacid, some Ativan. I fetched the papers and sat in the green chair after offering breakfast. When she'd finished the nebulizer I moved into a chair next to the bed and began looking through the papers at headlines about the war, feeling loathing and horror. My eye caught a picture of a mobile home burning. Los Osos, said the headline. I scanned down. Morro Shores – why that must be Diane's park, I told myself, and then my eye caught both her name and the word died. I read again. "Ann," I said "Ann – it's Diane, she's dead." She didn't understand instantly, so I handed her the paper and began to cry out loud, my head down on the bed.

As Ann held my hand, I let the knowledge come in waves, at first, maybe someone else, do they have a body? In a minute she was going to call me and say she was at a friend's house. Then, she was gone, and I was alone.

Then I began to theorize. It was the dog, she must have gone in to rescue the dog or the birds.

Then more tears, then recollection: her face yesterday outside the door, the long face, "Honey," her Southern voice, listening to me from across the table, week after week, blotting up my anxieties.

After the newly hired help arrived, I went to talk with Harvey, telling him about Diane. He began to cry a little, then held it back. After I left, he called Beth to tell her. Beth, crying so much she's almost incoherent, called Claire, who called me. Later, Noelle phoned, with promises of ideas for getting through this. I wondered myself, what effect this will have on me. How will I change? What wisps are going to pursue me, or am I going to pursue? Nothing now, in that other country without either Diane or Ann. I'm not going to be able to let Ann go.

At the end of the day, Claire came to be with me for the weekend.

March 22, 2003, Saturday

Last evening (Friday) Claire tried to help me fix the automated system for the porch light. It turned out, though, that all she could do was replace the burned out globe. Ann rose in her red pajamas, and shaky and bent, an old woman, hair straight, flying, fiddled with the timer. Click, click, click. I asked Claire to stand by in case she started to wobble because she's so weak. Claire glanced back at me, mouthed, "Don't you know how to fix it?"

Afterwards, because Ann seemed to enjoy Claire's company, we sat and talked, Claire with wine, Ann with scotch and water, I with water for most of the time. Claire spoke of the schools, the library, Annie's teacher, Annie's essay on dolphins. Ann for the most part listened, but two or three times chimed in to correct Claire's pronunciation or idioms. Claire smiled, made excuses: I wondered how this affected her. It's a change in Ann as far as Claire is concerned, but I recognized the old Ann, the Ann who ranged among her internet friends with rewritings and corrections, the critic her cousins remembered. I had arguments with this part of her personality early on, and had the power to win them, so Ann squelched it for me. But now it's coming forward. And I'm happy to think she's had this means of personal expression among her internet friends for years.

Later we listened to Brahms' Alto Rhapsody and following that some of his more light-hearted songs, staying up quite late.

I tried not to think of Diane. Save it for later.

March 23, 2003, Sunday

Yesterday, Saturday, Claire helped me gather copies of poems Diane had given me and passages of prose I'd saved on my computer and drove with me to deliver them to a close friend of hers in Los Osos, together with a note expressing my sorrow. Claire also spent time with Ann, helping her manicure her nails.

The day was so difficult for Ann she stayed in bed, except when the Hospice aide came to help her shower. She even ate dinner in bed, with me sitting in the green chair, tray on its stool. Then, in the night, at 2:30, I heard the buzzer, donned fuzzy robe and slippers, made sure I had my glasses, and came down to her. She was sitting on the side of the bed, breathing heavily. "I don't know who Maxwell is," she said. "Someone was asking for Maxwell over the intercom."

"The intercom isn't open for you to hear anything," I explained softly.

She disagreed and began to tell me how we have to be careful. "The boat must be in the North Sea, near those straits, you know the straits."

I didn't know the straits, but I nodded.

"They don't know I'm a Canadian."

"But you were born in Sacramento."

She shook her head, no.

"Your name is Ann F. You must be telling me about a dream."

"I don't know why they're calling me that," she said.

The discussion went on for ten minutes or more, while I tried to make her more comfortable with pillows and pills. She didn't know her name. She said she didn't know me. No matter how much I tried to tell her where we were, she refused to believe me. The Canadian boat story was the real one, and the Ann F one is the dream, she insisted. Still, she did know me well enough for me to take her hand, try to comfort her, when she said she was out of breath. But why was she out of breath, why did she feel the pain in her feet, the pain in her side? After a while, when the pills had begun to take effect, her breath slowed down, and she became more calm. I went upstairs to fetch a blanket and pillow and, sitting in the green chair, a little cold, a little uncomfortable, dozed off and on until 4:30, when I went back upstairs to bed.

Ann's loss of a common reality with me terrified me. Should I have called Hospice? I kept asking myself. Have we begun the final stage, when she's going to become agitated? Hospice and Diane had spoken of unresolved conflicts. Is Ann's sense of being a Canadian an unresolved conflict? Of course not. All during last night's long hours, I was conscious of pain for Ann – this is a constant now, I think – fear of more pain, of pain I won't be able to stop – a need to keep up my strength. There's also a terrible sense of my loss of Diane – yet rational thought tells me I wouldn't have phoned her or bothered her anyhow. I'm glad Claire is here this weekend: trust in someone I love, sense of reliability, someone I can talk with. It would have been the same with Noelle or Beth. We need our families at time of death, we need people close to us.

Last night was like a boat ride, and we were alone in our stateroom. I remember those lights I could see from the train that terrible night when I was sick and had a headache, the industrial area as the train makes its way along the bays, the delta, the river, toward Sacramento.

This morning, I've determined, I will phone Hospice if Ann isn't sure of who and where she is. When I came down just after 8 o'clock, "What's your name? I asked.

She answered Ann F and told me she remembered the night. "It was real, not a dream." She grinned at me.

"You didn't know me," I said.

"Yes I did," she disagreed.

"You didn't know your name."

"Yes, but it isn't real. Where I was was real."

Okay, if we want an alternate reality, let's have it.

March 24, 2003, Monday

Before dinner Sunday Ann was resting in her chair in the living room, green pajamas, blue robe, hair combed so that it falls gracefully down the side of her face, as if she wore it in a bun. (I often ponder how handsome she is in her illness, even as she loses weight and the area around her chin, beneath her mouth, wrinkles.) We'd spoken briefly about her Stanford friends, one of them having phoned during the day, causing Ann to feel she must respond. She'd spent some time with a piece of paper on which she'd written when she saw Dr. Borda, how long he'd told her she had, how many days she'd lived since, how many days left. I'd pointed out her math was wrong: 7x8 making 56, not 42, as she had written. It seemed the time, the first time it would not be so intrusive to bring out my obit, tell her I don't know exactly what her activities were at Stanford. She suggested I get an annual from one of her friends – 1951 – she didn't pick hers up. I read out to her some of what I've written, and she stopped me at the Mayfield teacher/graduate school/Lenkirt intersection, then made notes herself on a piece of paper, which I picked up and put into the book holding the obit draft – Proust's *Cities of the Plain*.

Dinner then, and listening to Janet Baker sing, and then Ann wanted to go to bed, before the CD was over. Settled, nebulizer done, pills taken, breath almost back, she held back tears, straining her head back against the pillow. I was chattering about keeping the light on in the hall so she'd know where she was when she wakes up, sharing the observation that the dreams don't bother her during the day, so it must be the dark and the strange surroundings that cause the fearful, strangely real ones. Then she asked, holding my hand, "Are you scared?"

"I'd be a damn fool not to be," I answered, wondering whether I was going to be able to handle what's coming, the shapes and forms of which are like strange shadows. After a while, I added, "I guess I'm afraid most of being alone. But I'm thinking: right now I'm afraid because I can't do anything or say anything to ease your pain or your fear of being afraid. Except, it occurs to me I can talk about fear of being afraid, ease that one. If you wake up afraid, or if something's happening that frightens you, buzz me, I'll be down and we'll face it together, I'll be with you. Even just call out, I can hear."

I don't know whether it's the Ativan that calmed her or my words, but soon she settled down. I went upstairs, slept restlessly until five, when she buzzed me. Slippers, robe, glasses, one foot, two foot down the stairs. She was out of bed and circling the room.

"Where are you going?"

"I want to see what hit me, something came down

and hit me on my head and shoulder." She bent down to look under the bed, with me looking too. Nothing there. I tried to explain the sensation by suggesting she threw up and then dropped the electric bed adjuster or flapped it up from where she'd been holding it across her lap. She crouched on the side of the bed. "If I'm hurt I can't get any jobs acting, and I won't have any money and what will I do?"

I settled her back into the bed, helped with meds, held her hand.

"Dreams," I said practically, describing one of mine, but she's not willing to let hers go. I asked her what her name was.

"In this life Ann F."

After a while, head down on the bed next to our held hands, I said, "Maybe you're right, like Navajo dreams, it's another reality, and maybe now a better one."

She thought about it. I got the nebulizer. When she'd finished and we were waiting for her breath to settle down, she said: "I got the word about lung cancer, terminal lung cancer, and I tried to cope the way Ann F always copes, but there's something else that hasn't been able to cope, maybe something I didn't expect."

Didn't expect? Neither of us expected this long breathless agony. No one told us about it. This is what she can't cope with, and I don't really know what to do to help, except to say I'll be with you. I don't say it right away though, I want her to think through and maybe get to where the deep fears are. Fear of suffocating in a strange dream, I should think, not going out easily ... finally I do say that Janet will help find ways to ease things. Or did I just think this? Not say it? Morning light began and I pulled the curtain so she could see the mist of the sprinklers on the garden.

Now I type and Ann sleeps, while I wait for this day to begin.

March 25, 2003, Tuesday

Yesterday morning (Monday) after the help arrived, I drove down to Benton Way to say good bye to Claire. Harvey was in the garden, cap on, unshaven. I felt remote, my internal crisis pulling in all my threads. After a few minutes, I asked Claire to drive me down to pick up the prepared income tax returns and on the way I described this sense of unreality. I seem to be making rituals of routine inside, but really there are no routines and the ghosts of Diane and Ann pursue me like furies. Yes, Ann's ghosts are here too: she is only very occasionally the Ann I knew. Illness has ravaged both person and personality.

Janet arrived not long after I'd come back from seeing Harvey and saying goodbye to Claire.

Before we went in to Ann, I asked about the dreams, the unreality Ann enters at night. Janet's basic answer was to keep up what I'm doing. I could have called Hospice, but it might have been better the way I handled it with loving kindness. I could rub her feet. Play soothing sounds of water – though we agreed the air compressor should be moved so it doesn't sound so much like the sound of a ship's engine. Light on in the room is a good idea –

And so it is. Last night Ann awoke at two, not at all disoriented.

March 26, 2003, Wednesday

Tuesday morning I visited Harvey about 11, mailed bills, stopped by the bank. In the afternoon I was tense. Ann has been controlling the breathlessness and wheeze fairly well, but she had a troubling sense of pressure in mid abdomen that made her feel nauseated and unwilling to eat. We had soup for dinner while we listened to country dances written by Playford, a 17th century musician. Only a few instruments – strings and harps, quiet courtly melodies and rhythms. From across the table I noticed tears in Ann's eyes. Sorrow at loss of beauty, or frustration with her body, or perhaps also sorrow at our not being the way we were? Loss. Loss. I went around to her. Hugged her. Later I told her to be proud of herself, of all she's given to people in her lifetime. She held her head up high, the white hair falling down gracefully back toward her ears, held back from her face by the cannula. I believed she was attending to me.

After dinner she asked what I would like to hear. I chose Brendel playing Schubert's sonata in B flat, and made it through the first three movements, only to fall sound asleep as the fourth began. Ann woke me up just as the Fantasia on the same CD thundered to an end.

As we said goodnight, she was quiet and not sad, but thoughtful and loving. She commented on how tired I'd been.

March 27, 2003, Thursday

Yesterday had a pleasant beginning, except for finding a newspaper article reminding me of Diane's death. Janet didn't arrive until 11, allowing me plenty of time to keep the household routines as well as to write out Ann's medication needs and symptoms. As she came into the shadowy living room, Janet stopped, carrying her bag easily, standing up straight – I notice this, an almost military bearing – to comment on the article about Diane. "What a wonderful person!" Then sitting down to talk with me before proceeding to see Ann in her bedroom, she asked, whether there had been any more episodes of confusion at night.

"No," I answered. "As a matter of fact, Ann told me this morning she hadn't turned the light on at night because she didn't want to disturb me upstairs."

Then I tried to describe Ann's complaint of pressure in her stomach. Janet explained: the body shutting down, perhaps, choosing which portion to dispense with first – digestive goes before brain and heart.

The home health aide, a new one, was to arrive at one. I waited, doing some filing for Ann in her office, walking back and forth to Ann's bedroom, wishing the aide would come so I could nap. Finally half an hour late she arrived, a big woman, narrow chin, sullen blue eyes. I described the routine for her, left the room, returned to file. I was called back three times or more to point out, to show and tell, and when she asked me how something worked, I had to demonstrate and do it. Not that I minded this, not half so much as her lateness. In the end, she determined to put the air pressure pad she was supposed to install under the sheet rather than under the mattress pad, as Janet had suggested. Ann and I allowed this because we believed in her experience.

The experience was in nursing homes, where no one has any come-back.

After she left and before I napped I felt the bed and wondered whether it's going to be comfortable for Ann. Later in the day I turned the level down to "soft."

That afternoon I slept on the living room couch, while Ann rested next to me in her chair, having risen twice to fix the pillow behind my head properly so my neck wouldn't hurt. Even after a forty minute nap, I woke up still tired.

We started for bed at 9:30, but it was 12 before I could settle down upstairs because the pressure pad made Ann uncomfortable, so uncomfortable she couldn't sleep. Tears began to roll down my cheeks as I removed it and remade the bed. I explained to Ann that my neck and back hurt, just little things, from tiredness. I felt awful, I told her, because I was letting her see my distress. I was crying for her, for myself, for Diane.

I can't say I felt any peace after this outpouring.

March 28, 2003, Friday

Thursday evening, after a visit from Anne C, Ann became nauseated, a condition that grew worse in spite of Ativan and oxycodone. At about 7 – I think it was – I phoned Hospice. Expecting they will want to take her to the hospital, Ann told me to make sure I had my power of attorney for health care and her black calendar book with cards handy. The on-duty nurse called back, first ascertaining what we had in the house to control nausea: Compazine pills, Zofran left over from chemotherapy days and Reglan. Since the cautions on Reglan suggested that nausea may be a side effect I said I didn't think that a good suggestion. The nurse laughed, then apologized, and finally suggested I check through the Hospice drugs in the refrigerator – the "comfort pack." There I found Compazine suppositories, which she thought would be better than anything by mouth.

I had a devil of a time getting one out for Ann; the foil wrapping isn't kind to short-nailed and fumbling fingers. Finally I scissored the foil away, handed it to Ann in the bathroom.

I wheeled her back to the living room, where she bent over a towel for about ten more minutes, I sitting beside her, just to be sitting beside her. After she seemed comfortably, deeply asleep, I decided it was best not to move her because getting out of breath was too troubling to her. So I lay on the couch next to her chair. Twice in the night I wheeled her to the bathroom. The second time, at four a.m. we decided she'd be more comfortable in bed. I went upstairs, fixed her some tea with sugar in it, brought it down, went back upstairs and got into bed to sleep another hour and a half not as relieved as I thought I'd be. This morning she seemed all right at 8 o'clock.

March 28, 2003, Friday
*continued, in pen, while sitting
in the green chair in Ann's bedroom*

This morning at about 11, Ann panicked as she became too hot around her face and shoulders, yet her feet remained cold. "What can I take?" she asked me desperately. I offered oxycodone and Ativan. They didn't help. Nebulize. I took her hand. Finally, I suggested a second Ativan. After a while her breathing slowed from 24-26 gasps per minute to 20 or so. I left her for a minute, returned, and she was asleep, the count down to 17.

First Suzanne (the agency help we'd hired) arrived, and then Hospice's new bath aide. We decided on a sponge bath. I went upstairs to try to sleep and when I came downstairs Ann was sitting up, eating lunch (applesauce, cottage cheese, dried fruit). She was feeling easy, impressed by the way the bath aide handled her. She demonstrated this for us with Suzanne guiding the wheel chair after she'd gone to the bathroom – her feet need to be lifted up into the bed for her, she told Suzanne.

Janet, who arrived at 3:30, was reassuring. Ann was amusing, her quick memory of facts sharp. Janet's comment on the pressure pad was that since it didn't work she felt we had to order another. I suppose this was a way of informing us that Ann will soon be bed bound.

Out in the kitchen she asked if I had KY jelly to help

with suppositories. I shook my head, no. She asked, "Will you be able to insert one?"

I think so. I thought it through last night.

March 29, 2003, Saturday

Ann has been spry all day, even walking to the hall bathroom from the living room. But since five o'clock she's been miserable, short of breath, nauseated, pain or cramping in her belly. She ate two mouthfuls of dinner and half a piece of very thin bread. In her bed she accepted the pillows I'd been told to prop under her arms readily, which she didn't do last week. When I left her just now – 11 p.m. – she felt pressure around the sternum, was short of breath and somewhat frantic about that. She took another oxycontin with my blessings.

4:30 p.m. the next day
March 30, 2003, Sunday

I can't remember all that's happened today, can't describe what is happening. At six I came downstairs in pajamas. Ann seriously nauseated after she went to the toilet. Compazine. I ran to kitchen to get the suppository, returned to her bedside, pushing the table out of the way. Slit the foil wrapping. It came off, for a change. Looked fruitlessly for latex gloves I thought I'd seen in the bathroom cupboard. Ann's breathing hard: gasp, gasp. I provided oxycodone, Ativan. Nebulizer. She insisted on inserting the suppository herself, got back into bed. We fussed with pillows and adjustments.

I waited – the Compazine wasn't helping. I called Hospice after a while, spoke to the call nurse – who said to use Zofran. I carefully peeled the paper back from the tiny cup where the white circle of medicine resided. Picked it up. Put it in her mouth. Still no change. She was suffering, wanting it to stop, wanting to leave the house – had to get in the car. I tried to find out about the pain – she just looked at me, her eyes narrowed, cheeks bright red.

"I've got to get shoes on" I said. She didn't want me to leave – but I had to go to the bathroom. Upstairs I dressed as fast as I could and grabbed an orange to eat, shoes. Downstairs again. Fetching my hot water bottle...

Then Ann developed a headache – couldn't tell me how severe – or wouldn't. (I see her face now, mouth pulled back, eyes green, maybe trying to talk.)

"Shoot me" she said.

"Where's the pain besides your head?"

"Everywhere. Can't we get help?"

I tried the hot water bottle. Too hot, she said. I got an ice pack, put it at the back of her neck. At first this helped, but after a few minutes, no.

I called Hospice. Morphine?

"I don't have any. She's agitated, has severe headache, wants to get out of bed."

"Shall I come?" the nurse asked.

"Yes"

She arrived in half-an-hour. Ann impatient for her arrival, continued to ask: "Why won't anyone help us? Why are you trying to do this all by yourself?"

When the nurse arrived, Ann was in the bathroom.

I'd been trying to help her get up from the toilet, and I had to tell the nurse I don't know anything about patient care. With one look, she agreed that indeed I didn't.

After settling Ann in bed, she checked out the Hospice pack of drugs in the refrigerator, asked about Ativan, ordered morphine, a hospital bed, and said to use the commode.

10:30 p.m. Sunday, March 30, 2003

Not the end of a difficult day, not yet. Ann lies quietly in the half light her bed receives from the light over my head. (I'm sitting in the green chair and have turned one of the track lights over the book case on.) I've given her two morphine tablets and 1 mg of Haldol; I'm supposed to stay up until 11:30 to give her 2 more morphine tablets. The night nurse said on the phone that two every hour seem to be what's needed to knock out pain. Working backward from this – the pain in her stomach had come on around 9 again and was mildly alleviated by Prevacid and Reglan.

Checking back over the afternoon notes I see that when she's awake, and she's been awake since 2:30 – she feels this "everything hurts" pain. I've been up and down helping her for about 16 hours now, with a few moments of looking at the paper, and 45 minutes napping in the green chair.

Just now I asked her not to get up and sit on the edge of the bed, because I was so tired. Every ten minutes or so she's been asking me to help her up, hoping what, I don't know, because she didn't express what she wanted or needed. Then after sitting up for a brief time, she needed help getting back down again.

I'd begun to sob. "Please, Ann, please stay down, I'm so tired. Does it help to sit up?"

"No, I guess not," she said.

Suddenly like a great wind, all the love I'd ever felt for her and felt coming from her, more than twenty-five years of being and working together, rushed into and through me, filling me with peace and warmth, a sense of its goodness and blessedness. I've never experienced anything so full of blessing.

She didn't try again that night to sit up.

March 31, 2003, Monday

Last night I waited until 12:30 to give Ann the last Haldol, what I hoped would be the last for the night.

The pain was strange – at one point, after the 11:30 morphine, she said her face hurt. About two minutes later, she smiled – it's better.

While I waited for 12:30 to come, she said, "Carol, it's close."

Close? I'm not sure – was she speaking of death? Later as I tucked her in after the Haldol dose, she tried to grasp the air. "Quickly," she said.

My mind, so accustomed to trading Shakespearean references with her, immediately thought of Dame Quickly speaking of Falstaff's death, how he spoke of green fields, and I wanted her with all my heart to think of green fields and flights of angels so I said the words aloud.

Also: all day long yesterday, two sets of thoughts –

great grief for all the human pieces of her left behind, the plans, the hedges against fate, the gifts to others, the information, the arrangements and the question, what is there to do next?

This morning at five I listened to her slow breathing. Fussing about the Haldol, I went into the bathroom to measure the dose in a dropper. It was hard to hold at first, but then I managed. Her lips and mouth were dry. I swabbed them. As the water touched her mouth, she stopped breathing for ten seconds. I shook her arm gently, felt her face, she didn't move. I'm going to have to phone Claire, take her offer to come down and be with me.

March 31, 2003, Monday
handwritten in my notebook

Our last trip. Beds side by side. Ann comatose, drugs or disease? Don't know.

Strange mix today. Work and worry. Ann awoke into a semi-conscious state at 9, refused to accept transfer into the hospital bed brought in (that's where I am now), often asked for – I'm not sure – relief or death, saying "Please, please, quickly, quickly." We moved her recliner in from the living room and she sat in it for a while, stiff and straight, long enough for Beth and the baby to visit for a few minutes. A little after noon there was a moment when Janet, who had come by, saw a swift change in her, thought she was going and both Claire and I lay on the bed with her. I embraced her and told her I loved her. Once I had to tell her who I was, and she winked at me.

Now, will she last the night – please yes, please no.

April 1, 2003, Tuesday
(written April 4, 2003)

I woke up at 4:30, lying on top of the hospital bed next to Ann's bed. Ann hadn't moved all night, not since five the evening before. She had her arms supported by pillows, her head was back, her mouth open, and she was breathing through her mouth. Sometime during the night, maybe before I went to bed, I added extra covering with her brown blanket, up to her waist, anyway. I'd been up a couple of times during the night, each time, feeling her arm, asking myself, is it cold? The way it had been last night? This time I got up to see if the aide had given her medication. Yes, she has, at 4:15. I went to the bathroom, climbed back into bed, then thought, she doesn't sound just right. I got up, stood next to the bed, kissed her forehead, whispered "Goodnight sweet prince, and flights of angels guide thee to thy rest." Thought of the green fields again, trying to project peace, lightness. But I had a hard time, because I was so upset. At about 4:50, I felt for her pulse – couldn't find it. Her breathing very slow and shallow. Then one breath. Then another one. And at about five, none. I waited ten minutes, holding her hand. Then I called Claire in to be with me.

April 4, 2003, Friday

It's been three days since Ann died. It's happened, yet it hasn't happened. I want to cry and cry, but can't. Except rarely, when I deliberately bring up the thoughts of Ann, and then I can't let them go on for long. I'm still stunned by the difficulty of Ann's last days, no matter how I try to assure myself Ann wasn't conscious of the anxiety she expressed. No matter how hard I try to push my mind back into days before she got sick, I don't succeed.

I discussed the memories of Ann's death with Claire at the breakfast table this morning, concerned that she might take scars away. She said no, that she felt good to be of use, that she felt Ann was at peace, that she knew there were people with her who loved and cared for her. This word eases my horrors and tremors, somewhat.

April 14, 2003, Monday

A peaceful weekend. Didn't move around much. Didn't sleep in the afternoons. In spite of waking up early. Saturday I did nothing much. In the early afternoon I hunted for and found the Lucia Popp CD with the hymn to the moon from "Rusalka" that always made Ann and me cry. We'd listened to that around the first of March, perhaps earlier, just before I wrote Ann's farewell to her friends on the internet. I remember holding her hand while we listened. This afternoon I lay on the couch as I had been that evening, reached out as I had that evening, and imagined that I held her hand, just as I had that evening. I'm able to recreate the hand, her dark sleeve, the bracelet, the watch – the tears.

Acknowledgements

This book would not exist without the long-time encouragement and support of Linna Thomas and the welcoming ambiance of Coalesce Bookstore, Morro Bay, California. The work of Brian Schwartz in seeing the book into print together with the technical skills of Robin Krauss have also been invaluable. Even though their real names remain undisclosed, I am grateful to the doctors, nurses, and other medical people who did their best to ease my friend's last days as well as to the friends and relatives who rallied round. I appreciate more than words can say the sensitive and understanding readings provided by Joanne Hand, Ellen Willis-Norton, Sharon Rooney, and Ann Edwards, and the careful work of Mary Hwass-Hay on the manuscript. Finally, I send a heart full of love to my three daughters, Noelle, Beth, and Claire Norton, who have always brought light to my life while standing by me "for better, for worse, for richer, for poorer, in sickness and in health."

www.ingramcontent.com/pod-product-compliance
Lightning Source LLC
Chambersburg PA
CBHW031402290426
44110CB00011B/236